S0-BEI-373

We Only Live Once

We Only Live Once

LUCIE K. BURTON

Copyright © 2018 by Lucie K. Burton.

Library of Congress Control Number:		2018902261
ISBN:	Hardcover	978-1-5434-0715-0
	Softcover	978-1-5434-0714-3
	eBook	978-1-5434-0713-6

All rights reserved. No part of this book may be reproduced or transmitted in any form or by any means, electronic or mechanical, including photocopying, recording, or by any information storage and retrieval system, without permission in writing from the copyright owner.

Any people depicted in stock imagery provided by Thinkstock are models, and such images are being used for illustrative purposes only.
Certain stock imagery © Thinkstock.

Print information available on the last page.

Rev. date: 07/04/2018

To order additional copies of this book, contact:
Xlibris
1-800-455-039
www.Xlibris.com.au
Orders@Xlibris.com.au
770717

For my husband, my children, my family, and my best friends.
I love you all more than you'll ever know.
I hope this story will help you live more mindfully.
Take care of yourself, your health and your loved ones;
they are what's important.
Nothing else really matters.
Lucie

Disclaimer: I have tried to recreate events, locales, and conversations from my memories of them. In order to maintain anonymity, in some instances, I have changed the names of individuals and places. I may have changed some identifying characteristics and details such as physical properties, occupations, and places of residence.

Introduction

Everyone has his own story; this is just mine. This book, long in the making, brings you along on my journey, which taught me that life should never be taken for granted and every single moment of it deserves to be lived to its fullest. Because at the end, it helps us understand the big picture, that everything happens for a reason, the best and the worst, even if it seems unfair or outrageous at times. Later down the track, we understand why it had to be that way. We are masters of our own destiny, within reason of course, but the choices we make will always condition our future. I've also learned that health and time are worth more than money, and I would give away all the money in the world to get more time with my family.

This book is for my children and my wonderful husband, who I love so much and who have been steadfast in coming with me on my journey. Somewhere along the line, they saved my life and I want them to have a reminder of it, something tangible they can keep forever. They are the three reasons I live for. They are part of me and I want to be with them every day of their lives, sharing precious moments along the way. They mean everything to me. Even in my craziest and most beautiful dreams, I would never have imagined being blessed by such an amazing family. They are everything I've always wanted in the deepest recesses of my heart.

I'm writing in English so they can read my story, our story. I'm not sure they will be able to read my French when the day comes, so I've tried my best to write down my feelings and memories in English, their language. Of course, I hope to be around long enough to tell this story myself, face to face, and also teach them their second language. But life can surprise you, so I prefer to be safe rather than sorry.

1

It's September 2015 in Sydney. I'm thirty weeks pregnant and definitely bigger than my last pregnancy. My belly is already so big that I can't walk, I can't see my feet and I'm like a giant bowling ball. I can't believe it. From now on, every day is a bonus for me and I really hope I will carry this baby to term and leave the hospital with my healthy baby, balloons, and presents like all the other mums... this time around.

Our first pregnancy started back in June 2013, a year and eight months into our marriage...and I was pregnant. I just did a pregnancy test and it was positive. I was nearly in tears. I was so excited, ecstatic even. My twin sister had just left from her long visit. She had come all the way to Sydney from Paris to meet John, my husband, and introduce us to her beautiful baby girl, Amélie, my niece. I guess spending two weeks with such a cute one-year-old convinced us to have one of our own, and we started trying as soon as the visit was over. It was a couple of months of trying and finally it happened. I had been feeling sick and very emotional for a week and was wondering if I wasn't pregnant. And I was. I gave John a present that evening.

"What is it? Why do I have a present? It's not my birthday," said John.

"Open it." I beamed with excitement.

He opened the small package and discovered a small jar of baby food, apple and banana puree.

"Is that it? Is that what I believe it is?" he asked with tears in his eyes.

"Yes." I was so excited, I showed him the t-shirt I was wearing. It had an Anne Geddes baby drawn at the place of my belly and the positive pregnancy test. "You're going to be a daddy."

He was so happy. Tears formed in his eyes and he brought me into his arms for a big cuddle. He kissed me with passion and bent over my belly to add, "You'll be a boy. You'll be a boy. Make a boy." It was funny. I love when he's happy and he was over the moon. He took me back in his arms and held me tight. My twin sister was the first to know of course. We did the test together over the phone.

I was smoking a couple of cigarettes a day back then, so I quit straight away. It's funny how easy it is to quit such a bad habit after so many years once you know you've got a human being growing inside you. Knowing that something is developing in your belly is actually a weird feeling and can even be scary at times. I spent the next few weeks wondering if I needed to eat differently, sleep in a different position, stop my daily gym workouts, or if I should go private or public in terms of hospital care. Life was changing for the better, except that I was getting very emotional. John and I were to become three and happily excited. He was helping me a lot at home so I could rest, giving me a very nice feeling of support. I wanted to keep the secret for the first three months as nothing is really certain until then. Yet, I told my parents and we decided to tell John's mum. They were happy for us and promised to keep the secret. Same thing at work, I didn't want to tell anyone, even though some of my workmates figured it out because of my "glow." John and I couldn't help but look at baby stuff and start thinking of our future family.

After eleven weeks, I had my first antenatal appointment. John came with me and together, we listened to the baby's heart. It was such a special moment. I was laughing so hard in my happiness that we had to stop the foetal Doppler; the interferences with the machine were too noisy to listen to the beats. The nurse thought I was fifteen weeks pregnant rather than eleven—a bit comforting for me as I had put on nearly three kilos already. I had to do the fourteen-week scan to make sure the baby's health was fine and rule out Down Syndrome. So, the next day, John and I went back to the hospital to meet our baby for the first time.

We arrived at the radiology department and couldn't wait to enter the ultrasound room, not only because I had drunk a lot of water and my bladder was ready to explode, but also because we were longing to see our baby. After a little while, the technician let us in the room. I was excited and a bit nervous. I'd seen ultrasounds done in movies before, but now it was us—we were at the start of parenthood...and about to meet our baby. We decided not to know the gender, as John wanted the surprise, but somehow I thought it was a boy. So we told the technician we didn't want to know.

She started to put some gel on my belly and pass the monitor on it to find the baby. We were looking at it. It was so magical to see our baby moving...his head, his little arms and legs. I was nearly crying with happiness. But after a little while, I realised that the technician was very quiet. At first, I thought it was because she was used to it and maybe bored, but then, I started to feel anxious. I was worried; something wasn't right. She left the room without a word to us.

"There's something wrong," I told John.

"No, you're worrying for nothing. She's going to come back. Everything is fine." He touched my hand, trying to comfort me.

"I'm telling you, she didn't say a word. This is so beautiful. I was so happy to see the baby, she must have been happier than that, even if she's used to it. I'm scared something is happening. I don't know what it is, but there's a problem."

"Let's wait and see, okay? Please calm down; we'll see when she's back." He touched my shoulder, trying to rub the tension out.

The technician came back in the room.

"You need to talk to the doctor," she said with no emotion.

"Why? What's happening?" I prompted.

"I can't explain myself. You need to talk to the doctor. I am showing you the way now."

We followed her to the maternity ward, then she indicated a room where we could sit. The wait was excruciating. I felt a knot form in my chest and as the minutes ticked on, John started to worry too.

"See, I told you. Something is not right. Why else would we see the doctor? I'm so scared John..." I sobbed.

The doctor entered the room quietly. She was wearing a surgical uniform, as if she just performed a delivery. An intern came in quietly behind her.

"Hi...Sorry, why are we here? What's happening with the baby?" I urged.

"The reason you're here is because there's a problem with the baby," she replied softly.

"What...What do you mean?" I asked anxiously.

"Unfortunately, the baby didn't develop his brain yet and he won't be able to grow properly if you pursue the pregnancy. It's a known condition called anencephaly."

The news was devastating. In a couple of words, she ripped our hearts apart.

"What does it mean? I don't understand...What did I do wrong?" I was in shock and started crying in pain.

"Nothing. You didn't do anything wrong. Unfortunately, it can happen; it's very rare and happens only in one in ten thousand," she said offering me tissues.

I was crying so much I could barely hear her now.

"In this case, the hospital can offer to terminate the pregnancy promptly. You can do it tomorrow if it's convenient for you. Usually, the earlier, the better," she added, clearly feeling for us.

"Oh my god. I can't believe this...One in ten thousand and it's for us...Why? Tomorrow? That's it? I'll have to say goodbye to my baby. I've just met him..."

I burst into tears. John held me tight in his arms, barely coping with his own emotions. I thought about the ultrasound; I was so happy I didn't see anything. I didn't see that his brain was missing. I just met my baby and he wasn't finished. I had to say goodbye already.

The tears couldn't stop coming up and were rolling on my cheeks. I was devastated. It was surreal. How could such a thing happen to us? What have we done to deserve so much suffering?

"It happens unfortunately and there is no explanation. Maybe a lack of folic acid but you're taking some supplements so maybe it's not that...or you should have taken a higher dose; there isn't much in these tablets. But as I said, it's very rare and it's unfortunate but there was nothing to do to really prevent it. Do you want me to leave you for a while?" the doctor asked.

"No, that's fine. We will come back tomorrow." I looked at John for approval.

"It's up to you, my love; whatever you want," said John, grief clouding his face.

"Yes, it's pointless to wait any longer. At what time do I have to come tomorrow?" I said, trying to stop crying and get some kind of composure.

"7 AM. Here, at the maternity ward."

We left the hospital devastated, weakened, and heartbroken. All the happiness and excitement we had at the start of this appointment was taken away by the terrible news. John didn't cry. He was trying to show strength and support; at least one of us had to stay strong. We went for a coffee and had a quiet walk on our favourite beach at La Perouse. I was still pregnant, my baby moving in my belly, alive. For now. I had to say goodbye. It was so painful; all these thoughts flooded through my head…I couldn't help but cry. John was emotional too; he couldn't help it. As strong as he was, we were in the same boat—a sinking one. We were losing our baby and all our hopes with him. I couldn't help but feel guilty. I was the one carrying him after all. Maybe something was wrong with me. I started doubting that I could have a normal baby. We went back home after renting a couple of movies. As always, we had our shower together and that night the water was covering our flooding tears while our four hands were holding my belly, giving our last goodbyes to our beautiful unborn soul.

"He still alive. He's still in me; he's still moving in me. I can't believe we have to abandon him. This is so painful." I couldn't stop thinking about the innocent life that I was about to leave, my first baby, our first baby. "We were so happy and now this. It's too hard." I was blurting out.

"I'll try to be strong for you darling. But it's hard for me too; it's so hard. Life is so cruel, another reason why I don't believe in God. Why would he do something like that? We didn't do anything wrong," John said through his tears. It was the first time he cried for our baby and the first time I saw John crying.

"I know, the only thing I prayed for, every day during this pregnancy, was to have a healthy baby. I don't understand either. You don't have to be strong for me; you're still human. I love you. I'm so sorry baby…"

And after a long and difficult shower, we quietly watched two movies before going to bed—the last night of my pregnancy. And again, John let go of more tears, but this time, I tried to be the strong one and comforted him.

The next morning, I was up at 4 am. I couldn't sleep anymore. I was in tears. I called my twin sister in Paris to explain what was happening. With the time difference, I hadn't been able to reach her before. Then, it was time to go. We arrived at the hospital at 6.45am and finished the paperwork by 10 am. I was finally placed in a bed an hour later. After getting some painkillers and receiving some non-invasive medical procedures, I started feeling some pain in my belly. I was afraid my baby was dying. Every time a nurse came to talk to me, she asked for my identity and I had to let her know why I was there. It was unbearable. I had to say "termination" too many times. I was about to terminate my pregnancy, my baby. They would take his life away because he wasn't how he was supposed to be. I didn't manage to finish him correctly. I felt guilty again. I was sobbing all along. John was there, holding my hand all the way until it was time to go into the theatre. He followed the team, rolling my bed into the anaesthetic room, but he had to leave me there.

It was so distressing for me to be alone, surrounded by the medical team moving around me, each and every one of them having to do something. They were about to take my baby away from me. I couldn't stop crying. It was my first time in surgery, under general anesthesia. From this first room, they transferred me into the theatre. The lights were blindly bright. They moved me from my bed to the operating table. I was terrified as they put a mask on my face and made me breathe into it. Then the anaesthetist injected something into my IV and I quickly fell asleep, tears still wet on my face. The only thing I remember from that moment was that I dreamt. It was a weird dream, very bright, but that's all I remembered about it.

The next thing I knew, I woke up where I started, on the bed I got when I arrived. I asked for John straight away. I wanted to see him. The nurse called him and he was by my side within the next five minutes. It was 1.15pm and it was over. I felt tired and disoriented, sad and lost. I was bleeding a lot down there. I just had lost my baby and I didn't have anything left in me, in my belly—just his memory and the pictures of the ultrasound. Before I left, a nurse came to talk to me; she wanted to make sure I would be okay. I was desperate but she said that time would make things better. I would never forget but the pain would soften.

The next few weeks were painful and sad. I couldn't get more than a few days off at work and my boss wanted me back. I was grieving while trying to come back to my normal life. I had to tell the people who knew that it was over, that I had to let him go, and every single time it broke my heart. Every time I broke the news to someone, it broke my heart just a little bit more. We didn't want to know the gender, thinking it would be easier to recover. We lost a baby and somehow it was easier not to know what he/she was. Angels don't have a sex anyway. John never really understood why it took me so long to grieve my baby, as he recovered quite quickly. After a couple of weeks, he told me to move on. Men and women are definitely different when it comes to emotions and life or death. For him, "you live and then you die" and as death is part of life, when it happens you just need to move on. I found that level of pragmatism harsh and insensitive.

Finally, a few months after the loss of our baby, the routine took over and we stopped talking about it. John started to get upset when I had to share my feelings, so after a few weeks, I kept my pain for myself. I decided it was time to go back to my home country, France; I needed to be with my family. I wanted to hold them all in my arms. Planning for this trip saved me. I was thinking of something else, something healthier that I could look forward to and I loved travelling and organising trips. It would be John's first time in Europe too. He met my sister when she came over in April that year and he met my parents when they came over after our wedding a couple of years ago. Now he was the one to come to my country and I was happy for him to discover where I came from, my roots, and the country that made me who I was.

In October, we went to Paris to see my twin sister for a week and visited the entire city. We enjoyed drinking beers at brasseries terraces, eating the delicious pastries and walking everywhere. I showed him where I used to live and the places I used to go to when I was living there. Then we went to the city I was born in, Nice, a beautiful small town on the French Riviera between Cannes and Monaco. We spent five days with my parents, visiting the surrounding old villages along the sea and savouring the local culinary specialties. I was revived. It was so good to be able to show him my home town and sharing all the things that I loved with him. He loved it too. We also went to Italy as I'd always wanted to see Pisa, Firenze, and Roma—where his auntie was living now—and so we did. It was fantastic. I was living again and John and I were happy again, loving each other like never before. The loss of our child was very painful and disturbing for both of us and each of us dealt with it in its own way; but at the end, we were still there, together. That romantic time in my country helped us get over it by bringing us closer.

I wanted to be pregnant again, quickly. Even if everyone around me was telling me to take my time, for me there was no time to waste. I wanted to move forward, turn the page, and try again. I didn't want to sit on this tragedy for too long. I fell pregnant again when we got back from our wonderful trip in Europe. I was due exactly a year and one day after we lost our first baby. That was when we met Jason, our rainbow baby. We would never have had this baby if we had the first one and somehow, it was the only good thing that helped me get over the loss of our baby angel.

Now I'm on my third pregnancy and I'm trying to do as little as possible, except at work, where my boss is pushing me to finalise the crazy launch of our new high-end brand. I'm a national brand manager for three brands, which means being under a lot of pressure and having crazy deadlines. In less than a month now, I'm launching a new brand on the market and there are still some major details to arrange for the biggest event of the year to be ready.

If something happens this time, at least my hospital bag is ready. We just bought a "big boy" bed for our son Jason and will use his cot for the baby. I try to explain to Jason that my belly is very big because I'm keeping his little brother or sister warm in there for now, but I don't think he gets it. I really hope for a girl this time. I'm a bit over pants and shorts, tees and shirts; I'd like some skirts, hair stuffs, and fluffy princess dresses and those sweet pink outfits.

The small lump I discovered in my left armpit is getting so big and painful that I had to see my General Practitioner (GP) and asked him to do something about it. I don't believe any more in his diagnosis of "maybe a swollen gland because of a cold" he gave me three months ago. Who's got a gland there for a cold, really? It's nearly a four-by-five-centimetre ball now and I'm having trouble closing my arm. I've really started thinking the worst. I'm in such pain that I don't think I'm going to wait two weeks to get an ultrasound done. There's no availability before that, so I will go to the emergency room at our local hospital tomorrow. Maybe they will be able to do one straight away. I can't wait any longer to know what else is growing in me.

I'm on my way to the hospital first thing in the morning. After nearly an hour wait, I am examined by a doctor. He seems quite worried and asks me a few questions while touching my armpits.

"Did you lose weight or have you been tired recently?" he asks seriously

"Really? I'm thirty weeks pregnant and I look like a balloon, so of course, I'm tired." I do my best to smile at him. "I've got a sixteen-month-old baby at home who always wants to be held and starts tantrums. And obviously, I put on weight, not the other way around." I'm now laughing.

He is not laughing at all. His face looks so anxious that I start to worry.

"I felt a little lump in my armpit nearly three months ago now. I was afraid it could be a lactic conduct obstructed, but my GP told me it could be just a swollen gland if I had a cold. What do you think?"

"I don't know. We have to do an ultrasound before any diagnosis." He continues his examination, touching my armpit.

"But I tried to get an ultrasound and that's why I'm here. I can't wait two weeks for it. This ball is so painful; I need to know what it is. I can't stay like this anymore. I want to get rid of it. I also thought it could be breast cancer, but apparently cancer is not painful, is that true? Or do you think it could be cancer?" I am now in tears.

"Like I said, I can't tell you until we do a scan. Wait for me outside. I'm going to see if we can admit you for the day and get an ultrasound done today."

"That would be great, thank you."

I spend the day worrying and waiting to do the scan. I tell my boss that I will work from my hospital bed. I've got so much on my plate right now—two new brands to manage. I don't really need that. I'm scared of what this thing can be...cancer? That would be so awful. My auntie passed away from breast cancer when I was seventeen and I remember how hard it was for my cousins. I don't want that for my kids.

By the end of the day, I have my ultrasound and get the results. Another doctor explains them to me.

"There are three inflamed lymph nodes and the biggest one is three-by-two centimetres."

"What is it? What does it mean? Could it be cancer?" My voice is shaky.

"Well, to identify exactly what kind of infection it is, we need to do a biopsy," she replies calmly, not really answering my question.

"Okay, can I do one now? I really want to know what this thing is."

"Unfortunately, we can't. As you are pregnant, you need to ask the consent of the obstetrician or your GP...because the local anaesthesia could slow down the baby's heart and it may have to be done with monitoring," she says, obviously very sorry.

I am devastated. Of course I don't want to harm the baby but I'm so desperate to know what this stupid golf-ball-size lump is. I'm calling my GP straight away for an appointment the next day. Unfortunately, he doesn't want to make the decision and tell me to see with the obstetrician when I'll go to my antenatal appointment next week. I'm just hoping I don't have breast cancer. If something like this happened to me, I would feel like I let my family and John down. I want to see my kids grow and live a long life by their side. My stomach twists as I hope it's nothing and that I can heal with antibiotics.

That morning, I'm back to work just after my GP appointment but I can't concentrate. I can't stop thinking of the worst-case scenario. My boss, who came into my office to get some updates about our big event, sees me worried and asks if everything is alright. And I tell him everything about the biopsy bullshit and how worried I am waiting for a diagnosis. When I talk to the new product manager and good French mate of mine, Stéphanie, I'm in tears in her office. She's also worried it could be cancer but since we don't know, it's pointless getting overwhelmed yet. She's right, I need to calm down and stop worrying. But not knowing and having this strange thing growing in me while pregnant makes me even more emotionally overwhelmed. I can't help it and my hormones don't help at all. I'm about to have a baby and I'm terrified I won't be able to watch him or her grow up. John is worried as well but as practical as he is usually, he doesn't want to worry too much until we know what this thing exactly is. Then, we will figure something out.

This pregnancy is definitely complicated for me. Thyroid issues, varicose veins, progesterone treatment, thrush, and now this. I'm just hoping that with all this pain, the baby will be perfect; it has to be the most perfect baby ever. We haven't found a name yet. I'm trying to find one, but every time I come up with something, John doesn't like it. It's tough. Choosing a name that someone will have to live with forever is very hard. We don't want a "stripper" name for a girl—John's words—and we have issues finding a boy's name since Jason was the only one we ever found good enough. I'm focusing on girls names though, as I really think it's going to be a girl.

2

I remember how hard it was being pregnant with Jason. I was hot all the time. I had headaches and above all, I was so emotional, like crazy emotional. I tried to eat healthy and not to gain too much weight. I was due on July 26, 2014 and I was working hard for a promotion that wasn't coming as quick as my boss had promised. Because, really, who gives a promotion to a pregnant lady in this man's world? I was exhausted and driving John crazy with my anxiety. I was very nauseous, but I survived Christmas. We just told John's dad, Stan, and his partner, Ellen, on Christmas Eve and they were super excited and happy for us.

During the first trimester, I was very anxious something would go wrong with the baby since my first terrible experience, while John was pretty much in denial about the whole pregnancy. He was waiting for the thirteen-week ultrasound to acknowledge the baby in order to avoid another painful moment. I couldn't deal with it and I felt lonely. We argued a lot. Maybe we were both scared of becoming parents; after all, it was a big step. But John and I were always so different and I started doubting we had the same values. He wasn't helping enough with the chores at home. I knew his work was very demanding physically but I couldn't do everything by myself anymore, on top of my job. Cleaning, cooking, washing the clothes, hanging the clothes, folding, doing his company paperwork, paying the bills, book-keeping for our budget, food shopping—everything was going through me since we started living together. It was okay when I wasn't working, but now I couldn't do it anymore. It was too much and I started to get upset all the time, especially when I came home to see my husband lying on the couch, sleeping, when nothing had been done in the house. My main concern was that if he was like that now, how would we function with a baby? I couldn't do it all by myself.

I started to get less worried only at the end of January, thirteen weeks in, when the ultrasound technician told us everything was fine with the baby. He had a brain, two arms and two legs, a beating heart, and that made me feel a bit better. But my placenta was a bit low so I had to limit my efforts until the next scan, six weeks later.

In February, we finally told everyone. Things were definitely getting better and John was helping me with the household since I had to slow down. We were also looking at buying a house for our family. Since we were both working, we managed to save enough for a deposit and started visiting houses every Saturday. But the auctions in Sydney were always about a hundred to two hundred thousand dollars higher than the market price our bank was giving us. We were disappointed every time. And with half a million dollars, you couldn't do much in the city, or even an hour away. I also had to start picking out a day-care centre because it was very hard to get a position for a baby; the demand was high for a very limited number of centres. John was working most Saturdays and wasn't home for days when he was up the coast, quite a few times. So I had to visit houses by myself and it was tiring and deceiving. After a couple of months searching, my heart wasn't in it anymore. The market was crazy and we tried to focus on the arrival of our baby.

We bought all the furniture for the baby bedroom and I booked a space in the parenthood classes the hospital gave every Tuesday night in order to be ready for the birth. It was exciting and scary. My belly was growing and I started feeling the baby moving. It was kind of a weird feeling—another human being in my body, like a little alien growing inside me. I was talking to him a lot. I thought it was a boy, but we wanted the surprise again. I was craving salmon and nuts all the time. I was listening to my favourite songs and dancing a lot for the baby to listen and feel the moves. I imagined how good life would be with our child, our little creation, the mix of both of us. He would have his eyes and hair but my skills to study.

Every night we talked about our baby, the way he would be and how he would probably drive us crazy, in love and in madness. But most of all, we wanted him in good health, boy or girl. All that mattered was a healthy baby and like for my first pregnancy, I was praying every night for it. I tried to organise the birth in the water, like I'd always wanted. But they didn't want to take the chance and considered that I was a pregnancy "at risk" because my placenta was a bit low and lacked fluid. I couldn't believe it. Nobody else told me that before. Otherwise, everything was fine. John and I were happy and excited to start our own little family. I was a bit disappointed not having my family with me here; it was hard to live all this without my sister and my parents and even if Skype and Viber were great, some proximity would definitely be better. I could never ask a software to babysit either.

With all the thinking I had done for the birth of our baby, I didn't find any presents for John's birthday. It was coming up soon and I was still looking for a present. I ended up in tears the Saturday before his birthday, telling him that I was still looking for something and couldn't find anything. He was so hard to buy for. But he told me that he couldn't care less and that I shouldn't cry for that. Well, I was emotional. This pregnancy was such a roller coaster of emotions. When we came back home that night, I was exhausted but I still wanted to prepare my hospital bag. We still had three months to go before the expected birth but I wanted to be ready.

John laughed. "You don't have to do your bag right now. There are ten more weeks to go. Don't worry; you've got plenty of time. Go to bed," he urged me.

"But, that way, it's done. I know there is still time, but we never know. I just want to be ready."

"Come on love, we had a big day. You need to rest. The bag can wait," he insisted

"Okay. You're right. I'll do it tomorrow."

That same night, at 4 am, I was rushing to the toilet thinking I was peeing myself. Once in the bathroom, I realised that my water broke. I actually thought it was a nightmare. I couldn't believe it. I was in the bathroom, alone, looking down at the water and saying at loud, "It's not possible. This is not happening. It can't be happening. What do I do? Oh my God. What should I do? John? John?" Now I was calling for John in a very shy voice as I felt guilty and scared. I started panicking. I never thought I would panic. John heard me and joined me in the bathroom and looked at me. I was shaking.

"Is that the water?" asked John surprised.

"Yes, I think so…or maybe not." I tried to convince myself it wasn't happening.

"No, that's the water. We need to go to the hospital right now." John said firmly.

"No, no, maybe we should call the hospital first. Do you have the number they gave us? I can't remember where it is…"

"No, we need to go right now. No need to call; the water broke."

"But I'm only at thirty weeks. It's too early. It's too early. The baby…is the baby going to be okay? It's too early. I need to pack the bag. I need to have a shower and change my pants, look at me…" My pants were wet and I couldn't stop the leakage.

"Please, we've got no time for that. Let's go," John urged me.

"Okay. I take a plastic bag to protect the car seat though." Even through my panic, I grabbed the bag and shakily let John lead me out of the room.

John helped me to run the two flights of stairs that separated us from the car and we drove to the hospital. He impressed me by his calm. I was nearly jealous but also a bit upset because I felt irrational being scared by the situation. My baby was about to come ten weeks earlier than expected. Having read that thirty-three weeks was the safe mark to have a premature baby, I was also wondering what happened for the membrane to break. I thought these three weeks would have made such a big difference. I was scared for my baby's life. I had weird contractions two weeks before but my GP told me I didn't have to go to the hospital; I just needed to rest and everything was fine…right. Note for later: never listen to your GP but to your own instincts.

We arrived at our local hospital ten minutes later and went straight to the Emergency Department. They rushed us into the maternity ward. Once there, they explained that we couldn't give birth in this hospital because they couldn't care for premature babies less than thirty-two weeks of gestation. They had to find another hospital with a Neonatal Intensive Care Unit (NICU) able to care for very premature babies.

To make sure that the baby's lungs would be open enough for the birth, I received an injection of steroids. I also swallowed a tablet to delay the labour. Apparently, a baby could survive up to three weeks after the rupture of the membrane, with minimal water. I was terrified. John stayed by my side until they found a place for us at a very good hospital of the eastern suburbs, about half an hour away from our place. I was transferred at sunrise and John followed the ambulance in our car. I was placed in a shared room and given more steroids every twenty-four hours and also more tablets to delay the labour for the following three days. That Sunday, John missed the first day he ever organised a remote-control car bash with his mates. I felt bad for him, guilty not to be able to bring a pregnancy to term so far. It was my second pregnancy and I'd been feeling anxious all the way because of what happened during the first one.

On Wednesday, May 21, 2014, I started feeling contractions at 3.30am; they got shorter and more intense throughout the day. After some back and forth to the delivery suite and lots of monitoring, I was back in my room. The pain was intense but the nurses told me it could last days like this. I couldn't believe it; I wouldn't last days like that. I couldn't sleep or even rest. At 8.30pm, John had spent the entire day by my side, so I told him to go back home. It was getting late and he looked bored, playing on his phone. Two hours later, I called the nurse and let her know that the contractions were even closer. I thought that I would probably give birth that night. After a quick check and the doctor visit, they said that it would be unlikely. I was sure they were wrong though.

Around midnight, the contractions were four to five minutes apart but very strong and painful in my lower back and abdomen. I was trying to breathe slowly to relieve the pain. I called the midwives again and after a quick check, they decided to get ready for the birth. They brought the resuscitation cart, the delivery pack, and prepared everything in my room because there were no delivery suites available. My poor roommate was forty weeks pregnant and massive; she probably freaked out when she heard me screaming my head off and breathing like an animal. I asked them to call John back, but he wasn't answering his phone and they couldn't leave a message. I asked him so many times to set a bloody voice-mail. I was petrified now. I had very intense and closer contractions and I was alone, except for the midwife, a wonderful one by the way, and the other nurses. I had no family, no loved ones, and I was about to go through one of the most important moment of my life…alone.

"Where is my husband?" I asked panicking.

"We try to call him but we didn't manage to reach him yet…"

"Try again please. I need my husband," I asked, hardly breathing.

"Calm down, breathe. If you feel like pushing, please try to keep it inside. We are trying to get a delivery suite…"

"What? Sorry…how do I hold it inside? …Are you serious?"

"Yes, just try to focus. Continue breathing and try to keep your perineum muscles closed."

"Are you kidding me? Oh my god…it's so painful."

"You're doing great. Continue breathing through the contractions."

"We've got a room, we can go now," another nurse interjected.

"Can you move to this bed?" My midwife questioned, showing me another bed.

"Hmm…no I can't. I can't move. It's too hard with these crazy contractions."

"That's okay; we will take your bed. Let's go, take everything downstairs to the delivery suite."

A guy was pulling my bed in the corridor and towards the elevator when I felt it…

"I need to push now." It was an amazing natural sensation that I had to push, like the baby had to come out and was pushing through me.

"Try to keep it inside."

"I'm trying. Oh my god. This is too hard. Where's John? Where's my husband?"

"We got him on the phone; he should be there very soon."

"Thank God for that. …I have to push sorry, I can't hold it anymore." The power of my body asking for that push was too strong to resist. I had to push, it was beyond my power.

"That's okay, go for it and push."

We just got into the elevator and I couldn't believe I was about to give birth there. I was about to push a second time when we arrived in the delivery suite. I was still asking for John and hoping he would arrive before the birth. The doctors asked me if I minded some students watching the delivery because such an early birth didn't come around often. When I accepted I didn't realise there would be seven of them. But I didn't care, the pain was so intense and I was in such discomfort; I just wanted my man. I was holding my midwife's hand so tight I could probably break her bones. They gave me some gas but I couldn't care less; it wasn't doing anything for me and I was trying to push the mask off my face with my mouth.

When they transferred me to the delivery suite bed, John finally arrived. It was such a relief to see him. I pushed a third time, the pain was excruciating. Every time I pushed, I felt the baby's head trying to come out of me, literally distorting me inside out. I could feel everything. They told me that I must push one last time to give birth; otherwise the baby could be in danger for staying too long like that. They didn't have to say more and in a last strong effort, using all the energy I had left—coming out of nowhere—I pushed him out of me as if it was the last thing I had to do in the world. I fought the pain and gave birth to my first baby.

Once his head was out, the rest of his body slid easily out of me. They placed him on my bare chest for a couple of seconds. He was so small, curled up on me, his bottom up, like a little frog. These few seconds felt like minutes; it was such an intense moment. I already had so much love for this little thing. John was by my side, holding my hands and telling me with a big smile and a tear in his eyes "it's a boy," showing me his genitals. I didn't even think of the gender. I was just happy it was over and that he was here and alive. But I was so happy it was a boy. It was a boy, like we wanted. I knew it. He was so tiny, I could cover his little body between my small two hands. He was the most beautiful thing I ever seen, my son. They asked us if we had a name for him. I looked at John and said "Jason?" It was the name he always had in mind for a boy. But he replied that we would think about it. For me, it was definitely sorted. They quickly took him away to help him breathe and prepare him for the incubator. Jason was born at 1.19am, measuring forty-one centimetres at one kilogram and four hundred and twenty grams. I called my sister and my dad in France and everyone was very excited to welcome the first son in our family in at least four generations. From my great-great grandma to my mum, none ever had a boy. I was the first and my dad couldn't be happier.

We waited another four hours, falling asleep in the delivery room before they finally called us back to see our son. John and I had enough time to agree on Jason, John's step-grandfather's name—a war hero and a role model for him—and I liked the idea of a strong name for our little boy. I couldn't take him in my arms just yet, so we were staring at him, lying in the small plastic box, linked to machines with wires. There were two on his chest, one on his foot. He also had a tube in his mouth and was connected to a respiratory machine helping him breathing normal air, because luckily, he didn't need oxygen. He also had one cannula in each arm, held by a sort of big plastic piece and bandage wrapped around.

He seemed so small in this box, but he was the most beautiful baby in the world to me. I passed my hand through one of the holes on the side of the incubator. The palm of his hand was the size of my thumbnail and he looked so fragile. John was sad and very impressed with all the tubes, wires, and noisy machines around us, but I tried to comfort him. I was sure he would be okay. I was a premature baby myself and even if he was very early, it was thirty-four years later; nowadays they could do miracles for sure. John went home and I went back to my room to try to get some sleep, even if I started pumping my milk every three hours! I would rather have my baby with me than being woken up by an alarm to express milk!

The next morning, I couldn't wait to see my beautiful boy, and as soon as John arrived, we went to see him together. I went down the NICU every three hours to give him my milk, the precious little drops of the first milk, colostrum, so important for his health. It was my mission, my way of apologising, and the only help I could give him. I was desperate to hold his little body in my arms, on my chest, feeling his skin on mine, heartbeat against heartbeat, mum and baby together again. After changing his nappy, it finally happened. The nurse helped me transfer him on my chest, trying to make sure the wires didn't get caught and everything was staying in place while positioning him on my bare chest and covering him quickly with a warm blanket. And what an amazing sensation it was to feel him against me. I couldn't help the tears of happiness and fulfilment as I felt like I was whole again.

I missed him so much, I needed to feel him. I was in tears, like every emotion I held since his birth was finally coming out. I was relieved to have him back; we were together again. He was so small, so precious. I could feel his heart while he was resting on my chest. I was happy again, crying in love. I was a mum. He was such a little thing, with the amazing power of making me feel so vulnerable. I was under his spell, in love like it was the first time. I actually understood what love was. My heart was growing and about to explode with so much love...unconditional love. From now on, he would be my blood, my guts, my everything, my reason to live, to fight, my baby boy forever. I had never been moved like this before. He took my breath away and I couldn't stop the tears coming up my eyes. It was like I witnessed a miracle, something coming from the gods, an angel, pure and beautiful. John and I were contemplating our beautiful son, discovering his traits, his thin face, and every detail of his little body. He was our little miracle. Gorgeous. He would just have to grow, get bigger, and stronger and we could all go home. I couldn't help feeling guilty for his early birth but I was so happy he was fine. He was my son and together we would conquer the world. Nothing else mattered; Jason was my new priority, my life.

Our daily routine was simple. I would come every three hours to do his care: changing his nappy, cleaning him a little, giving him my milk. He was in his little aquarium, getting fed by the extremity of the tube outside the plastic box, going straight to his stomach through his nose. Then, once a day I had the chance to hold him on my chest, skin to skin or *kangaroo care*, for an hour maximum so he didn't get cold. The nurses would take him away earlier if he was. Being by his side as much as possible was the only thing I could do to help him get stronger: be by his side the most I could, providing my care and my love, cuddling him daily. It was either John or me; we couldn't really share that moment as he was very fragile and we couldn't move him too much. John held him the second day and he was so happy I could see tears forming in his eyes. He was a dad and I could tell how much he loved his son already. He was so proud. I held him two days in a row after that, it was too hard to wait two days; I missed him too much. Jason could breathe normally without the machine after twenty-four hours but he had jaundice and stayed under a UV lamp for nearly three days. It looked like he was getting a tan, with his eyes covered. He looked so funny with his little mask. But I was glad when the jaundice was gone.

After five days, I had to leave the hospital without my son and that was heart-breaking. I saw all these mums going around in the maternity ward with their baby and later leaving the hospital with balloons, flowers, and their baby. I had nothing but my tears. At home, I was still expressing milk every three hours. I was exhausted and sad, missing Jason badly. John didn't understand how hard it was for me. I was going to the hospital every day, waking up early and driving for an hour before arriving at the NICU, washing my hands thoroughly and finally feeling a smile forming on my face when I laid eyes on Jason. I started a diary for him, writing every day on his progress and what he liked to do: smiling to me, stretching, yawning, and sleeping. It was helping me cope with the anxiety and the sadness of having my son fight for his life away from me. It was an idea from the NICU crew and I loved it. They helped me collect the little things to remember his journey: his umbilical cord, the little UV protection, some wires, and his name tag. Also, one of the nurses drew a lovely sign with his name for his incubator. After nearly a week without clothes, I discovered my baby wearing his first outfit. The nurses gave him a red bodysuit with long sleeves and legs with a little blue elephant embroidered on the chest. It was size five zero, still way too big for him, but by wearing it, he looked more like a *normal baby* and he was handsome.

I was exhausted but I had to go every day; I couldn't help it. I had to see him, to touch him, to take care of him. I knew that being there for him was his best medicine. When my twin sister and I were born, they didn't know how vital kangaroo care was. They wouldn't have taken the risk to take a premature baby out of the incubator for a cuddle with mummy. I stayed two months at the hospital back then, my twin stayed three. They didn't put us together either. Now they know how important it is for identical twins to stay together because they recover faster. It took us so long to get out of hospital, and we had five weeks longer than Jason did. I was hoping that with all my attention and affection, he would come home sooner, so we could be together faster. I was a bit depressed and anxious for him, longing to hold him tightly against my chest after the four o'clock care. I was so happy to have him in my life.

My entire vision had changed that night. I was now seeing the world like a mother and everything was so different; it was all scarier and deeper. I finally understood what all that fuss about babies was and how things were different when you become a mum. I was enlightened, after all these years. It felt like I could really see for the first time in my life. I knew what unconditional love meant.

After twelve days we were able to transfer him to our local hospital and even though it wasn't as modern, it was only ten minutes away and I could go back and forth at home while Jason was asleep. The transfer made him sick for a couple of days though. Every time he would suffer a little, I would break internally. I couldn't stand him being sick or weak, or even sad. I felt guilty for having worked so hard without considering my health better. I was outraged that in Australia there were no obligations for an employer to pay maternity leave. This is the twenty-first century, after all! That puts so much worry and financial pressure on young couples and it was physically demanding to work until the last minute. I had never seen that many premature births around me. I came from a country where maternity leave is compulsory; women had to stop working six to eight weeks before birth. The doctors there would probably have put me on rest bed at four months like they did for my sister's best friend. She was pregnant at the same time, put on bed rest at four months because she was experiencing the same pregnancy conditions as mine and her boy was born healthy at thirty-seven weeks.

I spent every day sitting next to Jason, looking at him sleeping and smiling, feeding him by the tube, then trying to breastfeed him; it was tough. Jason was not strong enough to take the breast properly so we had to bottle feed him as well. He would take an entire hour to drink eighty millilitres of milk. The doctors were also worried because his oxygen levels dropped and he choked sometimes while feeding, falling asleep most of the time. We weighed him every two days to make sure he was growing. Just gaining a few grams was a victory; growing a few millimetres was relieving. John joined me after he was done at work and we took turns bathing him. It was our little ritual; the few cares allowing us to touch him were unbelievably pleasurable. We were looking forward to every little moment we could spend close to him.

After a month, I started to get desperate. I wanted him home with us. I couldn't stand the hospital anymore. It was too hard emotionally. John and I were overtired, going back home after 9 pm every night, eating quickly, poorly, and looking at the empty crib in our bedroom. Jason was out of the incubator but he had to feed properly in order to get out of the hospital. Unfortunately, we still had to finish most of his feeds by giving him the milk through the tube because he was exhausted. Every night, we had to leave him after the bedtime routine; the last feed, the last cuddle, the last kiss. Every night, it was getting harder for me. When a baby was out of the NICU, the next baby would get his spot, one crib closer to the exit. Finally, it was our turn. Jason was moved to the crib the closest to the exit door. We were next. We were so excited and I tried to make sure everything was ready for him at home, including us. But Jason wasn't feeding properly yet and we had to wait another three weeks before finally being given permission to take him home.

On July 12, 2014, after fifty-two days in NICU, we finally left the hospital with our baby. We put Jason in his baby car seat, still too big for him, and we drove him home. That day was one of the happiest of my life. He was still very small but he was beautiful and healthy. I showed him around the flat and explained where his bed was and how things would go from there. I told him how glad we were to be finally reunited, all together, as a family.

3

It's October 8, 2015 and I finally had my biopsy today. It took me a while because I had to wait two weeks to see the obstetrician—who said it was perfectly fine to do a biopsy, even pregnant—but requested a referral from my GP. So I had to go to my GP again to receive the referral and finally book the bloody biopsy. It took a full month but I've done it. It was painful but nothing compared to the fear I had. I looked at the big needle entering this now massive lump and got my tissues out. Two biopsies later I was out. The surgeon wants to see me next Thursday, maybe earlier if needed. Don't ask me what it means, I don't want to know.

I'm spending the weekend filled with anxiety. I'll have to go to work on Monday hoping that everything's going to be alright. And it is…until I receive a phone call, at around 10 am. It's the surgeon's receptionist; the surgeon wants to see me this afternoon at 3 pm. I'm in shock. What does it mean? He's got bad news? I call John and ask him to be at the appointment with me. I'm afraid something is wrong and I don't have the strength to go by myself. I'm scared to death.

While waiting to leave the office for my appointment, I talk to Stéphanie again. My thoughts are driving me mad and I need to vent to someone. She's scared for me; we both hope it's going to be fine. We will cry when we know and hopefully they will be tears of relief. I advise my boss that I have to finish early today and I leave the office after lunch. I pick up John at home and we walk together to the surgeon's private hospital suite.

The wait feels like forever. I'm touching my belly, praying it's going to be fine, holding onto my baby to compose myself. While waiting, John tries to make me laugh to divert me from thinking about what's happening next. The surgeon is a breast and thyroid surgeon at St. George's Hospital. After a couple of ladies, we are next.

"Mrs. Burton?" the doctor asks.

"Yes," I answer anxiously.

"You can come in now." He invites us to follow him.

"So we've got the results of your biopsies," he says, closing his office door behind us.

"And? It's bad...Isn't it?" I ask.

"I'm afraid so. You have melanoma."

"Melanoma?" I'm a bit confused as I'm not sure it's cancer. I look at John who's holding my hand tightly.

"Yes, it's a very aggressive skin cancer. And you're unfortunately at stage three, at least. Apparently, there's no primary cause. I'm sorry."

I turn towards John, my lips clamped tightly together in speechless terror. I feel tears slowly coming up in my eyes but I don't let them out. I want to stay as focused as possible. I want to make sure I understand everything. I just let a few gasps out and try to swallow the ball forming in my throat with much difficulty. I'm wiping the stray tears away as John tightens both my hands in his. "And the baby? Is the baby okay?" I asked worried.

"Yes, the baby should be okay. Usually the placenta protects the baby. But you will have to deliver it as soon as possible so we can determine your stage and start a treatment. I'm going to refer you to a very good surgeon, specialising in melanoma, at the Melanoma Medical Centre."

"But we wanted this baby to go full term. My son was already premature; we tried so hard to keep this baby inside me..." Again, I was looking at John who was now in frozen mode.

"I understand but melanoma is very aggressive and you need to get treatment as soon as possible. So, next time you see your obstetrician you'll have to tell her and start organising the birth. Do you have any questions?"

"No." I just want to get out of here, fast.

"So, here are the details of the surgeon I'm referring you to. My receptionist will organise an appointment with him for next week. Meanwhile, don't hesitate to contact me if you have any questions." He hands me the surgeon's business card.

"Thank you."

He opens the door and we leave his office. I'm paying the receptionist and she lets me know the details of my appointment with the other surgeon. John and I leave the private suite in silence, shocked, like someone just died in front of us. It was me. I'm dying. A new life is growing inside me and I may not be there for her or him. After a few steps in the hospital corridor, we stop and fall into each other harms to cry like we never did before. The world around us is falling apart and we are devastated. We held onto these tears for what seemed an eternity, trying to stay composed in front of the specialist but now we're exorcising the fears and the shock out of our systems, freeing all the tensions. We're out of breath, not able to move anymore. The weight of the news is so heavy, the consequences so big. I can die in the next few weeks. My life is at stake and so is my family. All I ever wanted is right in front of me now and it may be taken away from me. It's so surreal and confusing.

I ask my husband again, "Melanoma is cancer, right?" He just nods and we cry again so hard, holding each other, leaning onto each other to avoid falling. Devastated. Powerless. An excruciating pain in my guts is trying to come out of my mouth, but I choke and I'm overflowing with tears, unable to control myself anymore, I let everything out. I'm relieving all the fear, the pain, the extreme sadness and realise that what I thought impossible just became possible. It's happening to me.

So that's how it feels to be told "you have cancer." I would never have imagined that. Your entire world is shaken; everything around you seems so superficial. People live their life and you're dying, inside and out. You don't look sick but you're dying and nobody can see it. And you don't know when it's going to happen. Nobody can imagine what is happening in your head. It's like you've got a deadline, literately. You feel under pressure for time and a lot of questions come through your mind. I feel terrible for my family; I don't want to let them down. Two babies are hard to handle. I need to stay and help John, otherwise it's going to be so hard on him. Now that I have so much to live for, I hope I will have time to enjoy them.

When we arrive at home, I ask John for one night of crying, one night to be able to feel sorry for myself before trying to have positive thoughts tomorrow. Because I know how he is; he doesn't believe that feeling sorry for yourself helps anyhow so, after the loss of our first baby and when I came home without Jason the first night, he didn't let me cry long. But tonight, I need it. I ask him to understand

and somewhere I think he needs it too. So we're crying together after putting Jason to bed. We don't want him to worry or wonder what's wrong with mummy and daddy. I let it all out. I empty myself of the pain and sorrows. I completely let myself go and I'm going down. I reach the deepest darkness of thoughts possible.

I'm overwhelmed by the worst fate scenarios possible. I bring myself so deeply down that I can feel how dying could be nearly relieving. And when I reach the darkest edges of my mind, I can feel the light within me, all the things that I am not ready to lose shining brightly through the darkness. I think about all the things that I achieved since I was born, all the obstacles I had in my whole life, now shortened. If I survived all this and got stronger because of it, then it was for this very moment. It was for me to be strong enough now to fight this shit. I won't die without a fierce fight. John, my kids, my sister and parents, they need me. I can't let them down, not now.

I'm scared. I'm feeling guilty for abandoning my family, for leaving them behind me one day, too early. I don't want that. I can't believe it's happening to me. I don't have my family here and I came here so my children could have a better future. I don't want them to live without their mum. Somehow I lost mine too early and now that I'm living so far away from my parents, it's rough enough; I don't want that for my children. I want to be there for them and for their own children. I don't want to leave John with two babies to raise; he's got enough trouble to take care of one for a few hours, so two for a lifetime. No way would I do that to him. He needs me; they need me. I have to survive this beast.

★★★

During childhood, life was all pink and happy. I guess children have a great ability to look at the positive side of things. I had a happy childhood, a lucky one too. I always had food on the table and even though my parents didn't want me to wear brands—a waste of money for a kid growing up—I had clean and proper clothes on. I've always been a good student and loved school. I used to share all my time with my twin sister and we were inseparable. We didn't bother talking to the rest of the world until we were two years old, probably because life together was pretty good and we didn't need anybody else. My twin, Lali, has been my half since our conception and even with the distance between us, we stayed close and couldn't live without one another. So, sharing my childhood with her, my best friend and confidante, I didn't really need to develop my social life very much and I was living for my marks and to make my parents proud of me.

Lali and I loved each other like ourselves but we were quite different besides being identical twins. She was creative and I was more analytical. I performed very well at school when she didn't seem really interested. We were very competitive and being compared all the time didn't help, so my parents decided to place us in separate classrooms after two years at school because the competition had a very negative impact on us. Still, we were the best accomplices at all times. School was for learning; outside, it was for us and family.

I've always been a very driven person, so I spent the first thirteen years of my life learning and trying to always be the best in class. It was all about books and even the small things in life were about getting some learning out of it. I also enjoyed holidays, spending all my summers in a holiday camp managed by the company my dad was working for as an engineer. Since I was four years old, every July, I used to go somewhere in France, hours away from home by bus, with my sister. It was hard at the beginning being without Mum and Dad, but I had my sister and we loved spending time riding bikes or ponies, climbing or just playing games with the other kids. They were the same kids, year after year, sons and daughters of Dad's workmates. Growing up, I was looking forward to this time of adventures and independence.

I stopped going there when I was fourteen. I was going to secondary school then and felt like I was getting too old for it. So my parents thought it would be good for me to improve my English skills by going to London and living with an English family for a month. Lali and I went there and spent July 1995 with a very nice couple and their dog, going to English classes in the morning and spending the afternoon visiting the big city. We loved it so much that we did it again the year after, this time in two separate families and without lessons. We visited every inch of the capital, immersed into the English culture for two weeks. It was such an adventure and such a change. Different country, different money, different language, different architecture, different shops, and different way of life. We spent the third and final week apart as I had to follow my family on a weird holiday in Clacton-On-Sea. We lived in the caravan they owned in the local caravan park. Their twelve-year-old daughter was gambling while her mum was playing bingo all day, every day. I didn't understand how she could waste all the money she had been saving all year long, just for fun. But these two episodes of London getaway gave me the taste for adventure and new horizons.

So overall, my childhood was pretty good, lucky even. We were a close family, spending winter holidays skiing for a week together and usually the first two weeks of August in the Alps, hiking together. Mum was the affectionate one and Dad was the teacher. Sandra, my big sister, was kind of a loner and Lali and I were the inseparable pair. But all together we had great times and even if the daily routine was often full of arguments, we had lots of love for each other.

I had my first crush at summer camp, Thibault. He was a very confident boy with dark hair and a pretty face, always ready to lead the other boys into some kind of game. But I didn't know that you had to ask someone to go out on a date with you. I didn't even know what going out meant. I missed the boat with him and a very popular girl asked him out first and he accepted. I was shocked when he said to me that he would have accepted if I had asked first…but I thought these things happened naturally, like in the movies. Anyway, I learnt my lesson and it was my first step in understanding men. First lesson: they are weak. It took me two more years to actually date someone. I think I was about five years old when I realised that I wanted to find the One, get married and become a mum. And since that day, I never stopped looking for the One. I had two objectives in my life: be a successful businesswoman and find Prince Charming.

It was 1995 and I was at the end of secondary school. I was raised with no real knowledge of fashion style and I was a sort of tomboy up until then. I was dressing up casually, with no brand names and no real effort. I wasn't wearing any makeup either (back then, not many girls would wear makeup at fourteen anyway). I was wearing glasses (the not-so-pretty ones), I was first in my class (not so cool at the time), I had a twin sister (it was hard when you get compared all the time), my mum was working in the same secondary school I was, and we were living the flat above the school building as it was part of her salary package. Let's just say, I didn't have it easy with my schoolmates.

I wasn't popular. I didn't even understand what the point of popularity was and I focused on my studies. I didn't know what I wanted to become and I was projecting myself into the future only for a couple of weeks ahead. However, I decided to change my look because I realised that my appearance mattered if I wanted to get some positive attention. I begged my mum to get me contacts instead of glasses and she gave up after a month of resistance and a devastating letter to explain how I would feel so much better in my skin without the glasses. But after a few re-looking lessons from my best friend Mélodie, I was getting a bit more confidence. André, a tall bloke with dark hair and brown eyes, was already in my classroom that year, but we started dating only the year after. He was all my first times: first kiss, first date, first pubs, first clubbing, first intimacy, but really first love. I felt lucky to have found love young because the nearly four years I spent with him shaped the woman I became.

When I think about it, I couldn't be that bad because at least eight boys asked me out before he did. But I respected my mum's rule about no dating; I was too young. Until one day, André, who I really liked, asked me out. And this time, there was no way I was going to answer with, "sorry, mum doesn't want me to." I didn't want to lie and I still can't believe I was actually giving this answer when the boys I liked asked me out. You can imagine their faces and their laughter when they heard my excuse. Anyway, the day André asked me out, I answered in the affirmative. For him, I justified my rebellion and didn't tell my mum straight away. Until two weeks later, when mum was cooking us some beef patties for lunch.

"You know you said I couldn't date anyone because I'm too young? I'm fourteen now and some of my friends have been dating since they were like twelve years old. I mean, if someone asks me out now, can I say yes if I want to?" I was pretending that it didn't happen yet and just checking on the status of this rule.

"Are you dating someone?" she smiled with surprise.

"Maybe…and if I was, would you be mad at me?" I hesitated.

"You're still young; that won't last anyway," she said, clearly amused.

"Yeah, right," I said, trying to stay neutral. "But it's not because I'm young that it won't last. I don't think my age has got anything to do with it."

Somehow she gave me the green light but I was upset she didn't realise how important it was for me. It was only a couple of weeks I was dating André and I was very much into him already. I was so proud it was mutual and I was so happy he asked me out. Later that day, André called on the home phone and, even if I rushed to get it, my mum took the call first. We didn't have any mobile phone then and there was no such a thing as privacy for us teenagers.

"Hello?" She said with a smile, hearing obviously André asking for me. "It's for you...it's a boy," she said, clearly excited for me but with a question in her voice.

"Thanks Mum," I replied trying to stay neutral. I had a quick chat with him about our plans for the afternoon and hung up the phone.

"Who was he?" Mum questioned.

"It was André." I answered.

"André who? Is that your boyfriend?" She asked with way too much enthusiasm.

"André Du Chateau and yes, he is. Now, stop questioning me." I felt embarrassed.

"Oh, he's a noble?" She asked surprised.

"No, I don't think so, but who cares really. What kind of question is it anyway?" I stopped the conversation and started to get ready for my date.

And she was wrong, finally. It lasted. The more we spent time together, the more I thought we were meant to be, we understood each other so well; we were happy and in love. After a first kiss sealed at a girlfriend's party, weeks and then months went by, going out at the movies first, then cafés, fuss ball, then pool, and after a couple of years, it was clubs, car trips, and weekends in the country. We were at the end of high school already. We stayed side by side all these years, even becoming a popular couple without asking for it. We were the record-breaking couple in terms of our relationship lasting and the other teenagers were inspired but envious somehow. We used to love talking about anything and everything, about life and the world, about society and relationships and about our plans for the future. He was a sort of revenge on the insecure child I used to be; with him, I was becoming a woman, still focused on my studies, but also socially respected and even popular. I finally had a proper social life. But the most important lesson was that I could finally understand a man by observing his behaviour closely. I was figuring out what was going on in his head as I witnessed the transformation of a boy into an adult.

André was my age. He was sporty and passionate about squash. He was a below-average student but a funny guy and an opinion leader. He had two brothers, fourteen and ten years older than him, which gave him some advantages when it came to intimacy. We were telling each other everything; we were loyal and crazy in love. Yet, my twin was part of our life and he knew how important she was for me. After all, we knew each other since we were seven years old, as we started school together, all in the same classroom. We only got separated because my family moved to another suburb two years later. After all these years of social difficulties, I was finally happy. And my grades were fantastic too.

André was also my boyfriend when my life took a dramatic turn. So far, life was pink, happy, like in a fairy tale. Happy family, great grades and love...the future was looking good for me. But on June 6, 1997, pink changed to black when I was pushed into the cruel reality. Everything around me started to turn into darkness and I wasn't prepared at all. So far, I had managed to spend my life without any trouble and my vision of the world was pretty naïve. I was living in a Walt Disney movie when everybody else was living in reality.

I was the only one of my family to wake up that morning to go to high school for a math class and it was an exam day. As always, I was prepared but I decided to wake up a bit earlier so I could check my notes before leaving home. I went to the toilet and I was shocked by the sight of my mum lying on the floor.

"Mum? What are you doing?" I asked, worried. She wasn't answering, yet her eyes were open and I could tell she understood what I said. "Mum? Are you okay? Let me help you..." I tried to lift her up but her body was as heavy as a dead body. It was too hard; I needed help. "Don't worry, I'll get Dad. Stay awake." I went to my parents' bedroom to wake up my dad. We weren't allowed to wake him up on a day he could actually sleep but I rushed to his bedside to ask him for help.

"Dad?" I tried to wake him up calmly. "Dad, I'm sorry to wake you up but I really need your help now. Mum is on the floor."

"What?" My dad asked, rousing from sleep.

"Mum is lying on the floor. I've tried to get her up but she's super heavy. I can't do it by myself, it's too hard, you need to come."

"Is she conscious?" he asked while following me.

"Look, her eyes are open. She's conscious but she doesn't answer..." I explained reaching the bathroom.

"Okay, let's bring her to our bed." And we moved her and placed her on her side of the bed.

"Do you want some water?" he asked her but she wasn't answering.

"We need to call the firemen, Dad." In France, they are the best ones to call in case of medical emergency.

"No, that's okay. Go to school, I'll take care of her," my dad said firmly.

"But Dad...Are you sure? I can stay. I'm worried for Mum."

"That's fine, get ready and go. You'll be back soon anyway." He was right; I only had class for three hours and I would be back for lunch.

"Please call the firemen, Dad," I urged him.

"I will call SOS doctors," he said to reassure me. They were a sort of emergency GPs.

I was worried because my dad didn't seem too anxious and wasn't very quick to call a doctor. He didn't like doctors. The further away he could be from them, the better. I wasn't like that, and looking at my mum, I knew something wasn't right and we had to do something fast. But I listened to my dad and left for school. After a bad diagnosis from the SOS doctors, two hours later, my dad called our GP who rushed them to the Emergency Services of our local hospital. She was the victim of a stroke. Sometimes, I wonder if I shouldn't have stayed that day, if I did well listening to my dad.

I left overwhelmed not knowing what dad was doing. André was waiting for me downstairs with my daily breakfast, some Nutella pancakes his mum cooked for us. I wasn't hungry. I told him what I just witnessed and he tried to comfort me while we were walking to high school.

This tragic episode changed us—my sisters, my parents, and I— as individuals and as a family forever. From one day to the next, at sixteen, I became a mum, transferring from childhood to adulthood in only a couple of months. I had no choice. With Mum spending more than eight months in hospitals, not being able to talk, the right side of her body disabled, my family balance was shattered. Mum wasn't there anymore to hold us together and there wasn't such a thing as family after that. At this point of my life, my dad was only a banker for the misunderstood teenager I was, interacting with me just to give me my pocket money every month, never really talking to me except to ask about my grades or help with my homework. He didn't arrange anything as he was visiting mum after work and never used to come home before 9.30pm anymore. I felt like my big sister Sandra was trying to replace Mum and Lali shared the same feeling, which got them into so many arguments. Sandra was spending her time studying in a nearby city, seeing her boyfriend Rémi at night or helping me with the home chores before leaving again on the weekends to be with him. I was feeling trapped in the house and alone. I didn't see my mum or my dad very much anymore. My big sister was always with her boyfriend and my twin, Lali, was too sad to accept what was happening and preferred going out with her mates and the Swiss Italian boyfriend she was seeing at the time. Nothing was the same anymore; I was discovering the dark side of reality.

André and I didn't have much time together anymore as it was hard to get away from chores and homework. I felt lonely, even if I was going out with my friends. I felt misunderstood and guilty. I even wondered if it wouldn't have been easier if Mum died that day; life was so painful since her hospitalisation. André didn't understand how hard it was for me and didn't help the tragedy of the situation by breaking up with me, a few months before our high school exams.

After nearly four years together, in April 1999, he drove me to our favourite beach and told me that it was over. He was crying so much that I nearly felt sorry for him and didn't quite get why he was breaking up with me if that made him sad. A very nice touch by the way, since I wasn't able to go there anymore without thinking about that day. *Note for you guys, never break up in a nice place if you care about your future ex.*

Mum was still living at the hospital then and I was overwhelmed by sadness, studies, and chores. Every night, I was crying like crazy in the shower so no one could hear me. I felt stupid and hopeless. It was even worse once I realised he was a cheater. I didn't know it at first, but six months after our breakup, a common friend told me that he slept with another girl at his place, after planning the thing for weeks. Meanwhile, I was studying and I didn't see anything coming. He wasn't even brave enough to tell me the truth. After this episode, I definitely had trust issues with pretty much all my boyfriends. Still, he was the only guy I dated who knew my mum before and after her stroke.

I was missing Mum. I wished I could talk to her, but every time I visited her at the hospital and in intensive care at first, I couldn't really communicate with her. I was talking to her, telling her about school but I never really got any answers because she couldn't talk anymore. One day, I saw her about to eat one of her anti-wrinkles cream and I figured out she was in a very bad shape. She wasn't the same anymore. She wasn't the positive, tough, active, and strong woman I used to know anymore; she seemed weak, distressed, and sad. I started to confront her; I didn't accept the sad reality anymore. I wanted her to make efforts, stop feeling sorry for herself all the time. She had to fight for us. We tried to give her a paper so she could write some answers with her left hand but it was difficult for her, especially since she was right-handed. With time, she started to talk again, like a kid would start talking, the brain finding other ways to reconnect the synapses. Walking was harder and she never recovered her right arm. These eight months without my mum at home were distressing and I had to confront my dad for the first time in my life.

Since I was born, Dad was the "Sunday guy." We never really did anything together except for Sundays and holidays. Growing up, he wouldn't accept me having a boyfriend, always thinking I was too young. With Dad, it was all about school, grades, work, and learning, because everything must be educational—"No fun Dad." And I was trying hard all the time to be the boy he never had, spending years of my childhood perfecting my rock climbing or my soccer skills. I wanted him to be proud of me so I was working hard to get good marks at school, then in high school, but he never told me that he was. It wasn't until I passed Business School that he said he had always been proud of me, but the most important thing was for me to be proud of myself. Note for dads: tell your kids you're proud of them; don't wait twenty years. I always felt that with Dad, the answer would always be "no," regardless of what I asked. But that time, I wouldn't take a no for an answer. I would tell him how I was feeling, even if I wondered if he was sensitive enough to get it. I was about to go to bed and I came to the lounge room to say goodnight. He was doing his daily crosswords in the newspaper.

"Dad?" I asked a bit shy.

"Yes," he answered undisturbed, head down in the paper.

"Can I talk to you please?"

"Yes." Finally, he looked up at me.

"We need to talk about what's happening..." I said seriously while I took a seat in the chair next to him.

"What's going on?" he replied, stopping his game and moving the newspaper away from him.

"I am not sure you're going to like what I'm about to say. But it's important to me and I really need you to understand because we can't continue like this. It's not sustainable for me." I was trying to keep my calm and talk like the sixteen-year-old adult I was.

"Well, tell me and we'll see then," he said, almost like a challenge.

"You know, I understand that the situation is very hard for you too, mum being your wife. It must be awful going through this. You nearly lost her and now she's so different. But as painful as it is for you, it's hard for me and my sisters too. It's our mum. She's always been there for us; she always used to talk to us and now we don't have anyone to talk to and we're growing up too. I mean, we're teenagers. Look I don't ask you to talk about all these girl things, that's okay. I can manage by myself, but you need to be a dad."

"But I am your dad. I am here." He acted like he didn't understand what I meant.

"I'm sorry, you're not here. It's not because you're here that you're with us...and you come home late and don't even thank us for dinner. We cook, we clean, we do everything in the house to help you and when you come home, you barely talk and most of the time we are already in bed. I mean, I am happy to help but I want you to understand that this situation is painful for us too. We didn't ask for that. We have to do things that most sixteen-year-olds don't have to do and I'm sad to see what's happening to our family too. Sandra is always with Rémi, Lali is never here anymore, and neither are you. And I am the one trying to keep up the place and bring us back together. We barely know each other and you're more a banker than anything else to me at the moment. Look, I just want you to be my dad okay?" I was now in tears. These words required so much strength. Saying that to my dad was excruciating.

He was trying to swallow his tears. It was the real first conversation we ever had and I had been harsh on him. But I needed him more than ever and if I wanted things to change between us, it had to be said.

"I understand. I will try to do better. But you know, you can talk to me anytime," he said gently.

"Can you give me a hug?" I asked, nearly begging.

"Of course I can." And we fell into each other's arms, crying like we were relieved of all the stress and anxiety accumulated over the past few months. I can see now that this conversation actually changed everything. Over time, and as we had more open conversations, we learnt to know each other better and we managed to develop a healthy and close relationship as father and daughter.

Mum wanted to come back home instead of going to a specialised rehabilitation centre that could have helped her get better faster. She was the administrative officer of my secondary school and had a flat above it as one of the benefits of her position. Since her stroke, she was on sick leave and because it was a very damaging condition for her, she couldn't go back to work and had to take an early retirement. The flat wasn't set up for someone with a disability, and we had to move back to the apartment my parents bought a few years before, after our tenants moved out. She was back home after so many months away. I was happy to have her close to me but so upset to see that she was changed forever into another woman.

She was constantly feeling sorry for herself and unable to pronounce a sentence. She was barely walking and forgot all rules of good behaviour when interacting with others. The brain connections were slow to repair and she appeared to me like a toddler, learning to speak, to walk, to count again but also to behave socially. And I was now the mum, trying to help her with everything. She was like a young kid in an adult body. Still, she kept her memory. I wanted to see the mum she was again. Now that I was old enough, we could have been shopping together, like my girlfriends were doing with their mums. She could have helped me with my Spanish lessons as she had a degree in this language; but she could barely speak French and remembered only a few Spanish words that she was placing sometimes in the middle of French sentences. I was angry at her because I had to teach her everything again—to write with her left hand, to pronounce words properly, to put the correct word on what she wanted to describe, to recover the rules of calculations, recognise and name numbers, and simply to walk, moving one foot in front of the other. But what annoyed me the most was that she didn't seem to understand anything I said and we had trouble communicating.

4

On the same night, after the surgeon appointment, I decide to tell my family I have cancer. It's delicate and very difficult. I call my sister first. She's devastated, saddened, and horrified. She's also scared it can happen to her now, since we're twins, but I reassure her, it's apparently not genetic. I also tell Mum and Dad, who weirdly take the news very well and don't seem to worry at all. Denial maybe? I'm not sure but somehow I'm sad they don't reflect the gravity of the situation and how badly it's affecting me and my family. I hold onto my tears when I let them know, trying to stay strong and practical to protect them. Maybe that's why they're not freaking out…or maybe they are trying to protect me. Now that this is happening, I actually wonder how I'm going to do this without them, being so far away. I wish they could be here, by my side. I wish I could hug my sister and cry in her arms.

I remember why I came to Australia five years ago, leaving them behind. I wanted my life to change when I left France and I changed every single aspect of it in less than a year. This country called to me for a very long time and I finally flew the twenty thousand kilometres that separated me from the land of opportunity. Something I can't explain was attracting me. For more than seven years I was trying to find a way to come or maybe just the courage but every time I was thinking of leaving everything behind and go, I found a good reason not to; if it wasn't for my family, my grandma, my job, I was staying for a boyfriend. Until the day I ran out of excuses. I didn't have any boyfriend, I didn't have the job I wanted, and I was close to thirty years old. It was time, it was my time to be selfish and live my dreams.

Back in March 2010, I had a three-month contract selling advertising for a monthly magazine in German and English distributed on the French Rivera and overseas. This sales job saved me from depression but it also made me realise how much I wanted my life to change. I was nearly thirty and dreaming of a different life; mine was unsatisfying and heavy. I was still looking for a marketing job after eight months of unemployment, struggling to pay my bills and the rent of my studio apartment. I was going to Paris every month to attend interviews. I was geographically flexible, ready to move and get a lower salary package. The problem was that I wanted a job in marketing but companies didn't trust in the future anymore; there weren't many head offices and most of them had already their marketing team, composed of one or two people at most. After passing a Bachelor Honours of Business and Administration and achieving so much to give myself the keys to success, I felt like I hit a brick wall. Also, I was still searching for the One Love, now definitely late for our date. Maybe was he overseas? Maybe he wanted to stay in his country. If he couldn't find me, I would have to travel and find him myself.

At the office, everyone was living their normal day-to-day life, nothing interfering with their routine, comfortable and so predictable. I found it depressing. I was dreaming of so many things…I wanted to achieve great things, being adventurous, feeling useful, I wanted to use my life for something bigger. I didn't want to be like anybody else…I had to start over. People at work were German or English and spoke in their own language; I was the only French. That triggered me. I realised how much I was thirsty for new cultures, new ways of life. I felt trapped in my small country, sinking in its own too-conventional and conservative ways of doing everything. I was desperate to open my mind to new horizons. I wasn't the problem anymore. France was my problem. I loved my country, its food, its culture, and its beautiful landscapes, but on an economic point of view, some work had to be done. On top of feeling trapped in my own country, I didn't want to be stuck in a routine yet. Just the thought of a daily routine made of: wake up, go to work, come home, eat, sleep and back to work again…every day, one day after another…having kids—if one day Mr. Right finally showed up—and doing it all again, until I die…made me sick. I had to do something about it right now as I wasn't getting any younger. But this "normal" way of life that I was raised into, just like anyone else, was trying to catch me from every corner.

I didn't want to be like everyone else. I wanted to see the world; I didn't want to stay trapped in my hometown forever. I had enough of feeling that my life was managed by those surrounding me—my family, my twin sister, and my parents. They wanted the best for me but didn't realise that the way they were trying to help was bringing me down. I was feeling like a marionette following their plan for my own life. I was playing nicely along so far, always asking for their recognition, their approval, their praise, but feeling like I was never good enough and on top of that, I was always there for everyone else, putting them first. I looked around and noticed that everyone was settling down and moving forward with their lives, their career, their partners, getting married, having kids, everyone but me. With time, the heavy weight of my situation started to become a burden, slowing me down day after day. Now, I wanted to free myself from it.

I was miserable and felt like nothing retained me on this dying planet anymore. I might as well die too. I didn't have anything worth staying alive for...Until I figured out that I didn't realise any of my dreams. I couldn't die without doing all the things that I ever wanted to do or at least the ones I could afford. If I really wanted to die, I could still die later. Now was the time to make my biggest dreams come true in order to die peacefully, with no regrets. After three months selling advertising, my contract was over. I told my boss that I didn't want to pursue this job because I had other projects in mind. My decision was made. I would leave. My life was going to change and I wasn't scared, just a bit anxious and very excited. It was my last day at work; I was leaving the magazine and turning the page over. I cleaned my desk and closed my files in order to leave the job completed. I was free for my last summer in France and I would leave the country before the end of the year. After a couple of days, my paperwork was sorted and my passport renewed.

I started my bucket list. Skydiving was the first dream to tick off for my 29th birthday, then I would explore the world. My parents were about to offer me the sky, its immensity, its beauty, and the feeling of being smaller in the universe on my birthday. I was finally about to realise one of my teenage dreams: jumping from a plane from four thousand metres high. And it was so exciting. It was even better than when I went for my first concert, to see the epic U2 on my 25th birthday with my twin sister. It was a small step to start making my biggest dreams come true. I was about to take back the control of my life, jump into space to start filling up my existence with decisions made by me. I would throw myself into a new world, a new life that I was choosing, overriding my past failures. It was a small symbol for a big start over. A little death for a new life. These four thousand metres between me and the ground were the distance between me and the life I was dreaming of. Every single metre flown would be a step closer to my forever goal—a happy life.

I felt like I had spent my entire life observing other people's adventures. But I was about to truly start living now, to enter my body and to be reborn. After that, I could enjoy the rest of my life, achieving what I had never done. After all this time taking care of others, watching over other people's lives, I forgot myself. I was so involved in helping others with their problems, that they became mine. I forgot my own issues, my own desires, and finally my own life. It was time to live for myself, even if it was easier said than done. I had to be alone, in a country where nobody knew me or my past, so I could build a new future, my own future.

I had an entire year of thinking and questioning. I got sad but I also understood the deep mechanisms of my personality. I got to know myself better, my faults, my qualities, my behaviours, and reactions and why I was the way I was. I had high expectations for myself; I had to follow the principles, beliefs, and values inherited from my family. I liked my soul. I just had to become the person I was dreaming of becoming in this world—an accomplished woman with a career and a love life, married with kids one day, blooming in all aspects that society asked us to be invested in. I had the foundations, solid enough to succeed in getting there. Moving away seemed to be inevitable. I was done here.

Unfortunately, skydiving was postponed by three days, so I didn't dive for my birthday. But I still spent it with my mum and dad. Despite the stormy weather and the bad news, we had a good day. I smiled and laughed with them. We were a family and most of all, happy to be together, knowing each other so well. My mum and I exchanged smiley stares while Dad was showing us the photos of their last holidays; his dad used to do that too and we would all fall asleep on his lounge. My dad was mimicking and using his body language to talk to me while screaming on the phone to my grandma so she could hear. And finally that was the most important for me: we loved each other and we demonstrated it to each other, sometimes in awkward ways but love was there. If I was to live overseas, I would definitely miss them.

The night before the jump, my friend Nicolas picked me up and brought me back to his place where we talked about everything and anything before he started asking me about my future plans and refreshing my memory with Australia. He was there for three months the year before and knew it was my dream for the past seven years. As we talked about my bucket list, skydiving being on top, Australia was second in line.

"So if you're not sure about going to the United States, are you sure you want to go to Paris? Paris, again, France, still, same streets, same mentality, that won't provide you with a real change..." He asked concerned.

"I know. Look, my family wants me to have a job before I leave so I don't have many options really. My internship in the United States doesn't seem to be happening anytime soon and I've got nothing else. I wanted to go overseas so badly, improve my English, discover new horizons, new cultures. I would like to go far away from here, very far away from everything I know, from my past. Everything here reminds me of my past. I am so over this. I want to change air; I don't want to see France anymore, same negative mentality, same politics, same economic crisis and same bull shit day after day."

"Why don't you go to Australia then? It's your dream since like forever."

"I know right? I thought about it a lot lately. I think I just tried to convince myself that my family is right, that I should settle and try to find a proper job. But deep down I'm boiling. I want to free myself, I don't really care if nothing is sure beforehand. A bit of spontaneity won't kill me. But it's scary for them; it's so far away too...I love it," I replied excitedly.

"Ha-ha, it's such a great country. You're going to love it for sure." He was laughing now.

"And I had an online chat with one of my friends who lives in Melbourne with his wife yesterday; one of his friends is the president of the French Alliance there; it could be helpful. And I've got a Bachelor of Business from La Trobe Bendigo. Maybe I could ask them some help once I'm there..."

"Go then, just go... What is stopping you? You've got a diploma from an Australian University, you even know some people there. What are you waiting for this time?" He was so obviously excited for me.

"Yes, I know right." I was laughing with excitement too. "After all, except for my family, nothing is really in my way this time around. I mean, I always had a boyfriend, or my mum's health, or my grandma, or a job getting in the way of me doing this for the past seven years. Today I've got nothing stopping me and nothing to lose really. I should do it; you're right."

He showed me his postcards of the faraway country, telling me stories and things he experienced there. Listening to him reminded me of how much I wanted to go somewhere else, to experience new things with people who knew nothing about me or my past. I was seduced by the idea that I could start over, be like brand new once I arrived. It was nearly midnight and I had to go if I wanted to be fresh the next day because I had to wake up early for my jump. Tomorrow, I would make my decision as soon as I landed on Earth again, after travelling four thousand metres, including a free fall of two thousand five hundred meters at two hundred kilometres an hour. After that, for sure, I would know and my new life could start.

The next day, my alarm rang at 8 am, waking me up slowly with one of Pink's songs. I smiled for the first time in a very long time, thinking of the day I was about to live. It was the third day of my thirtieth year on this planet and everything was going to be different after what I was about to experience. Because, for sure, after such an adventure, I would be transformed and I promised to myself to be finally happy and live every day to the fullest, without worrying about what people would think about my decisions. I rushed under a relaxing shower, put on a pair of jeans and a printed T-shirt of Mickey—it was a fun day after all—before finishing my bag. I also packed a lighter outfit and a pair of flip-flops because it was 35°C outside, the day would be very hot and I didn't want to sweat during our picnic but enjoy the hours after my jump comfortably.

My dad finished packing everything into the cooler and we were ready to go. I was happy, but less enthusiastic that the first time because I was scared the jump may be postponed again, even if the weather was supposed to be fine for it. We arrived at 10.30am at jump base in Le Luc. The wide plain was surrounded by mountains like an arena, offering the promise of a wonderful view once I would be high in the sky. On site, the mood was relaxed and parachutists were laughing together while having a coffee at the local cafe. It was a beautiful warm day and I felt the adrenalin in the air. We looked for the man in charge of my skydiving to check when I will jump. A tall, slightly bold, man in his forties welcomed us.

"Hi guys, I'm Damien, I will be one of Lucie's instructors today," he said with a smile.

"Hi, I'm Lucie; this is my mum and dad. Do you know when I'm going to jump? I think it should be soon, isn't it as it's already 11.10am." I asked wondering if I wasn't too late.

"Look, we're a bit late in the schedule, but I think you should be able to start around 12."

My mum seemed to get impatient already and we killed time with a drink at the cafe. I was looking at the guys jumping in the sky. They looked like pinheads, so high that I had trouble following the plane, big as my pinkie's nail. My god, it was so high and far. How brave was I going to be once I was up there? I would be in the sky, in the atmosphere, higher than the birds…it was exciting and terrifying. The longer I had to wait, the more excited I was getting. My time was approaching, a wonderful moment where tons of emotions would melt together deeply in my soul. Finally, I would make a new step, reach a new stage, and realise a dream. Finally, I would have a proper start in the thirtieth year of my life.

The heat was so high that it could affect the balance of the parachute and it was too dangerous to jump, so we had to wait until 4 pm and decided to go for lunch. We walked to the nearby forest and set our picnic spot close to a small creek where wild tortoises liked to rest. I felt guilty making my parents wait for so long, to fill up their entire day just for my own pleasure. I knew my mum was impatient and I felt even worse. My dad reassured me and tried to change our minds by placing the picnic on a large blanket. I went away for a minute in order to swap my pair of jeans and runners with a lighter dress and a pair of thongs. It was very warm now and I felt better that way. We were sitting peacefully in the middle of this lovely décor, savouring our delicious salads. I took advantage of a quiet moment to tell them about the idea of going to Australia later that year.

"By the way, I wanted to talk to you about my projects for autumn."

"Yes?" Dad prompted.

"Well, I put a lot of thoughts into it and as I'm still waiting to hear from this internship in the US and it doesn't seem to be going anywhere, I was thinking I could still go overseas instead of Paris. Because, after all, the real goal was to improve my English skills and get some international experience to help with future employment. So I thought I could go to Australia, like I've always wanted to..." I said neutrally, trying to show some kind of reasonable thinking.

"Yeah, I guess. Why not?" Dad replied in between bites of his salad.

"Really? You would be okay?" I couldn't help but get excited. "Because you know, I thought about it and it wouldn't cost me more than the US. I mean, I would have to pay three thousand Euros to the company providing the internship in the United States, and that doesn't include the flight ticket. For Australia, it's actually cheaper. I just have a flight ticket to purchase and once there, I can find a casual job while I'm looking for one that matches my skills and degree. Also, I would speak better English so if the US internship finally comes up, I could fly directly from there. I should be able to manage moneywise and most of all, it's my dream for so many years. You know how hard it has been lately for me and that's why I wanted to take this year for me, to realise my dreams."

"Yes, we know how it's important for you and anyway, it would be certainly better for your resume to go overseas." My dad was smiling at me. I was nicely surprised by his new enthusiasm. He must have seen how much I was suffering while trying to do things their way for so long, sacrificing what was most important for me, to do what seemed to be reasonable for them.

We started talking about this continent country, the Asian Pacific region that I studied for two years with my Bachelor's degree, its economy, all the research that I'd done for so many years on how to live there, what to expect, and the paperwork. I also told him what Nicolas and Sébastien said about this supposedly amazing country: the great culture, diversity, modernism, ecology, and the youth of this country where so much had still to be done. I was satisfied and I told him I would check the price of flight tickets before making my final decision.

After lunch, I put my pants back on and we walked back to the base to wait with a coffee. Then, I walked to the folding room to observe the parachutists working hard on packing their parachute and a professional team practicing on the acrobatic figures they would do once in the sky. It was beautiful to watch. At 4 pm, the manager decided that it was safe again to jump. This time, it was my turn and my legs started shaking slightly. I was nervous but I couldn't be happier.

"Hi, I'm Marc," a young blond guy in his thirties said.

"Hi, I'm Lucie." I returned his smile.

"I'll be your instructor and teammate for the dive; you will be attached to me in the plane and we will jump together." His confidence was palpable.

"Great. Where do we start? Are you going to teach me how we do this? I'm so excited. But a bit scared too…I mean that's a crazy fall right?" I wanted some kind of reassurance.

"I will explain everything you need to know once we are in the plane, okay?"

"It won't be too late in the plane? Shouldn't I get instructions beforehand?"

"Don't worry. I have done more than five thousand five hundred jumps. I know what I'm doing. You just have to relax and enjoy." I found him cheeky. Getting high and hooking up with a cute dude was pretty fun for me.

Marc helped me put on a full harness, to which he would attach himself once in the plane. I also got a pair of glasses, specially made for skydivers, which I would have to wear just before diving. He didn't really tighten my harness so I was still able to walk to the field where the plane would pick us up. It was time to go. I kissed my parents before joining the others on the launch area. There, Marc tightened my harness and I followed him in the plane with all the excitement and anxiety I accumulated so far. That was it! I was there, in a tiny flying bird, stuck with seven men in two square metres, but I was there, in my flesh and blood, ready to face the dizzying space of our atmosphere! I would finally discover what it felt like when every single part of you is detached from the ground, surrounded by space, by nothing! I had already jumped in the sea, from about fifteen metres above sea level, so I knew how it felt to fall in space but it never lasted more than a fraction of second, and I always landed in the water screaming and breathing again once the fall was over. The fall would last forty seconds this time around.

The plane took off and it was the first time I wasn't attached on a proper seat in a plane, this time, it was a very small plane compared to the commercial flights I was used to. I felt the turbulences like never before, I was right next to the sliding door and trying to relax by listening to the jokes the guys were making. I noticed that I was the only woman on board, except for one cameraman, here to film another tandem; I was also the only newbie to sky dive today. I was a fighter and a modern woman, not afraid of adrenalin. The mountains and the lands were getting further away from me, I could see the sea now, and the coast from Fréjus to Toulon…we were getting very high.

"At what altitude are we now, Marc?" I asked.

"Two thousands metres," Marc replied, showing me the altimeter attached to his left wrist.

"Is that all?" I said with surprise, because it already felt so high that I was shaking…so going twice the distance further up would be massive. "When are we going to be attached to each other?" I asked nearly yelling to cover the noise of the engine.

"Let's do it now. Climb on my knees like you want to sit on me, as close to me as possible," he said smiling.

"Okay." I executed the manoeuvre, a little anxious as the big jump out was coming up next. He tied me first at the bottom of the harness, right and left side, then he did the same with the top and checked that everything was fine.

"I will go first and place myself on the sliding door so I can film you when you're jumping out of the plane," said Damien, the camera operator.

"Put your glasses on," said Marc when we reached three thousand metres. "When we jump, you'll have to curve yourself, pelvis to the front while your body will be outside the plane, okay?"

"Okay." I was terrified now.

He opened the sliding door. As the wind went through the passenger compartment, I startled and let a quick scream out of my chest. I could be brave, but I was still scared. But I stayed strong and focused. Marc gave me the signal once Damien was outside, waiting for us. That was it, my turn. I was hardly breathing now. I stood up, shaking, and curved my body into space, outside and looked down... And I saw it—the height, the void, the four thousand metres between me and the ground. I was in the atmosphere of planet Earth and it was so high. I couldn't believe I was doing this; it was crazy. I really had trouble breathing now and tried to catch my breath like pregnant women do in the movies when they are delivering their babies....I was delivering me today. It was pure awesomeness.

Marc didn't warn me and propelled us out into this giant space... Wow, what a fall. At this moment, I wasn't thinking about anything anymore, I was screaming so hard with my mouth wide open. I had never screamed like that. It came out of my deepest flesh, from the bottom of every single one of my organs; it was the scream of relief. I wasn't linked to anything anymore. I was in the immensity of air, belonging only to the birds and I was above everything. I wasn't feeling my body anymore, lighter than ever, I couldn't hear myself screaming, there was nothing around me, within me. This crazy fall took my breath away, literally.

"Breathe," I said to myself. "Contemplate, enjoy every single second of this amazing moment, the hardest is behind you. Enjoy. Look, you're falling at two hundred kilometres an hour, you still have thirty-eight seconds to savour this amazing moment."

I felt Marc's hands taking mine off my harness and opening my arms. Then, he passed his hand under my chin, moving my head up so I could look and see Damien filming my fall. I felt like Superman. I wasn't screaming anymore; I was reborn. I was happy and enjoying the present moment, mindful of each second. It was the first time of my life I was actually enjoying every second passing. Carpe Diem. What a kick.

Then, we turned around for a three-sixty view. The curve of the horizon was so evident from there, I noticed the different layers of colours in the sky. I was going through the light clouds and there was no sound but the air buffeting me. I was still enjoying the magic when I saw Damien waving goodbye. I waved back at him and Marc opened our parachute. Like a powerful elastic rebound, I felt like flying once again, backward because of the breaking. What another amazing feeling. It was definitely worth making this dream come true. What a revelation!

The extreme sensations gave way to a relaxing moment. Everything was quiet and we were going down peacefully, under the parachute.

"How do you feel? How did you find it?" Marc asked.

"Oh my God. It was amazing Marc. What a crazy jump. I thought I would never manage to breathe again after such a scream... but it all went great. It was massively impressive, what a joy to live this." I was happy like never before.

"You've been great, Lucie," he reassured me. "Now how do you feel? It's nice to sail isn't it?"

"Oh yeah. Now I can really relax and enjoy the ride," I said, finally unwinding.

"Tell me; are you sick in the car?" he asked with a cheeky tone.

"No, I'm not...Why?" I was surprised by his weird question.

"Look..." He started to make us turn from right to left and gave me control of the sail, showing me how to turn, to the right, to the left, making closer turns. I was looking at the ground spinning and twirling. I was enjoying peacefully, trying to take mental pictures of every single detail of this experience, just in case it would never happen again. My head was empty, without any thoughts, only focused on living every second as they came, enjoying mindfully the beautiful present that my parents offered me. I felt so lucky, capable of facing anything. I had jumped into the depth of the sky and I was still flying high...Until I saw the ground quickly coming towards me. It was time for landing.

Marc had slowed us down heaps and in three little steps, I was standing on the mainland. Damien was already there to immortalise the moment with his video camera.

"Wow," I sighed with relief.

"That was great," Damien said giving me a high five.

"Congrats." Marc kissed me on the cheek and I hugged him, giving him back his friendly kiss.

"That's a proper kiss. What a kiss." Marc exclaimed, giving a high five to Damien. He didn't hide it and was flirting with me from the ground to the sky. I was flattered and happy.

"High five guys. High five." I ordered them, giving them my round of high five.

"How was it?" Damien asked while filming my debriefing.

"A-ma-zing." I was ecstatic.

"So tell us!" Asked Damien, like a journalist, holding his camera in front of me.

"It was incredible! Incredible! I don't know, it feels like a massive void and after to be like this, and then it's like Wow." I tried to explain laughing and mimicking my body going from standing curved in the plane to falling down into space. "It was so good. I have trouble finding my words; I still can't believe what I've just done."

"You'll come back then?" Damien asked.

"Oh yes," I answered enthusiastically, even if I knew it wouldn't be right away as my emotions were still shaken and knowing the high cost of this activity, but I had done it and really, it was a memory that would last a lifetime.

We walked back to the base, still talking about this incomparable experience and laughing. My parents were waiting for me and I rushed in their direction to kiss them as hard as possible. I thanked them for offering me so much support and making one of my dearest dreams come true. My dad was glad to hear all about my adventures and my mum was listening with a smile. We waited for Patrick to finish the montage of my video and we left once I was given the souvenir locked in a DVD. I kept a wide smile on my face until we arrived home. We packed our stuff away and we watched the video of my skydiving experience. My dad was so happy. I found him smiling and cheerful, like he hadn't been for a while. My happiness was contagious, which made me feel even better.

After dinner, I took out some pictures of the video so my sister could measure my fall and acknowledge that I had done the crazy jump myself, too. Besides, when we chatted on the phone, she was describing her skydiving with as much enthusiasm as I was describing mine and we laughed for a while, living again through all these emotions together through the device. I also told her about Australia; she thought it was a great idea because, having been there herself, she knew how this experience had transformed her in many positive ways. I went to bed satisfied with my day and promising myself that I would make my dreams come true this year. After a jump into space, nothing was scary anymore; I was free and I wanted to live. I delivered my own self today. I transformed into a butterfly and the chrysalis of my caterpillar was lying on the ground with my past. I fell asleep, with a smile still on my lips.

The next day, I started to figure out how to make the Australian dream happen. I didn't lose a minute and started writing an email to my friend Sébastien, an expatriate in Melbourne, to see what kind of advice he would have for me if I had to land in his city. I also asked some people on LinkedIn who were French or working in marketing there to give me more advice. Then, I sent an email to Leslie, the lady I was in contact with at Internabroad, the company supposed to find me an internship in the USA. After these quick updates, I checked my budget, the availability, and price of a flight to Melbourne in October, with the return a year later for the duration of my working holiday visa. A week later, I had my flight ticket to Melbourne; I was leaving on October 28, 2010.

5

I find it hard when people greet me with the casual, "how are you?" It feels like a blade in my heart and I don't know how to answer. It seems wrong to reply, "Well, not too bad considering I've got cancer." That would be awkward. So I'm keeping the secret for now, except for the delivery team at the hospital and my family. Nobody else knows. Somehow, not telling anyone feels like it's not real, that I'm just in a nightmare and I'm not ready to accept it yet. And I look healthy. I imagine people out there, walking in the streets, maybe some of them have cancer too and we don't know. We can't see it on their faces; they don't look sick. What a weird feeling to be dying from inside, betrayed by my own body.

Also, I'm upset at my parents since my sister told me that she would come to visit me anytime if we couldn't make the trip to France we planned for April, but my parents didn't even mention the eventuality of coming at all. I don't want to scream that I've got cancer to anyone, but at the same time, I'm desperate for some comfort. I don't want to tell everyone because I don't want people who don't care about me to show some kind of fake support, or pity, but I do want my parents' support, their empathy. I'd like them to feel sorry for me, telling me that I can count on them if I need anything. I've got none of the above and I'm hurt. And I'm pregnant. I just want to be happy for the birth of my baby. I should be excited and euphoric but instead I'm scared to give birth to a future orphan. But I've got John. We're in this together and so far, he's been quite supportive. I feel closer to him than ever before; he's always been there for me, since the day I met him, nearly five years ago.

★★★

After I arrived in Sydney in December 2010, I quickly found two jobs: waitress in a café in the city centre and barmaid in a pub in Glebe, where I lived. With these two jobs, I hardly had any spare time but I loved it. I was working and making money, saving too. I sacrificed on food and paid a hundred and fifty dollars a week for my shared bedroom, so I could save heaps, something I couldn't do in France for sure. It was so easy to save money here...life was easier in so many ways. People were nicer, except for the two regulars who were coming daily at the pub and always complaining because I was French and a real Aussie would pour their beer better. In general, people were nicer, more generous, easy going, and genuinely honest. What a change. Back home I was so depressed by people never smiling, barely acknowledging you, always complaining about how life was terrible. Don't get me wrong, all this negativity was so contagious I became one of them and I hated it. In Australia, it was like I was on another planet. People gave you a chance; they didn't judge you straight away. They tried to know you as another human being and not only in order to get something from you. Overall, they were less defensive, less argumentative, less confrontational, and more generous, more charitable, more helpful, more ...human.

My daily routine was to wake up at 5 am, get ready and take the bus to the CBD. I would arrive at the café at 7 am and start preparing my work zone for the morning. About two hundred slices of bread toasted and spread later, I would finish at 11.30am. I discovered the various types of bread people get for their morning toasts: white, brown, multi-grain, sourdough, Turkish, Turkish raisin, raisin toast, bagels. And also the weird mix they could do and how important the mention of light or extra was: Light Vegemite, extra peanut butter, jam, peanut butter and jam, peanut butter and Vegemite, cream cheese, avocado, cheese, ham and cheese, butter, the weirdest I ever had was probably Vegemite avocado and cheese.

I realised how Australia was such a coffee society. I mean, back home, we loved our morning coffee, made of an espresso, but very rarely would people add milk in their coffee. Working at the café, I noticed that every person had their favourite way to take their coffee. The French popular long black and espresso were the least ordered here. Latte, cappuccino, macchiato, mocha, chai latte, caramel latte, were more popular, followed by tea or hot chocolate. And again, the size was very important, if it was weak or strong, or even decaf. It was a science. I discovered that a good coffee was not only about the type of coffee or the brand you chose, but also about having a good barrister to make it…an expert who didn't burn it, didn't make the milk too hot but silky. It's such a disappointment now when I go back home and ask for a coffee with milk, so I always order my old friend espresso and now I can tell if they burn my coffee.

After working at the café, I would get a bite to take away and rush into the bus to go back to Glebe. I would work at the pub from around 2 pm until late at night. So I would go home to nap for an hour before walking to the pub. This nap was so important to me, and most of the time it felt like I had two days in one. I would work behind the bar at The Point Hotel for the rest of the day. Cleaning, serving, and talking to my customers. Also, after a couple of months, I passed my RCG, a certificate required to work in the gaming room. I loved working there, not only because I could work there from 12 to 6 pm and therefore get my evenings back, but also because it was more about customer service. It was a dark place though and I missed the light of the day, also all these noises were painful to deal with at first. I never gambled; we didn't have gambling machines back home, except in casinos. So, again, I discovered a new thing. I didn't really understand how some people could be so addicted to it. Once a guy threw the stool he was sitting on into the screen of the machine because he lost big money. He freaked me out.

On a Thursday in January, I was working behind the bar when a guy came up to the counter. He was of average size, with wide shoulders and muscled carves. He was wearing one of these yellow shirts that labourers and tradies wore –another thing that I noticed here; they were everywhere and I found it great because it reinforced the popular feeling that we need these people. In France, they were devalued, yet here he was smiley and seemed happy.

"G'day. Can I have a VB please?"

"Hi, sorry we don't have VB on tap. Do you want something else?" I replied politely.

"Do you have a bottle of VB then?" he said with a confident smile.

"No, I'm sorry. Maybe you'd like something else?" I asked after checking in the fridges. I was a little dismayed I couldn't give him what he wanted.

"Oh, I'm sure you've got VBs in the bottle shop. Can you please have a look?" Okay. Now this guy was getting under my skin and I found his behaviour nearly rude, telling me how to do my job. Anyway, I went to the bottle shop to check it out…and found it. I came back to the bar a bit confused. "You were right. I'm sorry, we have VB."

"Great, thanks," He said happily. I couldn't believe he didn't seem upset by my short attitude. Maybe it wasn't that bad if he didn't notice anything, after all, I stayed polite the whole time. I went to the till and looked up for the bottle. I found it in the bottle shop section and asked for the payment.

"It's four dollars please," I said with a smile.

"I don't think so. I think you gave me the bottle shop price. You have to add the pub fee." Still so friendly. I couldn't believe my ears… Oh my god this guy was honest. In France, he would have gotten away with it. Nobody would have told me that I made a mistake by giving a cheaper price. I was shocked and definitely confused. I looked up in the cash register and find the fee he was talking about.

"I guess you should work here. You're right again; it will be six dollars please." I told him with a cheeky grin.

"Thank you." He smiled at me giving me the change. "And that's for you…" He added, giving me another two bucks. He took his beer and left to find a seat in the smoking area.

What did I just witness? That was so surprising. Not only was he very nice about the entire situation but even generous, giving me a thirty per cent tip. No one ever gave me such a tip at the bar. Okay, I had a lucky fifty dollar note at the café on my first day but otherwise people rarely tipped. And this guy, who I was nearly rude to, smiled and tipped me. People were definitely different here. With time, I realised he was a regular and was coming every Thursday. And when I started working downstairs in the gaming room, where my boss put VB on tap, he was happy to come and chat a few minutes with me, ordering his VB. After a couple of times, he finally introduced himself. His name was John and he thought I was Swedish, certainly because of my blond hair and blue eyes. He was very surprised to learn that I was French, because he didn't think I had the typical French accent.

When I started working at the pub, back in December, I met Dean, a tall Aussie bloke with light blue eyes and messy dark hair. He used to come regularly with his mates and was always very flirtatious and smiley to me. He had a kangaroo in a triangle tattooed on his back, the made in Australia sign, so I nicknamed him "kangaroo." We started dating at the beginning of January but after a few dates, I figured that this wasn't going anywhere. He was rude, unreliable, and such a player. He also used to gamble and drink too much for my liking. He was also very jealous and didn't trust me if I was going out without him. We argued a lot and I couldn't stand it anymore. It had to stop. After three weeks of dating, we didn't see or contact each other for a week and I thought it was over when he came to the pub on the last Thursday of January. He walked downstairs to see me in the gaming room, followed by his mates Robert and Owen, a jug of beer in hand.

"How are you, babe?" He said like everything was fine between us.

I couldn't believe he was in front of me, like everything was sweet between us when it was a week I was in shut down mode, raging he couldn't care less not seeing me.

"What babe? You're not happy to see me?" He seemed genuinely not understanding my surprise.

"Well, of course I am, but you're not at work? I didn't have any news and you're here now, like last time..." I replied hesitating. Because it already happened once; he was unreachable for days and would show up by surprise at my work.

"No, I had an early day, so I came to see you," he said smiling.

And they played the rest of the afternoon, waiting for me to finish my shift. At 6pm, I found them with David, one of my regular customers too—who knew how bad the situation was between Dean and I—drinking a beer, outside in the smoking area.

"Hey guys. I'm sorry I can't stay drinking at the pub in my uniform. I need to get changed." I said when I joined them after work.

"No worries just go get dressed and we'll wait for you here," said Dean casually

"Are you sure? Are you still going to be there when I come back?" I asked, knowing how reliable he was.

"Yes of course babe." He replied confidently.

So I run back home to get changed and pass a casual dress and some sandals. I tried to stay casual because he was always complaining that I was overdressed. Each minute passing by made me doubt even more that he would still be at the pub. And I was right. When I finally came back after a short twenty minutes, I looked everywhere in the pub but there was no sign of Dean. I asked David, but he told me he left just after me. He didn't answer my first phone call and just had the time to say hello on the second one before the line cut off. No more battery. I was upset and outraged. He sent me a text asking me to meet him at his place in the city. John was drinking a beer with his mates inside the pub and I was about to go outside when we both reached the door at the same time.

"Are you okay?" he asked, knowing that I was looking for Dean.

"Yeah, I guess." I replied disappointed.

"If you want, you can join us for a beer, I'm with some of my mates," he said genuinely friendly.

"No, that's fine; I need to sort something out, maybe next time…"

"You're sure? I just need to grab some cigarettes and I'll be back in a minute. You can wait or you can come with me if you want," he insisted.

"Thank you very much, it would be great, but my boyfriend just let me down, again, and I really need to tell him it's over face to face. I don't want to let this go like that. I'm so upset he was supposed to wait for me and he didn't." I explained sad and upset.

"You should be treated like a princess…Maybe next time then. Good luck." He said nicely.

I took the bus to the city and after another disappointing night, I left Dean for good. After a lonely week working my arse off—it was probably the loneliest once since I arrived in Australia— jogging in the park next door and trying to enjoy nights out with my mates, I finally forgot him. I was more upset than sad, so once I got over my frustrations, I got over him. In this difficult time, I missed my sister a lot, my family, and friends too but I wasn't ready to go home. I loved my life here and I wanted to stay. I felt like maybe going back home for holidays would be nice but not forever. Not yet anyway.

Thursday came and like every Thursday, I saw John.

"How do you feel?" He asked, knowing that it had been a couple of weeks since I broke up with Kangaroo.

"Good." I was happy to see my smiley friend. "VB?" I asked with a smile.

"Yes, thanks. So that's it, you and Dean, it's officially over?" he asked, a bit shy.

"Yes, it's been two weeks now and I'm done with it. He was driving me crazy." I said like comforting myself.

"He didn't deserve to be with someone like you anyway."

"Yes, you're right...I should be treated like a princess, isn't it?"

"Exactly." He gave me a smile and left for the smoking area.

He came to see me for another two rounds, each time more chatty and smiley. Until that third time.

"Another VB?" I asked seeing him standing in front of me, an elbow on the bar.

"Yes, please." He smiled. "Lucie?"

"Yes?" I replied casually.

"Do you like coffee?" He asked me with hesitation.

"Of course I like coffee. I'm French."

"I was wondering...would you like to go for a coffee with me, maybe on Sunday morning?" He asked me knowing we were both working the six other days of the week.

"A coffee? On Sunday morning? Like for breakfast?" I asked again, surprised that for once, someone didn't ask me out for a drink, at night.

"Yes, you know I just would like to know you better, so I thought we could get to know each other around a coffee...don't worry, no expectations." He said, probably thinking I just came out of a disappointing story and didn't want to start anything else yet.

"Yes why not, no expectations right?"

"That's it."

"...Okay then..."

"Do you have a pen, I'll give you my number..." He asked with a smile.

My bag was on the ground, underneath the counter, so I bent over and grabbed it to find a pen. At this moment I had an intuition; if he gave me his number, I would never call him and somehow I felt like I would miss out on something big. It tickled me, I didn't want to miss out on happiness just because he wasn't my type...He had lovely hazelnut eyes, seemed genuine and definitely honest. He was always nice to me and always behaved as a gentleman. After all, he had said "no expectations" and I could trust him.

"You know what? I'm going to give you my number." I said with a smile. "Because to be honest, if you give me yours, I'll never call you."

"Okay...I'm not sure how I should take that..." He replied a bit confused

"Don't worry, it's better for you. I never call when guys give me their number and I'd like to go for a coffee and get to know you, so please take my number and call me, okay?" I tried to explain my behaviour.

"Okay, even better then, I'm ready." He was ready to type my number in his phone.

I gave him my mobile number and he left happy, a big smile on his face. Also, he probably had a couple of beers before in order to find the strength to ask me out.

It was Sunday morning and I was up early. John was supposed to call me to let me know where in the city we would meet, so I decided to go there for breakfast and he could join me later. As the weather was getting fresher, I put on a nice pair of jeans and a pink sleeveless top. I had to be casual but still pretty. I straightened my hair and put on some makeup. We should have met at 11 am but by the time John finally arrived, it was already one in the afternoon. He called earlier to let me know he'd be late and I didn't mind anyway. I barely recognised him when I saw him, for once outside the pub, in "civilian" clothes. He was wearing a pair of jeans, a shirt and casual shoes. He had cut his hair and shaved his light beard; that's why he was late, he was at the hairdresser. A red rose in hand and a smile on his face, he came towards me while I was waiting in front of the World Centre on George Street. It was nice to see that he'd gone out of his way to impress me.

"Hello. Sorry I'm late. That's for you." He said offering me the flower with a smile.

"Hey, how are you? Wow, you look so different in real life. Did you cut your hair?" I said nicely surprised.

"Yes. I wanted to make a good first impression for our first date."
He replied a bit shy. "But no expectations…" He smiled.

"No expectations at all." I smiled back at him, flattered that he
considered this a date.

"Where do you want to go?" He asked me.

"I'm not sure…I know we said coffee, but I had two already, so
do you mind going for a beer instead?" I asked him. I started to get
a bit shy with all the efforts he made and was genuinely touched by
all his attention. I needed a drink to relax.

"Whatever suits you. A beer is fine for me too." He replied.

"Where do you want to go? I'm not sure which pub is good
around here…" I was asking for help.

"Well, I don't know, I'm not really used to the city…Look, there's
one just around the corner." He pointed a pub with a terrace a level
above ground, a hundred metres away from us.

"Let's go then…" I said smiling at him.

We walked to the pub where we spent about two hours chatting
about our lives, why I came to Australia and what I had done so far. It
was so easy to talk to him…but I noticed my English wasn't as good
as thought because I could barely understand him. Except for when
he asked me if I wanted another beer. He was swallowing his words
and speaking with lots of slang. He had to explain to me a few words
and I had to repeat some sentence as he struggled to understand my
French accent. John was a very smiley thirty-two-year-old man, a
labourer, who spent most of his time working. He left his hometown,
Wollongong, at sixteen to start working in Sydney. And it was only
recently that he'd started living with his younger brother Jacob and
his Italian mum so they could afford to rent a better place in the
expensive city. He seemed amused by my trip and pretty interested
in what I was saying; at least he was listening. He also shouted me
two beers without blinking and that was a nice change. We had a
great time; we laughed and didn't stop chatting. It was so easy to
feel comfortable with him and he made me feel very special. He paid
attention and looked at me like if I was shining. After two and half
hours, it was time for me to go to Town Hall station to catch up
with Calum, my Scottish friend from Melbourne. We had planned
to do a pub crawl that day, since I broke up with Kangaroo. I had
never done one before and I wanted to experience it. John walked

me to the station and waited with me there…for forty-five minutes. Calum was late. All that time, he stayed with me, chatting and telling me how he preferred to be with a beautiful girl like me rather than going home to his brother. He was so sweet and a true gentleman. That's how we started dating.

During the week, he used to pick me up after my shift at the pub and we'd go for a couple of drinks in another pub, up the street. On Sundays, he used to show me around Sydney. At the end of February, we went to the Chinese Garden and Darling Harbour for our fifth date and we finally had our first kiss. It was a quick one, at my front door when he dropped me off.

On the next date, three days later, we were all fire and passion. With him, I wanted to use my Grandma Lucienne's advice: he had to wait. He had to chase me and prove to me that he was worthy. I wouldn't be an easy prey; he had to seduce and court me, like a gentleman. He was already a gentleman though, always holding doors for me, complimenting me, listening to me, paying for our meals and drinks, picking me up and dropping me off at home. I was happy.

He was so different from the guys I used to date. He was patient and sweet. He had such a great heart, always so positive and happy. I learned to know him and we got better at understanding each other. He even downloaded a dictionary application on his phone so he could write words I didn't understand and get the French translation for it. He was caring and affectionate with me. The way he looked at me made me feel so special; I trusted him.

We spent so much time talking about our lives and everything else in seven dates that I felt like I had known him all my life. He actually said to me that I pretty much knew him better than anyone else ever did. He was a good man from a low-income background. He had spent his childhood in housing and commission, raised by very young parents who ended up separating. He had also been raised by his mother's parents for a while. He never met his mum's dad as his Italian grandma left him after they arrived in Australia with their six kids. His step-grandfather, Jason, was his father figure and he had lots of admiration for this war hero. He finished school at fourteen because his teacher told him not to sit in the front row of the classroom if he wanted to stay in class. He left. He knew that if he was at the back he wouldn't learn and would be distracted; he wanted to do the right thing and she thought he was insolent. He never went back.

He left his hometown for Sydney and started over there, working hard as a labourer to make a living. He used to date a lot and he nearly got engaged, thinking it was what she wanted. It wasn't. He didn't believe in friendship saying that friends always disappoint you. He was such a beautiful soul. He had been hurt badly by family and friends. I had too and somewhere we were together against the world.

He introduced me to some of his mates when he took me to a barbecue. There, I met a French bloke who was married to an Aussie; he was a chef and told me his story. Like me, he loved Australia and wanted to stay all his life there, even after only a couple of months. Talking to him, I realised how I would love to stay here my entire life. I loved the cosmopolitan aspect of this amazing country, the various cultures, everyone bringing to the table their own cultural inheritance and differences to enhance this country where everything seemed possible. I loved the way the small business and the economy in general was managed and also the way they still understood the human side of things. The community spirit—which didn't really exist in France—the way they used any occasion to party, the way they would catch up or meet at the pub, the social life. Here everything was so different from what I knew, from the opposite seasons, the fauna and flora, the driving on the left side and the left gearbox, the space and houses versus tiny flats and overcrowded streets, the optimism…even the moon looked different.

Of course, everything went well and this barbecue was another good time spent with John. He had never introduced any girlfriend to them, which made me feel even more special. He drove me home after a quick introduction to his mum and brother. Things seemed to get a bit more serious for him but I didn't want to rush into anything. We spent our first month together sending affectionate text messages and beautiful love quotes to each other. John was hard to compete with. I nearly thought he looked up online to find most of his words as they were pretty good.

6

I spend the rest of my week going to hospital for various appointments.

Tuesday. I have an appointment with my obstetrician and my first injection of steroids so the baby's lungs can start to open. Also I have an ultrasound to see how big the baby is. It's so painful to look at my baby and think that because of me, he or she will have to come to Earth earlier. But apparently the baby, now weighing two and half kilograms, should be big enough to avoid the NICU. The technician is very nice and shows me the baby in three dimensions; she even gives me some printouts of her face. This baby looks like a girl for sure; she's got voluptuous lips.

Wednesday. Second injection of steroids.

Thursday. John and I are seeing my new surgeon, specialising in melanoma, at the Melanoma Medical Centre in Crows Nest, an hour drive away from home. He seems like a very good one. He tells us that if I felt a lump back in July, the melanoma started at least six months before that. So I'm already nine months in. He's still hoping the cancer is only at stage III, so hopefully it hasn't spread to other organs yet. Otherwise it could be a lot worse. He doesn't want to talk about this option and prefers to let me know that at stage III, they do surgery to get rid of all the cancerous lymph nodes and those around. He also reassures me about the fact that having my baby at thirty-six weeks and three days should be fine because it's only a few days before full term. So the plan is to have our baby on October 26. After that, I will have a PET scan on the 30th to make sure I don't have other tumours elsewhere and finally I will have surgery on the third of November. He also adds that if they saw three tumours at the ultrasound, there were more than likely twenty of them underneath. I'm terrified. He seems to think that the tumours are localised only under my armpit, and if I'm lucky, they're only there. I'm hoping so.

On our way back home, I check online and Dr. Google tells me that the odds to stay alive after a stage III melanoma at five years are only twenty per cent...but at stage IV, it's horrific and my eyes get blurry looking at the four per cent rate. I'm just hoping we will get rid of it with the operation and then, with treatment, it will never come back again. I can't help but think about John and what a life he will have if I'm not here to help him with the babies. I'm trying to stay strong and positive for them. I'm living every day as it comes and find some joy in welcoming my beautiful baby to the world soon.

What a birth though. I'm trying to enjoy myself, stay focused and happy about the birth, because my baby doesn't have to suffer the circumstances of his birth. I have to be happy and I have to enjoy the moment, like the day we welcomed Jason in our life, a tough one too but such a beautiful memory. On October 26, a beautiful baby will be born, healthy and perfect. It's weird to know the birthday already. The baby will be a Scorpio, a water sign. John being Taurus, Earth sign, Jason being a Gemini, air sign, and me being a Leo, fire sign, we will have the fourth elements, a perfect combination for our family, hopefully. I pray to have a girl so she could help John at home if I'm not there anymore. This thought makes me sick. I want to stay alive for them, at least until they are old enough to be independent because Jason and this baby will need their mum for a while.

If there is a God up there, he can't just do that to them. I'm praying so hard for a beautiful and easy baby girl. She will be my rock since she's sharing this cancer journey with me from the beginning. I've already relied on this baby to find strength and positive thoughts. John and I found a name: Rose. One night, I asked him to stop everything for half an hour so we could focus and find one. So we were lying on the bed, looking at the ceiling and saying names out loud, brainstorming. And even though he wasn't too convinced at first, we thought it was nice to find a name with the same pronunciation in French and English. And that was it. Like for Jason, we only have one name, so it has to be a daughter or it will be awkward. The good thing about having an induction is that I don't have to take my progesterone treatment anymore and we don't have to avoid intimacy because after all, if baby wants to come naturally, it will be even better.

Friday. I have lunch with my workmates to celebrate my last day. I haven't been at the office but it's my official last day and since I missed out again on the baby shower they usually do. They were nice to organise a lunch Botany Bay, an Italian restaurant not too far from my place. We don't talk about my health, since only two of them are aware, and it's nice to focus on the flowers and presents, talking about the last ultrasound I had, showing off the three dimensional print of my maybe daughter. Everyone has a guess on the gender and I'm glad to see that only one of them thinks it could be a boy. We have a good time laughing and joking about parenthood and soon it's time for me to leave.

I have to go to our local hospital, at the maternity ward, to see my obstetrician and plan the birth details. I will go to the maternity ward on Sunday at 3pm for a 6pm start. John and Jason will have a room in the paediatric ward so John will be with me for the delivery while Jason will be under the nurse's supervision. It's such a nice gesture from them to organise that, since we don't have any family to take care of our son and I feel better knowing that Jason will see the baby straight after the delivery. The baby will be close to term, so hopefully I will be able to take her home with me this time. I hope the baby won't have cancer either, but apparently it's very unlikely. They will still send the placenta for examination to be sure.

I'm trying to rest before the birth of my baby Scorpio because I will need all my energy and strength after that. I will have to take care of a new-born and a seventeen months old child while having my cancer treatment. I'm praying for my baby every night, for everything to go well...and also for John, Jason and I, asking for mercy after the most beautiful five years I had in my life. It has been too short to finish now. I'm crying for having thought one second of leaving this world five years ago, before leaving my country for good. I don't want that anymore, never. I have everything to live for now, everything to lose. I pray and beg every single day, with all my soul.

★★★

After welcoming Jason home fifty-two days after his birth, he never slept through the night until he was six months old; even after that he struggled. I was expressing milk every three hours for him, taking an hour to feed him on top of that. I wasn't sleeping and felt exhausted constantly. I was producing so much milk I had to buy a new freezer, a big one. I was a month of milk supply ahead and felt like a cow during my short maternity leave. So I tried to wean off in November to go back to work in December without having to express anymore. Giving Jason my milk was my way to help him having a good start in life. I felt like I spent most of my playtime with my son pumping my milk, which can be very uncomfortable. But the NICU nurses, as great as they were, kind of brainwashed me, saying how important it was to breastfeed your baby. It was my obsession and I felt very bad if I wasn't pumping. I think that things are hard enough for parents with babies at the NICU and the mums shouldn't feel that kind of pressure to breastfeed their babies, especially when their baby takes an hour to feed and can't take the breast. The rest and mental health of the mum should come first, before either the milk comes from their breast or a formula can, as at the end of the day, mum needs to be at her best to cope with all the issues such a premature baby brings into her life.

My parents came back to Australia for five weeks from mid-August until end of September to meet Jason. We were all living in the same small flat. It was nice to have them with us and we went for long walks on the beach, played with baby Jason and drove him to the Blue Mountains for his first getaway. It was raining like mad all weekend but we still rode the steepest train in the world, Jason attached to me in his baby carrier. I seized the opportunity of having my parents with us to baptise Jason and we had a small celebration on September 21, 2014, just before they left. During these five weeks, I thought about how hard it must be for them to live so far away from me and their grandson. Now that I was a mum, I got it. I couldn't imagine living that far away from Jason. I also thought about how hard it was going to be for us, not having my parents around for our kids, no one to keep them if we required some time off…and Jason was growing so fast. One minute he was small and the next he was crawling and eating purées.

Jason started day-care two days a week in November, then five days a week in January. I couldn't believe he was the youngest at the place or how unprepared the staff were for him. I understood that in Australia, many mums stayed at home with their baby for an entire year so that explained why most day-cares weren't used to young babies. In France, all mums go back to work and leave their baby at day-care after four months of maternity leave. Another difference I learned was how insanely costly day-care was here.

It was hard for me to go back to work full time after such a short maternity leave. I felt like I was missing out with Jason. Every morning I was telling him how I would miss him, how I had to leave him to go to work to make a living. Every morning, I would end up crying in my car after leaving him there. I was missing him badly. I wasn't really happy in my job anymore, resentful for this early birth. After work and on my weekends, I tried to spend all my time with Jason, playing with him, nursing him, enjoying every single one of his smiles and laughter. But as Jason and I were getting closer, John and I were drifting apart.

I felt like our bond was dissolving; we had trouble understanding each other. John spent most of his time on his smartphone, on the remote control car Facebook group he had created. He felt attacked for anything I said and I felt like he wasn't helping at home at all. I would be back to work soon, still doing all the household work and taking care of a baby on top of it. In October, just before I went back to work, I spent three days at my friend Stéphanie's house in Terrigal with Jason, leaving John alone for our third wedding anniversary. I wanted him to understand that it was too much for me, something had to change. After three days, I told him he had to come all the way up the coast to convince me to come back home. He probably wouldn't have come if I hadn't insisted. I didn't feel like he really cared but I couldn't abuse my friend's hospitality and I was hoping he understood my point. He didn't. As always, he just thought that he wasn't good enough and I had to take it or leave it. I took it; hoping things would get better once I would go back to work. I always found it hard not to work as after a while I start arguing a lot...Probably due to intellectual boredom or lack of self-esteem.

I went back to work in December and things got better with John; he tried to help at home and even if it wasn't much, it was helpful. I could have a quiet shower —the dream for a mum— and he woke up on weekends to let me sleep in. I was working very hard again, this time it was more so I could finish on time to come home to my son though. I had to launch a new brand and my boss didn't do anything during my maternity leave, waiting for the last minute again to request miracles from me with tight deadlines. My assistant had resigned the day I was admitted at the hospital, when the membrane broke, and the Product Manager resigned a month later. The Marketing team was just...him. I had a new assistant and she was a very motivated undergraduate, full of energy and a perfectionist like me, my saving grace. I thought about looking for another job after Jason's birth, but I wanted another baby quickly and it was better to stay where I knew all the ropes rather than diving into the unknown, especially when I had to adjust to motherhood. Plus, people are very nice in this company.

In February, Jason was starting to crawl and roll; within five minutes he could be on the other side of the room. He still had his blue eyes and dark blond hair and looked a lot like me. He was adorable, cheeky, affectionate, and so funny. He was very curious of his surroundings and surprised me every day by his behaviour. He started waking up at night again and between the sleepless nights and my job, I was exhausted. Maybe I was pregnant again? John and I wanted a second baby and we never use any contraception anymore.

Jason was so wonderful; even if I had to sacrifice my favourite hobby, sleeping, he was such a joy. Always happy and so innocent, just his smile made me feel good every day. Nine months after his birth, he was seven times heavier and thirty centimetres bigger, growing so fast that I was blown away. I thought many times about my sister and how it would have been nice to live in the same city or at least the same country, so the cousins could grow together. She got pregnant again, on Jason's birthday. The twins were born at seven months, in December, and Lenny and Alicia were happy and healthy. Twins, a boy and a girl, like my sister and I always wanted to be. We always thought it would have been mad having a brother instead of a big sister or just being ourselves a boy and a girl.

She was glad to be able to understand that as twins, they had such a special relationship. They also stayed about fifty days at the hospital, same journey, same pain, same long wait, same issues and long enough for her to understand my pain when Jason was there too. She lived the same thing, twice as hard and with a three-year-old daughter on top of it all. I felt for her and I was sorry I couldn't be there for her either. I had given my parents Jason's premature clothes and I was glad to see pictures of my nephew and niece with my son's little outfits. They were in the same incubator, same crib, and were always holding hands and looking at each other. It was a sort of painful for my twin and me, happy to see them so close, but thinking how we would have loved that for ourselves.

The first week of March I started a detox with a Lorna Jane recipe book to lose the rest of my pregnancy weight. I didn't have the chance to go through the last trimester and felt like I missed out on the big belly thing. I had already lost most of it breastfeeding and running along the bay, pushing Jason in the pram while on maternity leave, and I was back at the gym daily at work. Still, I wanted to go back to my pre-pregnancy weight as I always felt better when I was good in my skin, and my jeans. John did it with me too. He didn't have much choice in the matter and it was very funny to see his face while eating some of the new-age recipes. It was hard to cook all this fresh food—vegetarian as well—taking care of Jason and working... but worth it. I didn't lose any weight but felt pregnant that week.

Jason started to stand up already and he could walk with us if we held his hands. At seven months corrected, he was early. Within three weeks, he went from crawling and rolling to walking. He loved going to the park, laughing in the swing and going down the slide. He also loved watching the waves at the beach and playing with us at home. He was going through a separation anxiety period but I tried my best to cuddle him as much as I could for him to sleep better at night.

On the 12th of March, I found out I was pregnant and told John when he came back from work.

"Hi love, how are you?" I asked with a kiss.

"Good, what's happening?"

"I've got you a little something..." I gave him a little sachet in silk like the ones holding jewellery.

"Oh, what is it?" he asked surprised.

"Open it," I said smiling.

"What's that?" he asked, pulling out the dried little chickpea. He tried to bite it.

"Don't eat it. You wouldn't eat your second baby would you?" I told him with a smile, struggling to form my words because of the excitement of the situation.

"That's it? Already?" He was really surprised and almost worried. We were exhausted because Jason wasn't sleeping through and he was helping me at night.

"Yes. That's it. Isn't it awesome? I know it's hard at the moment with Jason, but hopefully it won't last. Also, we always wanted our two kids to be close, so that's great. Anyway, it's better to do all the nappy and baby stuff now, we'll suffer for the next three years and then it will be over, once for all. I'm so excited though…I'd like a girl this time. I mean as long as it's healthy, it's okay, but I've always wanted a boy and a girl, so it would be perfect." I gave him a kiss and curled myself into his arms.

"Me too. It will be a girl anyway and she will be awesome and super nice to her daddy and she will let him sleep." He laughed.

"Yes. I'm sure that giving Jason my doll so he could practice like if it was his little sister was a great idea. Even if he's still torturing more than taking care of her, he's got nine months to learn. And hopefully, it will be hers after. Are you sure you want a surprise again?"

"Yes. Otherwise what's the point really?"

"Yes, I guess, but I really would like to know. It's going to be even harder not to know this time around."

"It's going to be fine. Surprise is best."

"Yes, that's right." I was so glad having a surprise for Jason, considering the circumstances. That way if things turned bad again, which I hoped it wouldn't, at least we'd have that to save the day, again.

That day, Jason walked by himself for the first time, pushing the musical lion walker along. I had my first emotional moment as a mother and couldn't hold the tears of joy and pride coming up my eyes. He wasn't even ten months old and he was looking for his independence already.

My first trimester of this third pregnancy was exhausting. Jason was sick a lot, sleeping in our bed most of the time and always wanted me to hold him in my arms. Between work, the sleepless nights and my pregnancy, I never felt that bad. Five weeks into my pregnancy, I found out that I had hypothyroidism, which meant that my thyroid wasn't working as much as it should, which could be damaging to the baby. I hoped we didn't find out too late and started a treatment straight away. No wonder why I was so tired. That certainly didn't help me.

Jason had a good bedtime routine, but he still didn't sleep through the night. I didn't want to let him cry all night, as apparently it could affect him emotionally. We had to try the controlled crying technique and see if he could learn how to self-sooth. We brought Jason to Tresillian, a hospital facility for babies where we could learn controlled crying techniques. I spent four days and four nights there with him, trying my best to cope with letting him cry, but learning how to differentiate the distressed cries and the tantrum ones. It was difficult but it seemed to work and as I didn't want to waste all our time and efforts, I took some days off work to consolidate the technique at home, especially since I wasn't sure day-care would do it right at nap time. Jason slept through but woke up at four thirty or five in the morning. At least he stayed in his bed, which brought back peace and harmony between John and me.

In May, we celebrated Jason's first birthday. He was standing without help and playing all day with the balloons we decorated the garden with. We were bringing him to swimming lessons every Saturday morning and he loved it. Especially babbling with other babies. My first trimester went quickly, and I was already eighteen weeks pregnant. It was different from my second pregnancy. I had never been that tired with Jason but I was more nauseous. I had a feeling it would be a girl...I couldn't help myself; I had to eat chocolate and sweets on a daily basis. I tried to resist, but it was stronger than me. Both my sisters craved chocolate when they were pregnant with their girls and I was hoping it was a family sign for having a baby girl, even if it meant I had to gain a fair bit of weight on my butt.

At that point, everyone at work knew that I was pregnant again and my boss was getting very annoying. I was working hard and yet I felt like I had to prove myself even more. I had done so much in so little time—organising displays for the new brand everywhere in Australia, working on the catalogue design and the brand guidelines, organising a monumental national brand launch, and still dealing with two other brands, all with the help of only one assistant. I promised myself that after this pregnancy, he would never see me again. The only good thing coming out of this conference was the nice body massage I had on the activity day. Finally, I had a day for myself. Finally, I could rest a bit and take a breather.

I was happy to come home to my boys and nicely surprised that John coped so well for three entire days, taking care of our son by himself. Jason cried a lot after me but overall it went well and somehow this time off reassured me of my husband's capacity to hold the fort without super mummy.

Even if I was a bit emotional sometimes, this pregnancy was a bit better, but my body was going through hell. The thyroid was now stable and my treatment made sure it was acting like normal but I got varicose veins in my groin and on the top of my right leg. I could barely walk. It started back in July and the doctors told me to avoid moving too much and rest as much as I could. Right. Between my job and my one-year-old son who wanted to be held all the time, without forgetting the four flights of stairs I had to go up and down at home. Also, the obstetrician told me that maybe Jason was born early because I terminated another pregnancy not long before falling pregnant again, potentially leading to an early birth. So they started giving me a progesterone treatment in order to avoid another early birth. I couldn't believe my ears. If chances to have an early birth were higher after the termination, why didn't they do something for my second pregnancy? Why didn't I receive this treatment for Jason? Or at least why they didn't put me on bed rest? I was upset but happy that they helped with this one and I was praying every night to have a healthy baby, born to term this time.

Also, around the same time, I felt the lump in my armpit and I was worried about it. But my GP told me that it was surely nothing and certainly a viral thing, nothing to worry about.

The past six months Jason hadn't gained any weight, so I directed my worry to him. After further tests, we figured out he wasn't coeliac but might still have reflux, and since he started taking his medicine for reflux again, he started to re-gain weight. I couldn't believe it took six months for the paediatrician to believe that my worries were founded: his growth curve was flat from eight to fourteen months old. I was disgusted, but relieved we were finally doing something about it.

He was walking around everywhere now and had his first haircut. He looked like a little boy and had eight teeth already. He could clap his hands, wave goodbye, clack his tongue, throw the ball, take his shoes off, and spoon feed himself. He loved to draw, paint, stack up Legos, and talk to us. Even if we didn't understand, it seemed like real serious conversations. He would get a surgery to remove the hydrocele he had in his testis since birth in November, nothing too serious, but it could become a hernia so we had to do it soon. Since he was back on his reflux medicine he was waking up at night again and it was exhausting for us.

Even with his constant health issues, Jason was such a blessing. He was such a wonderful and special little boy and I loved him more every day, but he was taking so much space in our couple life that it was hard for John and me to adjust. I was always looking for ways to positively re-energise our couple and we tried to have a ten-minute chat every night or every second day at least to talk about us and avoid the baby talk. But it wasn't easy and John was tired too. He was getting shorter and shorter with me, swearing, and smoking cigarettes down the garage for hours at night. I was missing my gentleman. So I thought it would be nice for all of us to go to France in April, when the baby would be a bit older and before Jason turned two years old, avoiding full price flight ticket for our children.

I was already organising a week away in Normandy with my sister and her kids, so we could be all together in a big house close to the beach. I was missing my family. Even if they were far from perfect, I loved them and I wanted to be with them. It was harder since we had babies and I couldn't help myself thinking that it would be so good to live closer to my sister and my nephews and to my parents too. Home was anywhere as long as I was with my family. John and Jason were my family now but my sister and parents were family too.

Finally, Jason's surgery for his hydrocele happened on the last week of August. I was so scared waiting for him to be released from surgery. He should have been out earlier. What was happening? Was my baby okay? I started to look at the clock on the wall...Every minute. It was so long to wait for my sweet boy. I was holding onto my unborn baby, touching my belly to comfort me, when they finally called me. Unfortunately, he had a bad reaction to the anaesthesia and was given oxygen all afternoon. When we went home that afternoon, he had a very high fever and shook badly. I never saw him like that. I was scared and drove him to the Emergency the same evening. He spent another two days and two nights in the children's ward of our local hospital as they thought he could have had a blood infection, but apparently it was just a bad reaction due to a cold. They gave him oxygen most of the first thirty hours and he had terrible fevers. We slept in the same single bed; he was curled in my arms the whole time. He had to walk dragging along the perfusion on wheels and still wanted to play and enjoy like nothing happened. He showed so much bravery and he got used to his little disability so quickly, I was stunned. On top of that he had a black eye because he fell on the corner of a wood table at day-care that week…my poor baby was pitiful and looked miserable.

I was so happy to be pregnant and having babies close to one another, knowing they would be friends and accomplices.

7

On the weekend, I decide that it's time to enjoy and live mindfully, so we visit the Sydney Aquarium with Jason and have a wonderful family time. Okay, cancer and dying are always at the back of my mind, giving me a solemn reminder to take mental pictures of every single minute of the day. I enjoy each second of it, every smile and every laugh. After a lunch on Darling Harbour and a chocolate ice cream, my favourite, we bring Jason to the playground and play in the water. He splashes, laughs, and loves the water, the fountains, and the slides. He's so happy; we all are. It's funny how knowing that you may die soon makes you savour each second of your life. You see things like never before. Your whole world is brighter, more detailed, deeper, and somehow happier. We probably won't go to France now, but John promised me that we will go to Uluru and maybe Tasmania, like I've always wanted to.

One thing is sure for now. I'm reconsidering my job. My time is so precious that maybe I should do something with more impact on people's lives. I've decided to write my diaries in English from now on, so my children can read my memoirs if I'm not there anymore to tell them my story. I hope I will though. I'm looking at the world the way I used to when I arrived in Australia. With eyes wide open and no plan for the future, living in the moment and appreciating everything around me, feeling my heart pumping and my lungs breathing.

★★★

When I landed in Melbourne on October 30, 2010, my plane had twenty six hours delay; I was exhausted but happy I had finally arrived! I took my luggage and went outside the airport to figure out how to get to the hostel I had booked. After some troubles, I took a bus to the main train station and then a cab to the hostel. Looking by the taxi's window, I could see the skyscrapers lighting the dark night, the streets were quiet as it was already two o'clock in the morning, but I was overwhelmed by a wonderful feeling of happiness. I was there, after all these years, I was finally in Australia. My dream came true! I felt like breathing for the first time in my life. I was alone in an unknown city, with no many plans but a lot of opportunities ahead of me. A great feeling of freedom overcame me. I was in charge of every single decision I would make, no interferences, no one to tell me what to do or how to do it. I could be myself, I could try and fail; I didn't have to succeed straight away because I had a year in front of me. I could go picking and it wouldn't be a big deal if I didn't have a "real" job, I could "waste" time finding myself, it would always be worthy.

I had trouble sleeping between the jet-lag, the excitement, the stress and the happiness of being here by myself, so far away from everything I knew. All these mixed emotions were overwhelming. My brain was overloaded, unable to stop, my eyes were swollen and I was dreaming of a good night sleep. It was tough though; there were six other people in my room and the girl sleeping underneath my bunk bed was snoring like a monster.

On my first day, I woke up after only a couple hours of snoozing. The excitement was unbearable; I had to get out and discover. I took my breakfast in the city centre and went to the immigration department for my working holiday visa and asked for my tax file number. Also, I opened an Australian bank account and bought a sim card for the Aussie phone that my sister nicely gave me. In France, I would never have managed to do that in one day, but here, it took me three hours and I took my time. People were smiling at me too; even in public administrations, you were welcomed with a smile and some jokes too. People were so nice, so smiley. It was so different from home. I felt like in Care Bears land. I was looking everywhere at everything, like I had just been given eyes, and life was beautiful.

When I created my Tax File Number on the computers of the Taxation Office, I met two Frenchies from the Alsace region who had decided, like me, to get rid of the paperwork so they could start working and enjoying as soon as possible. We were all very surprised to have finished just in time for lunch. The only issue I found was that it was expensive to eat properly with a tiny budget, so we went to McDonald's as we knew what to eat there and we would need some time to get to know what kind of food and price point we could find in this country. We spent the afternoon visiting the CBD and going downstairs after a visit to St. Patrick's Cathedral. One of the guys asked for a cigarette from a very good-looking girl and broke his foot while watching her walk away. Yes, broken foot. He had to go to the hospital, get a plaster cast, and all the rest. He couldn't work for three weeks. Hard for a start, poor thing; typical male though.

But good news for me—I had a job, my first job in Australia. I would work five hours on Wednesday that week and get paid a hundred dollars to sell radios at the International Cricket Cup. I found the advertisement and after a few minutes talking on the phone—while my mate was falling down the stairs—they gave me the job. Finally, we finished the day with some food shopping. Again it was difficult to go through the aisles as I didn't have my marks and the products I was used to buying for cheap back home were quite expensive here, especially fresh vegetables. Everything seemed overpriced and I had trouble filling up my trolley. I came back to my hostel exhausted and slept for twelve hours straight.

The next morning, I left my dorm at twelve o'clock, happy and rested, to go to La Trobe University offices. I wanted to know if they could help me out with my job search as I passed my diploma at this University. The receptionist was very sweet and managed to get me a phone conversation with the Marketing and Communication teacher at La Trobe Bendigo, my campus. He would try to help me by giving me some tips and the contact details of some companies which could be interested in my profile. We never know. But in ten minutes it was pretty cool to get some kind of help, I didn't waste my time.

While I was in Melbourne I also wanted to visit the surroundings so I went to Peter Pan –the coolest tour operator and internet provider for backpackers like me– and I booked my trip to Philip Island on Friday 4th of November, the weather should be good for it. I went to St Kilda, a suburb in the South of Melbourne, which I heard a lot about. I took the tramway and was there twenty minutes later. I wanted to end my Melbourne trip there, close to the beach. But it was tough to find any hostel available when I looked up online. I met another Frenchie in the tram and he indicated me where was his hostel so I could directly ask. It was Melbourne Cup weekend and everything was booked out, especially around Albert Park, where the event occurred. Luckily, I managed to get a bed. Like I said, it was Care Bare land here. Awesome.

The next day was another story; I'd never imagined it could rain like that. The wind was crazy strong too and I visited the Docklands under a storm...I walked nearly six kilometres under the rain and my shoes, socks, and clothes were saturated. I was freezing cold and my umbrella didn't last long fighting the wind...otherwise, the Melbourne Bridge was beautiful. I was drenched and I already had a cold, which didn't help my mood. I finished my day in a massive shopping centre in the city centre. The way I found it was surprising too. I was jumping off the Little Circus—a small old school tramway that I took to come back to the CBD—when I saw someone going up a tiny escalator, so I decided to follow him; maybe he knew a place under cover to dry off a bit?

When I arrived at the top of the escalator, I discovered a stunning and massive shopping centre, with a sort of red bricks building in the middle, finished by a pointy top, the entire thing being underneath a glass and wrought iron vault, part of the shopping centre ceiling. It was such an amazing discovery! Also, I was desperately looking for some free Wi-Fi networks as it was about four dollars an hour for a very slow connexion...but thanks to Mac Donald's and libraries I could get free access! I was at the State Library off Swanston Street, a very big one with so many people there! Computers and Wi-Fi access everywhere, people with laptops, doing their researches or surfing online. I had already booked my flight to Brisbane from France, as my sister told me I would love it and should stay there. I just had the time to book my hostel in Brisbane and apply for a few jobs that it was six o'clock already and the staff invited us to get out. I was out in the rain again and I hurried to go back to the warmth of my hostel for a well-deserved bath!

Finally, the first three days went very quickly and my next week was planned so I wasn't sure I would be able to see everything but anyway Aussies were super friendly and tourists too. Everybody was very nice, only my wallet was sad but I thought it had to get used to it because I loved Australia! I'd liked the weather to be a bit nicer next week too because I had my trips to The Great Ocean Road and

Philip Island, but like they said here, you can have all the weather in one day.

While having a much-needed sleep-in, my French phone rang. I wondered who it could be as everybody knew I was in Australia and when I considered the time difference, it was night time there, the day before. When I answered, I didn't recognise the voice straight away and he didn't want to tell me. He was upset and cocky, saying that I obviously had many men after him. I couldn't believe it... it was my ex, Patrick. The guy who pretty much caused a year of self-questioning and was part of the reason why I wanted to leave the country. He wanted to apologise for what he'd done to me and that now he knew how he hurt me. I was in shock. I told him I was now in Australia, no thanks to him. I asked if he had the three thousand dollars he still owed me, because after all he'd done, the best apology would be to give me back what he owed. But he didn't, so I hung up. With all the pain he caused me, I had forgotten his voice and I was still shocked, sitting on my bed, awake all of a sudden. After nearly two years, he finally apologised but I had moved on. I was happy. I had my revenge and I had forgotten him, until his voice.

★★★

It was February 2009 and it was nearly a year since I had found a good Product Manager role in an International company located in Monaco. It was also a year and half since I had met Patrick, a carpenter, eight years younger than me. We were living together in a one-bedroom rental flat in the city centre of my home town, Nice.

I had spent an hour in public transport and arrived in our small flat. I rushed into the lounge room to catch up with my boyfriend after a hard day at work; it was a good job, but my boss was awful...

"Hello Darling," I said joyfully.

"Hello, how are you doing?" Patrick said, without much enthusiasm.

"Yes, not too bad. I had a very hard day but I'm okay. What about you? What have you been up to today?"

He wasn't working and I was upset he couldn't find a way to make money because I was over wearing the pants in this relationship.

"Not much…the owner came to inspect the flat and she said that it was our fault if there was mould around the window frame because we didn't aerate enough…"

"No way. Did you explain that it was because of the humidity and the waterproofing issues?" I was outraged. I had another dreadful day at work and didn't have a chance to drop my bag and jacket yet. Of course, we started arguing and Patrick didn't need much more to say that it was over because we couldn't continue that way. For once, I agreed, but I couldn't help feeling deeply saddened by this failure, another love failure. I thought there was still love between us, but it was only a lot of memories. Since I found out he was cheating on me online two months earlier—if there was such a thing—I opened my eyes and saw all the things that I couldn't stand anymore in this relationship. We were going nowhere but to hell.

We didn't talk to each other for two days. I was going to work every morning while he was sleeping on the lounge and when I came back home, I spent the night by myself as he came back only after I fell asleep. I couldn't do it any longer, so one night I waited for him and told him that if we had to live that way, we'd better live separately. He should move out. He got upset but finally accepted, after yelling at me. I felt awful and tried to apologise the next morning by leaving a note before going to work. I even kissed him while he was asleep, thinking he heard me and agreed to stay. I spent my day peacefully, without even thinking one second that a terrible surprise was waiting for me that night.

I rushed back home thinking about the great conversation we were about to have to arrange the situation. We had to stop the bullshit, cut the crap, end all these stupid arguments, and take responsibility for our actions. He owed me a lot of money now and I was getting sick of it. He was unemployed and spending his days playing Xbox. I wasn't attracted to him anymore. I was angry and I was tired of being his mum. I was too good for him, he had to change and take responsibility for his behaviour. But when I entered the unit, I felt a weird feeling of cleanness and tidiness; I was like in an empty space. I opened the cupboards to confirm this bizarre sensation. It was a fact: most of our stuff was gone, with him. And I looked everywhere; there was no letter or post-it, no message on my voicemail and no text message. Nothing. He simply left me there, like an idiot. He even took the cutlery and the plates. My Xbox as well of course. I collapsed in tears on the couch, still there, because, lucky enough, he couldn't take it in his bags. I called him again and again but he didn't answer. I had to threaten him to throw out the rest of his stuff on his voicemail for him to finally call me back. He screamed at me not to get rid of anything and said that he would come with his mum to pick them up while I was at work. Really? Anyway, I changed the locks because if he wanted to come, he would have to face me.

I called my ex, Quentin, for help that night. I was upset and had to vent. He drove to my place to pick me up and after getting a couple of beers on the way, we spent the night at his place. We talked all night. Drinking and smoking, getting closer and laughing about these twenty-year-olds we were with (his girlfriend was five years younger than him too) and of course we kissed and spent the rest of the night together, like every time we used to see each other before. It was a long time since I'd seen him and he helped me go through this tough breakup. I left the next morning with the feeling that Patrick was just another young and irresponsible guy I was wasting my time with anyway, and obviously not the one. No need to spare a tear either.

I gave notice to the owner for the lease and started looking for another unit, closer to my parents, in the East side of the city, where I grew up. I was overwhelmed; my job was getting harder because my management was putting a lot of pressure on me. I was looking for a new flat and my heart and my pride were broken. Even working fifty to sixty hours a week, I managed to visit about twenty flats before finding the right one. It was a very small unit of twenty square metres but with a nice garden of about the same size. Nice provided about three hundred days of sun all year round and I loved being outside. We could see the surrounding buildings from the garden but I didn't care; it would be awesome to have an outdoor living area. It was on the first floor of a newer building in one of my favourite areas, between Riquier and the Marina, east side, ten minutes away from the beach and from Old Nice. I had one neighbour on the left side of my garden and the previous tenant, a Lucie too, promised me that he was very quiet, so I signed the lease. I got my confidence back and I was moving on. I called my sister to tell her how happy I was.

Lali had already been living in Paris for six years and long gone was the time where she used to say she would come back to live in the south of France. Since we went back to Paris together, she stayed and found a job as Customer Service Manager in a supermarket, where she also found her new partner, David. She was finally divorced and started to study payroll, burying her dream to become a makeup artist in the filming industry. She never came back home except to spend Christmas with us every second year and sometimes for summer or Easter, but she was definitely settling in the Capital. She was my age and somehow she managed to have it all: the good guy, the career, kids, and the house. She didn't have the best start but she managed to turn her life around. I was so proud of her. I was happy for her. She went to Australia a few months before, to discover the country she wanted to visit since she was eighteen and dating her first love, a French-Australian named Marcus. They nearly studied there together but they broke up. Since then, her love for this country was contagious and when I had the opportunity to study at La Trobe University in Bendigo, I jumped on it. I could have studied the last year of my degree there, but I chose e-learning instead and I always regretted not going. Lali used to talk so much about Australia that I was glad she could finally see this beautiful country. Every time she sent me pictures or called me from there, I was desperate to be with her, discovering the big continent instead of being trapped in my job in Monaco.

I called her on the phone and told her how happy I was to finally leave the jail I was in with the cheater for this tiny flat where I would be surrounded by positive waves and no humidity. The flat with Patrick was so humid that I developed no less than three allergies. Phenyl Diamine, perfume, and mites. Great, like I needed more memories from this story. I was blonde but I had spent the past six years as a brunette, pretty much since my sister's exile in Paris. Everyone found me much prettier and sexy then. It was funny how just by changing from blonde to brunette, men looked at me differently. I was taken more seriously; all of a sudden, I was smarter, respected, but also more attractive. Unfortunately, I couldn't be a brunette anymore because I was now allergic to my hair coloration.

I was coming back home thinking of my new little flat by myself, even if I wanted to go to Australia and get over my regrets.

A couple of days earlier, I asked my parents to take me back home in order to save some cash and be able to go but they thought I should settle down in my own place and look for another job if I wasn't happy with mine. My job in Monaco was stressing me out; I didn't like the ambiance and the pressure. My colleague was awful, competitive, and after a few episodes of very rude behaviours, I couldn't stand going there every single morning. I was so sick of it I literally had pain in my chest as I approached the building. I had panic attacks and nearly ended up in hospital one night of March. It was the accumulation of too many months of suffering because of this stupid relationship with a young and immature boy and the crazy ambitions of a company with an extra-limited budget. I had enough. Even my body was telling me to stop the damage. I wanted to leave, go far, far away. But my sister and my parents were very good a convincing me to stay. Finding a smaller and cheaper flat and looking for a better job was their advice. After visiting this one, I had to admit I liked the idea of having my own flat in my hometown because I had always lived with my parents or with my boyfriends when I was in Nice. I missed living by myself since the two years I spent in Montpellier for my Business School and six months in Salon de Provence for my first Marketing Manager position, probably the best times of my life. I would have my own space and I was very much looking forward to it.

In April, after a few months of suffering and nearly a year and a half working for them, I was finally free of this job. I still had living overseas in the back of my mind, Australia being my first choice since I always wanted to go, but anywhere would do it really. I just needed a fresh start. Living in my flat, I still wanted to give a chance to the job research and they were pushing me to do so. I started looking for a new job a month before I left my previous job. Unsuccessfully. Now that I didn't have a job anymore, I had time to go to interviews easily and even look into other cities. Australia could wait another year. It was on the back of my mind for the past six years, so one more wouldn't make any difference. Therefore, I tried to find another job in Marketing, anywhere in France, for a year.

After a couple of months living in my tiny unit, my neighbour became my best friend. He supported me greatly while I was struggling with the stress of losing my boyfriend and my job. He was a very good-looking young man, but gay which definitely helped our platonic relationship. We became so close that we removed the garden fence and created our own big backyard, perfect for barbecues, parties, and sunbathing; we were always together.

8

On the second and third days of November 2010, I went on the Great Ocean Road trip and had all the weathers: rain, wind, and sun, but it was amazing. I actually used the same tour my sister told me about and had the same funny Aussie guide. She drove us around and we discovered the beautiful coastal landscapes, the amazing apostles, the long beaches and again, people were so friendly. We had lots of fun during those two days and I even tried the Vegemite. Yuck...I decided to stick with jam, since Nutella was super expensive here. We also tasted a typical Aussie barbecue; I saw my first koalas and kangaroos in the wild and fed colourful wild parrots.

Wednesday, I worked for the first time in Australia, selling radios at the Melbourne Cricket Ground. I had to wear a bright yellow T-shirt while carrying a big yellow bag full of radios and a big yellow advertising frame going above my head. What a look. It was hard to sell, but I stayed motivated and again the weather was cold with showers. The match was Australia versus Sri Lanka and it was awesome to see these supporters painted in the colours of their team, wearing their uniforms. Just watching them and their excitement made me feel entertained. I made a hundred bucks so I was happy. That night, I also went to the city to catch up with my French friend, Sébastien, and his girlfriend, Kathy, for some Thai and a beer. After a late night, I slept in the next day and sent back eighteen kilos of winter clothes to France to avoid being in excess weight for my flight to Brisbane the next Monday.

On Friday, I went to Philip Island and the weather was so good. I could wear my shorts for the first time. We visited the koala and kangaroo reserve where I also saw wallabies; they had a thinner head and longer legs than kangaroos, made smaller jumps and lived in the rocks. There were wombats, very strange nocturnal animals, as well as parrots, chickens, roosters, sheep, ponies, and peacocks. The best was being able to touch the kangaroos and see koalas from a closer point of view than in the wild. Then, we went to Wholemail Beach, a beautiful beach where professional surfers had competitions if they couldn't use Bells Beach (where I'd also been, near Torquay, on the Great Ocean Road), a long breath-taking beach. We finished by going to the Nobbies, at the very end of Philip Island peninsula, where thousands of seagulls lived and reproduced. It was so impressive to see them all flying around me, they were everywhere, on the green land, on the dark rocks separating the sea from the green grass.

A strong cold wind was fighting my body and I was freezing in my shorts. But the landscape was stunning with all the seagulls and their babies. As the babies grew, they lost their light brown spotted feathers for grey ones. After a much-needed warm pizza, we went on the beach to witness the penguin parade. After waiting forty minutes in the cold wind, watching for the beautiful sunset, small groups of penguins started to appear fifteen to twenty at a time, doodling to the ocean to eat fishes or shells they would give to their babies later. There were like four lines of them, parallel to the water. One group was facing the shore, while the group the closest to the water started to fish, once this group was out of water the second line of penguins went in, then the third, then the fourth, always leaving a last line, facing the shore to prevent predators. It was a glorious experience. When we finally went back to Melbourne around midnight, I fell asleep in no time.

On my last weekend, I went to St Kilda, walking around the area, discovering the nice food, all these lovely bakeries and visiting the Botanic Garden. While in the garden, discovering the flora of Australia, I imagined myself living here, walking in these rainforests with my family, I tried to see how I would feel if I was living here forever…in another world. The thought was nice and exotic, but it would be hard to be so far away from my sister and my parents.

When I landed in Brisbane on the eighth of November, I spent two days thinking that this city was lovely but not for me, too far away from the beach. Also, it was pouring rain and the city centre was very small, like the artificial beach that my sister praised so much, more like a fountain for me. I chatted with my friend Calum, my Scottish buddy from St Kilda, who was in Sydney now, to see if he was doing better than I was. Apparently it was nice there, and for sure, better than Brisbane.

On my third day, I went down to my hostel kitchen, to prepare my breakfast, and I met two French girls, Isabelle and Eloise, who were talking about picking. As they were burning their omelette, I joined their conversation by warning them and they talk to me about their plan for picking in Bowen, in North Queensland. They gave me the contact details of the farmer and within the hour, I managed to get a job picking capsicums, making sure I was paid hourly, not by the bucket and booked my flight and accommodation to stay with the girls. They seemed very nice and I was happy to leave Brisbane with a job and two new friends. We arrived in Bowen the same night, around nine o'clock. Bowen Wood was the place where they filmed the movie *"Australia"* and I was staying at the hotel where some scenes were done.

I discovered the outback on a cinema background. I loved this movie because I was dreaming of seeing these magnificent landscapes, deserted but green, I was living in a sort of ghost town, cut by large dirt streets, shaped by low one storey buildings, and where the population density was near one for a square kilometre. A sort of Wild West place, where men were the majority and there was alcohol for all. The main activity consisted in going to the bar in the hotel I was staying at. There was a nice outdoor area where the music, neither current nor country, echoed up to my bedroom, until very late at night. Here, men and few women lived on the rhythm of the work in the field. They woke up very early and sleep early too. I had to get used to it quickly as the next morning I started picking at six.

It was tough to start with but finally the day was so exhausting that I was in bed at nine anyway. But this first day was the same as the following ones. Wake up at five, I put on my combat outfit: an old pair of pants and t-shirt, because this job was so dirty that I had to take two showers at night —until the water stop being brown. Then, I had breakfast, put the lunch that I prepared the night before in my backpack —three sandwiches, an apple and four litres of water— put my hat on and joined the group in front of the hostel across the street. We all jumped in a thirty-seater bus to reach the farm, a sort of big shed in the middle of the fields, in the beautiful Aussie outback.

The trip was short but rocky on the dirt road damaged by the mud. The girls were pretty happy about this adventure and I had to admit that when I realised what kind of transportation we got to reach the field, I was quite excited. We climbed the back platform of a big truck where eight big red cubic bins of about a cubic metre were placed. We jumped in one of them. We could seat at four in each of them…I felt like a clandestine immigrant hiding with his peers in order to cross the border. Once the truck stopped, we jumped off quickly to go into our field. There was nothing else but working lands in this flat landscape, the air was warm and humid. The tropical climate produced a wild flora with ponds and forest. The green covered most of the ochre lands of an Australia that I didn't know yet. The fields were split by long lines full of capsicums trees. Each of us got five to six buckets and took a line where we placed the buckets every two metres. Then, we started picking capsicums, following the boss' directions. He was Turkish and macho, with limited English composed by action sentences and some: "Hey Boy", "Hey girl", "Go there", "Two lines", "More buckets", "Stop talking", and "Faster," all with a strong accent that rolled the letter "R." I was definitely an immigrant paid to do a slave job in the middle of the poisonous cane toads and brown snakes, the second deadliest snake in the world with a bite that kills in twenty minutes, leaving no time to reach a hospital.

The heat and the sun were burning me all day; the farmer didn't let us go back to our stuff at the end of the field in order to put back sunscreen as it was a waste of productivity and my fair skin got sunburnt nearly every day. I nearly got fired one day because I couldn't stand the burn any longer I had to apply cream on my skin. This hot weather made the task even more painful and we usually finished at 4.30 or 5 pm, that is, when our driver didn't forget us in the middle of the fields because he was at the pub. In general, the rain would take over for amazing storms, very fresh. I was happy in the fields though, listening to music and trying to keep smiling despite the aches in my body. After six days, we had a day off because it was raining. Our only way out of the action. That morning, I couldn't get out of bed; I was way too sore. My whole body ached—my back, butt, arms, every part of it was in such a pain that I could barely move. We waited for the next day to get our pay and finally left because the rainy season had started a month early. It would just get worse, with no guarantee to work and the hostel still required two hundred bucks a week; it wasn't worth it. Lucky me, ten days later, I would have been stuck in the flooding. I decided to leave with two French guys, Marc and Cyril, who were living in my hotel. They were going on a road trip to Sydney with their car and I never planned to go there, but why not? I always wanted to do a road trip, so I joined them. We left the girls knowing that we would spend New Year's Eve in Sydney for its infamous fireworks.

We left on the evening of Friday, November 19, bound for Sydney, for ten days of adventures and road trip. We slept at Airlie Beach, forty-five minutes from Bowen after we set up the tent because it was still raining. The next day, we went to the rainforest in Finch Hatton Gorge; we walked across four rivers and five kilometres under the rain—the best way to enjoy the rainforest I guessed—until we reached a high waterfall. It was stunning but it was nearly dark and we had to run to go back to the car. Luckily, a friendly young Aussie bloke driving a four-wheel drive saw us struggling to cross back the rivers and gave us a lift back to our car. It was definitely easier to drive the now dangerous waters; we were drenched and glad to change our clothes. We planted the tent in Eungella National Park, near Rainbow Beach; there, the weather was nicer and the light of the moon reflected on the white sand of the Park, it was magic.

The next day, we went for a walk in Great Sandy National Park, in the forest. After seven kilometres, we finally reached the beach and the rain joined us for lunch. We decided to take another way back, but we got lost. When we finally met a ranger, he was surprised to hear that we took the forest path, in tongues and bare feet, without any water, under the now warm and sunny weather. He advised us to ask people for a lift as they should have been lots of four-wheel drives passing by on the beach. He found someone to drive Cyril back to our car for him to be able to drive back to Rainbow Beach while Marc and I tried to get a lift...but there weren't many cars and the rare ones couldn't take us. So we walked another seven kilometres along the beautiful beach, discovering new colours to the sand and the cliffs that separate us from the forest. We arrived on our knees but happy to have enjoyed such an amazing landscape, very deserted finally. The same night, we drove to Noosa and tried to sleep on the beach but the rain brought us back to the car. Sleeping seating wasn't easy but at least we were dried.

The sun came back the next morning, perfect for us to enjoy the beach and a first surf session for me. Till Tree Beach made me feel like I was in a washing machine before I finally managed to seat on my board to wait for a wave. This first time was exciting but very difficult on a small pointy board. After some food shopping and a well-deserved barbecue, we drove to Caloundra, a lovely city on the beach, and went to the lighthouse before sleeping in the car again.

After some light toasts and a coffee made on our gas stove, we went to the Glass House Mountains, where we could admire from the top of one volcanic point, sixteen others. The hike was steep and again, the rain surprised us. We just had the time to get undercover in a limestone cave before the storm. Half an hour later, the sun came back and we finished climbing the high hill. It was a sacred summit for the Aboriginals and I could see why. The landscape was mesmerising, green until the eyes could see, sixteen summits, all different in shapes and sizes, some red from the rocks, some green from the grass, trees, and plants. We felt like on top of the highest summits in Australia. It was so good to go up in altitude when we were used to be on sea level. After contemplating the beautiful three hundred and sixty degrees view, rich in humidity and life, we walked back down. We ate a nice noodles picnic with the flies before hitting the road again to King's beach where I had my second surf session; I got better at it but standing on the board was still a challenge.

The next day we drove south to Brisbane where we jumped on the Internet Wi-Fi to update our friends and family on our lives and went for a jug of beer with two of the boys' mates. In the evening, we were back on the road to Byron Bay and managed to sleep on the beach, finally there was no rain. The sunrise was beautiful, watching the dance of the dolphins on the horizon, a hot coffee in my hand. I tried another surf session but I quit very quickly. My body was exhausted, beaten by the waves and pulled by the currents and my surfboard, leached to my left foot. We rested on the beach where we spent another night.

On Saturday, we arrived in Nimbin after a forty-kilometre drive through the country. It was a city where hippies and all sorts of artists were living like back in time, trapped in the seventies.

We found psychedelic décors, had been offered marijuana cookies and other magic mushrooms and weed. This small community had also its own fair: "Mardi Grass," a sort of peaceful manifestation for marijuana legalisation. This year, they actually called out the American President Obama when he came to Australia –this drug being legal in some US states for medicinal purpose. This little joyful town made me feel like time had stopped while I was walking around the two main streets.

After a couple of stops along the road, we finally arrived in the first largest city of Australia, Sydney on Wednesday, December 1. We struggled to find our way since Manly Beach and as we couldn't park in the city –way too expensive– we found a hostel in Glebe, a student area, where we could park the car at night for free. We spent the next three days looking for a job, between the library –where we could surf online for free– and the streets of the city centre to dispatch our resumes. By Sunday, the girls from Bowen, Isabelle and Eloise, had joined us and we all enjoyed a day out at Bondi Beach –typical tourists– walking along the beautiful coastal path to Coogee Beach. It was nice to be back at the beach after three days walking in the city, even if the ocean water was freezing.

The following week, I spent my first days looking for a job with Isabelle, giving about sixty resumes to cafés and restaurants of the city centre and the Harbour. I looked for a job everywhere, until Thursday, giving my resume to all the shops of our local shopping centre too, the Broadway Centre. I already had some leads and had passed two trials, so I went to the Aquarium Museum with the boys on Friday. There, we could discover all the species of shark existing in the world and living in Australia too, and how scientists tagged them in order to observe their behaviour. You could also walk underneath a big aquarium through two glass tunnels and discover the sea life and all sorts of species: stingrays, sharks, tropical fishes, turtles and my favourite manatees. We had three hours of amazement and loved discovering Australian sea life, moon jellyfish, phosphorescent corals, seahorses and pig nose turtles.

I passed my RSA training that Saturday in order to be able to serve alcohol in New South Wales. Here alcohol was everywhere, even if it was very expensive, and it looked like a lot of people had issues with alcoholism. To be able to serve alcohol responsibly, I had to pass a licence (RSA) if I wanted to work in a premise selling it, like a pub or a restaurant. If anything happened to a customer who drank too much, I could get fined up to five thousand five hundred dollars and even go to jail. Well, luckily the teacher was really funny and I felt like at the comedy club as he had a true story for each subject we studied. Even with his strong Aussie accent, I managed to understand everything and I passed it easily after paying the required fifty bucks. Anyway, it looked like anybody could pass as long as they paid...all about business I guessed. On Sunday, I woke up early to go surfing with the boys at Maroubra Bay.

I got better but I also got a bad sunburn. Here, after half an hour, you could get burnt, even with sunscreen. I've never seen that before. I went to the chemist to get some ointment to soothe my skin and he freaked me out saying that after three sunburns you could get cancer, that here in Australia, the sun was different and I had to be careful. I got sunburnt so many times in my life, but even more since I was here, with picking and all. He was so serious he really got me scared.

On Monday, I wanted to make sure I had two jobs as my bosses should have called me on Friday but didn't. So I woke up at 7.30am to go to the pub in Glebe first and then go to the café in the city. Finally, I started the next morning at the café, from 7am to 12pm, Mondays to Fridays and at the pub on Friday night. I was happy to be finally integrated into the society, even if it wasn't my dream job, it was a start and I could really improve my English.

The Good Co. Café was located in the NAB bank building on George Street in the city centre; it was always full and one of the fifth most productive cafés in the city. I had to wake up at 5.30am all week for a 7 am start and would also close at 5.30 pm sometimes, being alone all afternoon to manage the seated service. I also worked at The Point Hotel —one of the oldest pubs in Sydney— located on Glebe Point Road, ten minutes away from our share house. Because I was now in a shared house—definitely living the Sydney life like a normal Sydney sider. We found a nice townhouse in Glebe, with two bathrooms, where we could all fit. Isabelle and I in the bedroom upstairs, Cyril and Marc, in one downstairs, on top of two Aussie brothers—twenty and eighteen years old students who just moved in—in another two bedrooms upstairs. The house was renovated and very nice to live in, especially since I'd been living all my life in a flat. There was a nice backyard, internet and all bills included. I should stay until my departure for Thailand with the girls in February. I loved Sydney, it was more hectic, dynamic and modern than Melbourne, but I loved the food and the kindness of people there too…I could see myself living here now. And job research was definitely easier than back home.

9

Next Wednesday, I have an appointment with my oncologist, who is apparently one of the best, if not the best in Australia for melanoma. We're about to leave home when I fall in tears thinking it could be the end, that I may not be here for my newborn, my son, and my husband. I get upset with John because he lets me cry alone.

"Can you come and comfort me please? I'm so sad," I ask him, sobbing.

"Why are you crying? I'm sorry we haven't left home yet. I'm ready now." He looks at me, baffled at my emotions.

"I'm not crying for that," I snap.

"What are you crying for then?"

"Because I'm scared. I'm so scared of dying. I want to see my babies growing; I want to be there for you…" I can't stop crying.

"I'm scared too. Oh, darling." And, taking me into his arms, he falls in tears too.

"Are you?" I asked surprised.

"Of course," he replied gently.

"Why?"

"I'm scared because I'm not sure. If something happens to you, I don't know what I will say to our kids, how I'm going to tell their mummy is not there anymore…that she's gone forever…" He's struggling to articulate. "What would I do without you? I'm lost without you. I won't be able to do anything without you." He is sobbing now.

"I'm so sorry love. I'm sorry this is happening to us." And I cry even more.

"You don't have the choice, you have to survive. You have to live. You can't leave me. I'm nothing without you, I need you," he replies wiping his tears.

"I'll try, I promise, I will try my best, but I can't guarantee you, I'm sorry. I don't want to let you down; I feel awful to do that to you and the kids. I'm so sorry."

And we're crying for a while, in each other's arms, until we realise it's late and we have to go. We dry our tears, swallow our sobs and leave home. It's by far the hardest and saddest conversation I've ever have with him, with anyone in fact. One of the most painful moments of my entire life. But the truth is that this surreal situation is indeed very sad. All the doctors, all our friends told us what a tragedy it is to be pregnant and have cancer. How sad it is to think that what should be one of the happiest moments of my life, the most wonderful moment of happiness for our family, is threatened by my own death, by the fact that I may not last long enough to see my babies growing.

If some director wanted to make a movie out of this, it would probably be a flop because people would think that it's a bit intense and way too much to be realistic. But it is real. And John is right, I've got no choice in the matter, I have to fight this with all my strength and survive. I can't let them down. I hope I'll survive and never have cancer anymore, never again, this one or another; I want to live happy forever with my little family, my lives. I don't want to tell anyone else, like John's family, unaware of the situation, I just want to survive and pretend nothing happened. I want it gone as fast as it came. I hope that if it began with my pregnancy, hopefully it will go away after the delivery, by miracle.

Once with the oncologist, she gives me two options, two different clinical trials if I'm stage III. Like any cancer, the determination of the gene mutation in the cancerous cells is crucial to find an appropriate treatment. I have a BRAF mutation, like forty per cent of people with melanoma, so I can participate in a clinical trial that would allow me to take a combination of two drugs, a therapy that target the cancerous cells, already approved for stage IV melanoma. In ninety per cent of cases, it helps to shrink significantly the tumours, so if I decide to take this trial, the surgery to remove the lymph nodes would be postponed for at least three months. The surgery should also be easier because the tumours should be smaller. Then I would continue to take these drugs for another nine months. The other clinical trial is randomised. I would have surgery and then

I would be either in a placebo group, so with no treatment, or in a group receiving immunotherapy. Apparently, immunotherapy boosts your own immune system to fight the cancer cells, limiting the reoccurrence. She gives me all the paperwork to read and study. Before anything, I have to do a PET scan to make sure I'm stage III. If I'm stage IV, it's another story and we will have to discuss again my options.

Once back at home, I discuss my options with John. All these pages of medical trials are difficult to understand, even if my oncologist did pretty well explaining most of the medical jargon to us, it's new to us and I want to be sure I make the right call; after all, my life is on the line. The reality is that I'm terrified. I'm scared because I don't know how long I have left. John doesn't want to know my prognosis and convince me not to ask my oncologist about it. It's too scary. But knowing how long I could last without treatment wouldn't be helpful anyway because I will have a treatment and there is no statistics available yet for the results of these new clinical trials. I hope I'm only stage III. I'd rather have twenty per cent chance to survive at ten years than only five. I want to see my kids growing and go to school, at least, getting married would be fantastic. I'm so scared and confused right now. I came to Australia because it was my dream and it's only been five years. I want to spend more time with John and the kids. Now that I have everything I ever wanted, I may lose it all? I remember when John and I fell in love, it was only a month we were dating and it all started with a weekend away in the Blue Mountains.

★★★

John decided to show me the Blue Mountains and organised a weekend away for me; he knew that no one ever organised a getaway for me before. It was a coincidence that this weekend fell on our one-month anniversary but I was happy it was and found the gesture very sweet. It was also a month we were waiting to be more intimate...It was my call and I was so glad I made it as our relationship was more intense that way. Things were getting warmer between us and we were like two teenagers falling for one another. Of course, this first weekend would be special, the next step in our relationship. Also I was excited to see this part of New South Wales as my sister told me it was beautiful. I had a cold but nothing would take the magic of this weekend away. He picked me up early and after a stop in a café for some takeaway beverages, we drove for two hours, chatting about the things we would do once there.

We arrived in front of the magical Three Sisters in Katoomba, appearing slowly underneath the morning fog coming from the rainforest underneath. We contemplated the view and took some pictures to immortalise the moment. Then, we walked in the rainforest and walked closer to one of the three rocks. It was beautiful. Later, we went to the local RSL Club for a beer and a quick bite while waiting for the check-in time of our hotel room. I didn't know what a RSL Club was, so he explained to me that at the start it was a place where war veterans met but now everyone could attend and get cheaper prices than in a local pub. At 2 pm, we dropped our bags at the hotel he booked for us; country style, a bit kitsch but comfortable. We left the room quickly to visit the area and we did all the tourists attractions. We took the Sky View, a sort of cable railway going across the valley, offering a glass bottom view to see the beauty of the Blue Mountains panorama: Three Sisters and the beautiful Katoomba falls with their over two hundred metres drop. It was short but impressive. Then we walked to the bottom of the falls to have a closer look and John told me he loved waterfalls and fireworks like me.

We took pictures, walked in the rainforest, he helped me walk across the river on the stones, discovered the beautiful landscapes of the Blue Mountains and the valley covered in a dense green forest. I love rides and I was so glad he took me to the steepest train in the world. It was fifty-two degrees of inclination with a very fast drop down the valley. It was awesome. We walked through the rainforest up to the coal mine and realised it was already five o'clock, time to go if we didn't want to walk all the way back to the top of the mountains. So we jumped on board of the last train and went for a beer in a local pub where the view of the mountains surrounding us was mesmerising. We talked for more than an hour. It was so relaxing being there with him and I had so much fun. When the sun was slowly going down, we got closer and looked in the same direction, watching the sky changing his blue colours to pink and bright orange and the mountains becoming blue, all sorts of blue depending on the distance they were at. I felt closer to him than ever. He had been a true gentleman all day, satisfying my thirst for discovery and adventure. I didn't think he realised how touched I was by what he was giving me, what no one else ever gave me: a wonderful weekend and most importantly the company of a genuinely generous and romantic guy. He had such a good heart and he was so patient with me. I had never encountered such a person...

We went back to the RSL Club for dinner, as the best restaurant in town was fully booked. John seemed a bit disappointed but I didn't care as long as we ate something and we were together. After a very basic dinner—I realised why he was disappointed bringing me there—we stopped by the dance floor and sat at one table to watch an old couple dancing a waltz. John sat me on his lap.

"See this old couple dancing?" he whispered in my ears.

"Yes, they seem so happy..."

"I love to watch these old people; it's so beautiful. They spent all these years married and are still together. Yet, they seem so happy; look at the way they look at each other..."

"You're right, it's beautiful. My parents used to argue so much when I was growing up, sometimes I wonder if they wouldn't be divorced if my mum hadn't had her stroke. These guys make it look so easy to be happy forever."

"Yes, they do. But I'm sure if you find the right person, you can be happy forever."

"Yeah, probably..." We were now looking in each other eyes with intensity and a long kiss followed.

"Do you want to go to the pokies?" I asked with enthusiasm.

"Do you play pokies?" he replied surprised.

"No, I don't but you're going to teach me."

And we went to the gaming room. I had some very basic knowledge thanks to my RCG. I picked a machine with lions pictured on the front and as I was Leo, I thought it could be of good fortune; my favourite animal would sort me out. I put a two-dollar coin in the slot and we played for nearly two hours. John couldn't believe it. We were talking about anything and everything while he was trying to explain to me how the lines worked and what was a feature. I won nearly thirty dollars and I insisted to pay for another round of beers for once. We laughed a lot and had so much fun. It was such a long time I didn't feel that good with a man, that I could be totally myself. I was lucky at the poker machines, certainly the beginner luck, but I felt even luckier to have this man in my life.

Then, it was time to go back to the hotel, the time to sleep in the same bed had come...I really felt like a teenager then, excited and shy, confused and anxious. We started to kiss passionately, caressing each other and finally the pressure was so big on us that after great foreplays, we stopped. We were a bit disappointed but happy to sleep for the first time together. We were tired and fell asleep very soon after, in each other arms.

We woke up the next morning, a bit tired and went for a coffee in the main street of Katoomba. We spoke about what happened the night before and I was trying to make him feel better because he seemed pretty upset about it. I didn't want him to feel uncomfortable all day and most of all, I didn't want him to think that I made a big deal out of it. We drove to the Victoria Falls, but once there, we noticed that we had to walk for six hours to see the actual falls. So we gave up and enjoyed the beauty of the valley. He also made me drive his car on the dirt road. I knew how to drive a manual car on the right side of the road, with the wheel on the left...but it was weird to sit on the right side and drive on the left. It was also uncomfortable using my left hand for the manual gearbox as I'm right-handed. But I did pretty well for my first time and we laughed a lot, John joking about the fact that I was a blond, a woman, driving on the wrong side of the road. I couldn't blame him, I thought the same.

We drove seventy-five more kilometres to the Jenolan Caves and the rain was pouring down when we reached the magnificent place. We couldn't visit the cave we wanted because of the weather so we went for a walk in the biggest one, accessible to everyone, above ground. It was close to a stream and we decided to follow it. We were like two adventurers. The rain was just a drizzle now and we could walk without being too annoyed. The stream brought us into the rainforest and we walked passed a nineteenth-century dam, and lots of dragon lizards. It was beautiful and we were happy to be there, enjoying the décor and each other's company; we laughed and poked at each other. After the dam, a beautiful waterfall gave birth to a nice little lake. And as the sun came back, a rainbow formed above the waterfall; it was magical. Lizards were everywhere and there was no one else around. It was just the two of us in this amazing landscape. We took some pictures up close, now so comfortable and happy together. Finally we went back to the car and I felt something tickling me on my ankles. I mentioned it to John and he became unsettled.

"Quick, show me."

I showed him my feet and he rubbed my ankles.

"What is it?" I asked, getting worried.

"Leeches. Look all over you. Shake your feet and check your shoes and pants. You need to take them off before they suck your blood," he said calmly, as if it were the most normal thing in the world.

"Whaaat?" I said panicking. "Leeches? Oh my God." I made sure he took them all off me.

"That's fine; the bloody suckers aren't that bad. Don't worry. I had one or two on my ankles too. Just make sure you don't have any more and we can go...I don't really want you to jump while I'm driving." He laughed.

"Haha, very funny. I'm not that scared come on. That's okay, I got rid of them. Anyway, I thought they were bigger from what my sister told me," I said with a relieved smile.

It was nearly night time when we reached Sydney, leaving the sunset and the Blue Mountains behind us. We had to stop for fuel and a quick sandwich.

"Can we stop by your place? I'd like to stay a bit longer with you tonight." I gave him a smile.

"Are you sure?" He replied surprised but happy.

"Yes, of course I'm sure. I'd like us to have another chance maybe..."

"Okay then, if you want, I am happy to have more time with you too."

We watched a movie together, loved on his couch and made love for the first time that night. It was a sweet, passionate, affectionate, and tender moment, full of loving cuddles. Then, we had a shower together in each other arms and enjoyed the hot water running on our shoulders.

"I had a very nice time with you this weekend," I said softly smiling.

"Me too." He replied kissing me on my forehead. "...Lucie?"

"Yes?"

"Can I ask you if you want to be my girlfriend now?"

"I'm already your girlfriend." I laughed. "I mean, I know how here there's this thing about dating someone and then becoming girlfriend boyfriend, but it's not like that in my country, so for me, from the moment we started kissing each other, you were my boyfriend."

"Really?"

"Yes, really. You know in France, we don't date."

"How come you don't date?"

"No, if you kiss someone and see regularly someone, you shouldn't see anyone else. This person is your boyfriend or girlfriend; you are supposed to be exclusive straight away."

"Really? That's weird."

"No, the other way around is weird." I laughed. "If you choose to be with someone, you shouldn't kiss or sleep with anybody else. It's how we do it anyway. Did you see anyone else while you were dating me?"

"No, I didn't. I was seeing someone before you but I stopped seeing her after our first date."

"Oh really. That's fine I guess." I laughed again. "So, this entire dating thing is not that good finally. I mean if you find someone interesting, you really don't have to see anybody else at the same time."

"Yes, I guess so. Can I tell you something?" He hesitated.

"Of course, what is it?"

"I'd like to tell you something but I'm not sure if it's the right time...maybe a bit early." He was shy suddenly.

"Don't say anything then, that's okay. You'll tell me later." I said thinking he would say the three big words and even if I was falling for him, I wasn't ready for it yet.

He drove me home reluctantly as if we wanted to stay together... the week would start again and we both had to work the next day.

John and I spent the next two months seeing each other as much as we could, despite our busy weeks. I was working fifty hours a week and we really had only a couple of nights together and Sundays. He guided me around Sydney—the north coast of Bondi beach, with its Fish and Chips shops on the harbour, Centennial Park, an immense park with black swans and ducks swimming on beautiful lakes and its trees full of bats. I was spending most of my Saturday nights at his place and we loved waking up on Sunday morning in each other's arms.

On the last Sunday of March, he introduced me to his dad, Stan. I was a bit anxious as he never had been very positive about his relationship with him. He was living in a housing and commission house of Maroubra, a Sydney suburb close to the beach. His German Shepard dog was barking when we were about to enter through the main door. It was dirty with stuff everywhere. The house smelt of dog and I hated it. There was dog hair everywhere and I felt quickly uncomfortable, even though his dad welcomed me with a big smile and a cup of tea. I was sitting on the edge of a very old and dirty couch and tried to keep appearances. They were talking in English but I could barely understand their conversation; it was way too fast for me and they were swallowing their words. His dad was skinny yet toned, average size, in pretty good shape for his age but his face was aged and full of wrinkles, his hair was blond and long, worn in a ponytail. He found me pretty, that was all I understood. There was a lot of slang and familiar Aussie language in their conversation so I gave up and looked around. The house was in a bad shape and his dad seemed to be a bit of a hoarder. He seemed nice though but poor and not very attached to cleanliness. I couldn't help remembering what John said about him and his troubled past. I had trouble breathing in this atmosphere and the situation made me feel more uncomfortable. I felt bad thinking that way though. What a petty, arrogant Frenchie I was. I should be less judgemental; that was the reason I also left France, all these people judging the book by its cover. I thought that if John was his son, at least he had done one thing right. I didn't want to punish John for his *"old man"* —what a weird expression. I was with John, not with him. I didn't choose my parents; neither did he. My *gentleman*, as I was calling him, didn't seem to notice my discomfort, just that I was quiet. At some point, I had to ask when we would leave so he would finally make the move. I was happy to get some fresh air and decided to leave this awkward experience aside for now. I didn't want to ruin a potential love story because of his family.

The next weekend, while I was spending the night at his place, after our usual movie night, John started to be sick. We were lying in bed and he was shaking, with fever. I started to be very worried because he was always so strong and fearless.

"What's wrong John?" I asked, very worried now.

"Nothing I'm okay, it's okay," he said shaking.

"I'm sorry that's not okay. You're boiling hot and you're shivering. Please tell me what's wrong? Are you hiding something?"

"No, it's just that I don't really want to talk to you about it." He sounded weird.

"Come on, what it is? You can tell me anything, trust me. Is that because you stop smoking weed for me?" I asked hesitating.

"Nooo. What a weird question. It's going to be fine, don't worry." He was in a weird foetal position.

"Okay, I'm starting to get upset now. Tell me what is going on, I am worried for you." I said, holding his chest in my arms.

"It's just that I am in such a pain…I've got haemorrhoids and it's getting worse…" He said a bit embarrassed.

"Are you kidding me?" I laughed. "Really. And that's what you didn't want to tell me." I couldn't stop laughing.

"It's not funny. I'm in a terrible pain," he grimaced.

"You're right sorry, it's just that it's a bit childish really…but I understand. Look, I'm very worried, you shouldn't be that bad. We need to bring you to hospital."

"No, that's okay really. I can't drive anyway…"

"I can; it's just that I don't know the roads, you'll have to guide me…"

"No, I'd rather stay here, not that I don't trust your driving skills…" he said trying to laugh through the pain.

"Okay, I'm going to ask your brother to drive us to the closest hospital."

"Okay…I'm not sure he will be willing to but you can try."

"Jacob?" I called while walking outside the room through the corridor.

"Yes…" He answered while I arrived at his bedroom door, obviously surprised to see me there that late at night.

"I'm sorry to bother you but your brother is very bad, he needs to see a doctor immediately. Could you drive us to the nearest hospital?" I said quickly.

"Oh yeah, of course, what's happening?" He asked now looking worried.

"Well, I'm not sure; I think it's because of his haemorrhoids..." I said with a smile. I never had haemorrhoids but I was just amused by all the suspense John went through to avoid talking about his butt.

"Okay, I'm ready, so we can go now if you guys want." He replied taking his car keys.

"Thanks, I get your brother. I was relieved we would do something about it."

And we all went to our local hospital in Kogarah, about fifteen minutes away. It was my first time in an Australian hospital. *I didn't know I would deliver my babies here one day either.* I spent the night by his side, waiting for the doctors to reduce his pain. He seemed embarrassed but happy for me to stand by him.

"Here, some chocolate for you." I just bought some Cadbury chocolate from the vending machine and thought it would be nice to show him some attention.

"Thank you but I'm not hungry...sorry."

"That's fine; just keep them for later, I bought them for you."

"The doctors may not see me before a while...You don't have to stay."

"I want to; I don't have anything better to do, except sleeping of course. Unless that makes you feel uncomfortable..." I was tired but I wanted to be there for him, he would have done the same for me.

"Exactly, you could sleep. You work tomorrow and you're going to be exhausted."

"That's okay. I'm fine, anyway it shouldn't be much longer now... it's been more than an hour, I'm sure the doctors will come back soon."

They had given him some painkillers and we were waiting for a doctor to examine him. Ten minutes later, I let him alone with the doctor and once he opened the curtain again, I could ask John what was the next step.

"So, what's up?"

"They will organise for me to go into surgery. I had many episodes like that and surgery will eradicate the problem once for all."

"Okay. I guess it's better to get rid of this issue as it seems very painful."

"They want me to spend the night in observation. So I'll ask my brother to drive you home okay?"

"Yes, thank you. I will try to get a couple of hours sleep before going to work. I hope you're going to be okay."

"Yes, I will try to rest, I'll be fine. Thank you for caring for me like you did tonight, I really appreciate."

"That's normal; you're my boyfriend isn't it?"

"Many wouldn't have done that. Nobody has ever done that for me."

"Well, I'm special, so I did," I said kissing him.

His brother drove me home and we had a quick chat in the car. He was single but had three kids from a previous relationship. They were now in foster care because he had a conflicted relationship with his ex. He seemed okay with it but I felt bad, as I couldn't imagine not being with my children if I had some one day.

I took a bus and two trains to go to his place the weekend after and we spent the weekend watching movies together, loved on his couch. He was in a bad shape after surgery and couldn't work for a month. His uncle came to pick me up the weekend after and we spent it watching movies again. It was nearly weird being in normal life with him, not visiting anything, like I wasn't a backpacker or a tourist anymore, just a permanent resident like everyone else. John seemed very pleased that I sacrificed my time doing nothing with him and staying by his side, taking care of him. I thought it was the right thing to do and I was missing him during the week so I was happy to see him after work and spend my time in his arms. John made an effort the next Monday and picked me up after my shift at the café. We had a romantic walk through the botanical garden, circular quay and enjoyed the sunset on the waterfront at the Rocks. It was a very revealing time, as he couldn't work; it was my turn to finance all our date nights. I even helped him paying his rent as his own mum didn't seem very happy to help him out. It reminded me of the story with my last ex back home and I hated money issues in my couple. But I knew that John was different and far more honest and humble than my ex. He hated that I helped him pay the bills. I hoped it was the One this time and that I wasn't making any mistake investing in this relationship.

On the 14th of April, after two months spent together, John picked me up after my shift. As usually on Thursdays, he was at the pub with his mates until I finished and then we went to the Toxheys pub, further up on Glebe Point Road. We ordered a beer at the bar and sat outside, in the smoking area.

"So how was your day?" I asked happy to finally relax after work.

"You know, the usual work day. What about you?"

"Yeah, good. Good. You know, I wanted to tell you that I am glad you don't smoke anymore. I know it was a lot for you but I really appreciate you quit for me. I didn't want another boyfriend smoking weed; it's just a source of conflict really."

"I understand, no worries, it was pretty easy to stop actually," he said happily.

"Yes, talking about that…I found it strange that it was that easy…I mean I used to smoke a bit too, and not since I was fifteen like you but it was hard for me to give up. So, I'm really surprised you dealing with this pretty well…" I trusted him but I couldn't help doubting.

"There's nothing strange. It's just a matter of willpower, and usually when I make a decision, I never come back on it. I did that for you because I know you wouldn't stay with me otherwise, and I'd rather be with you."

"Yes, I know, thank you. You know I like you a lot and I really want this relationship to work out. I mean, you're special to me and I don't want anything to ruin what we have."

"Yes, me neither…what's wrong then?"

"To be honest, I don't like that you still get the weed for your mates. It's weird. You shouldn't do that. After all, you quit, so you shouldn't be near any temptation…"

"So you don't trust me."

"Of course I do…"

"Well obviously not," he said, getting upset.

"Don't get mad. I didn't want you to take it the wrong way," I begged.

"Well, how do you want me to take that?"

"I just don't think it's a good idea, that's all. I'd like to trust you on this but I'm not sure I can really…why would you persist on helping them for that, it's their problem, they can deal with it." I couldn't stand this argument, our first argument.

"I know the guy that's all. I quit for you; what more do you want from me?"

"Nothing. It's just that I'd feel better if you stopped. Why should I trust you on this anyway? Why would you insist otherwise?"

"You should just trust me."

"No I shouldn't. Give me a reason why I should. Really... Give me a reason why I should trust you with this? Who knows if you're not still smoking when you're not with me?"

"Because..."

"Why? Tell me? Why?" I was pushing him to tell me.

"Because...I love you." He said these words meaningfully but like he wanted to shut me up at the same time. Great success.

"What?" I was shocked.

"I love you. That's why you should trust me. I would do anything for you." He was comforting me so well.

"Oh, really? I love you too John." I said smiling now.

I trusted him. It was a week I was desperate to hear these words and somehow I managed to extract them out of him. I was happy, we were happy. All of a sudden, there was only the two of us in the courtyard of the pub, staring at each other with watering eyes and a big smile on our faces. It was like both of us needed to hear these words and we felt even closer after sealing the love deal. We spend a lovely rest of the evening, closer than ever.

We spent the following weekends visiting around: Parramatta markets, Balmain, Balmoral beach where we had a little dance in the garden kiosk, Shoulder Bay, George Head. We loved spending time together, he was showing me his beautiful city and I never had that much fun and that many romantic walks. Also, we were awkwardly followed by brides and grooms everywhere we went. It was probably due to the fact that these romantic and beautiful places were also chosen by the newlyweds for their wedding pictures. So when it first happened, we just noticed it, saying something like, "look there's a bride and a groom." But one date after another, it became random. Every single time we met, there was a couple in their wedding outfit. It was like a sign following us.

So, early on, we started talking about how important marriage was for us and figured that we both wanted the same thing in a relationship and this one was serious. Also, we both wanted to marry our soul mate, for the forever commitment of love, because marriage was one of these sacred things that we wished to succeed, divorce wasn't an option. The old couple from the Blue Mountains was our model of happiness. I was glad to have found someone who shared my values and my thoughts about true love and marriage. He also wanted two children, just like me.

Soon, it was Easter and John brought me to the Sydney Royal Easter Show. I had never seen anything like it. It was like a mix of the Paris International Agricultural Show, the International Home Show we've got in Nice and a giant Luna Park, with trophies and all sorts of brand promotion in between. A massive field covered with stalls and animals, rides and show bags, all sorts of food and a giant arena with horses and old-school cowboy performances…we had a wonderful time there on the Monday before Easter. John came and picked me up at the café at lunch before heading to the show. It was an amazing surprise and I felt like a little girl, my eyes looking around everywhere, amazed by every little thing I'd see. We enjoyed all the craziest rides and bought all those stupid pictures they sell you a fortune. I had seen a cute purple teddy bear and John decided to win it for me. What a mistake. He nearly spent fifty bucks on this strong man hammer thing and didn't get it. I had to beg the guy and negotiate another ten bucks to get it, but we got it.

Once back home, after the great fireworks in the arena and a long time kissing and talking at the front door of my house, I was walking back upstairs to my room and while opening the staircase window, I dropped the teddy bear outside. I couldn't believe it. After so much effort trying to get the bloody bear, I lost it. He fell over the neighbour's fence. I had to get it back…I run downstairs, open the front door, opened the front gate, got out of my house and went straight to the neighbours. Nobody seemed to be home, even if I could see a light on. I tried all the three bells of the intercom, no answers. I panicked. I loved this bear and it was my gentleman's first present to me really, after all the roses anyway. I went back home, to the backyard, taking a chair from the kitchen on my way. I jumped on the chair and climbed the fence. I jumped on this other side, in my neighbour's yard. I was scared; this was so illegal. But Teddy was there, luckily not too wet, even after the bit of rain we had in the evening. I was glad to see a bin next to the fence and I climbed on top of it before climbing the rest of the fence and jumping back in my side of the yard. Wow, that was something. I laughed and walked back inside. I went upstairs, avoiding the dangerous window and got ready for a good night sleep. I had to tell John about the crazy events that just happened and we laughed over the phone. It was such a good day.

Easter was a very long five days weekend, a good opportunity for John and I to spend more time together and also for him to introduce me to the rest of his family. On Easter Sunday, we drove to his uncle's house in Wollongong for their family traditional lunch. His mum, her four brothers: Georgio with his wife and two kids, Tino, Luigi, Paolo and his wife, and his brother Jacob were already there. I found them very nice and chatted with all of them; they were nearly trying to marry us already. John never introduced them to anyone before so I felt very special and flattered once again. Later, John drove me through the city; we stopped at the lighthouse and admired the coastal beaches. He talked about his childhood here and decided to drive me around to show me where he used to live; his school and his childhood neighbourhood. Between the suburb of housing and commissions he used to live in, his troubled past and his complicated family, I could have run. But I loved him so much already, I stayed. He had gone through this and created a better life for himself, he left everything behind him and started over in Sydney, like I did; he was such a great guy and he didn't choose his childhood, nobody does. And that was what made him the amazing man he was now, the man that I loved. He was so different to anyone I had met before, he was special and we had so much in common. We were from two different and faraway worlds and we had finally met, after all these years apart.

Once at my place, I cooked two delicious pizzas from scratch and my favourite chocolate fondant for a diner with my friends. We spent the rest of the night in Newtown, drinking and celebrating Calum's departure. My last friend in Australia was about to leave. And maybe it was time for me to make the move too.

10

It's time. After spending the past two weeks organising the delivery of my second child, the day has come for me to leave home with my bag, my husband, and my son for a quick stay at our local hospital. I'm feeling anxious but prepared. After all, I already gave birth once and despite the circumstances, everything went well. It's my second child and third pregnancy. I don't think I've been very lucky so far with pregnancies, except for the fact that I got a boy like I wanted last time. I hope to get what I want this time again, it would be one good thing out of a pretty hard pregnancy...again. It's Sunday October 25, 2015, at one o'clock in the afternoon when I arrive at the maternity ward and I wait for the obstetric team to show me my room.

"Lucie?" A nurse asked me with a friendly tone.

"Yes, that's me," I answer with a bit of apprehension.

"So, you're here for an induction, is that right?"

"Yes..."

"I will show you your room and then we will start to prepare you. Hopefully by 5 pm you'll have your first injection. Did the obstetrician explain to you what is going to happen?" She asked nicely.

"Yes. I came last week for the paperwork and to prepare everything for the birth. I had my injections of a steroid to open the baby's lungs, and she said that once I will be here, you will monitor the baby and then you will apply a gel to provoke the contractions."

"Yes, the gel rarely works, but we'll try and if it doesn't work, we will inject a hormone to start the labour. Are you okay?"

"I have to say, I'm a bit scared. You know my first baby was very premature and somewhere I'm afraid to give birth to a premature again, after all we've done to avoid an early birth with progesterone treatment."

"You're going to be fine. It's very rare for the first injection to lead to labour; mums usually need two of them before feeling contractions. I know this must be hard within your circumstances, but you're in good hands." She reassures me.

She installs me in my room. They organised a room just for me, a very nice touch knowing that this birth was special. John and Jason spend the next couple of hours with me before heading to their ward. The nurse starts the process at 4 pm, but after two hours, nothing had happened and they give me the first injection of Prostaglandin. After six hours, still nothing. So at 1 am, I receive a second injection. Ten minutes later the contractions start...and how painful they are. I don't recall my contractions for Jason being that bad. They are violent and close to one another. At 1.30 am, I'm transferred to the delivery suite. John is by my side half an hour later. He's sleeping in Jason's bedroom in the other hospital wing. The children's ward is on the same level as the maternity ward and it's very comforting to know that this time he will be there for the delivery and no one would have to call him endlessly.

They're giving me some gas and even if it didn't do anything for Jason's birth, this time I feel like flying. It's working and I'm pumping on the machine like a maniac. John is laughing. But I have to take it, the pain is unbearable and I ask for an epidural. When the anaesthetist finally comes at 3.15am, I have to decide against it; I went from three centimetres to six in half an hour and they tell me that at this rhythm the epidural won't kick in before the delivery. I'm also very scared of the big needle because I will have to stay still while they perform the injection, even with the crazy pain and contractions I'm experiencing, I'm afraid it's going to be impossible. After twenty minutes though, I'm still at the same point, so I decide to go for it, whatever, the pain is too intense. I hope it will work, fast enough and hopefully before the birth. It's already painful enough, so thinking of pushing that life out of me—when I suffered so much for my tiny fourteen hundred-gram Jason—I don't feel like going through this with a nearly three-kilo baby. I had morphine and gas already, but it's not enough.

Another twenty minutes later, I'm sitting on the edge of my bed, trying to stay still, holding John's hand and praying it will be fine. I'm scared of doing this epidural with this cancer...it must be silly but after all, who knows what could be the side effects? I manage to stay fifteen minutes without moving, enduring the pain of labour, yet staying as still as possible, getting the pain out of my system through breathing and grunting. After the local anaesthesia comes, the massive needle. After a little while, the drug kick in and I'm glad I've done it. What a relief Okay, it would have been nice to pretend I was a warrior and gave birth with no painkillers, but I wouldn't have changed a thing. I can feel the contractions but without the pain. I even get the chance to rest a bit and nearly fall asleep.

Around 4.30 am, John has to go back to see Jason; our son woke up when the nurses came to bring John by my side and since then, he was playing. John explains to them how to put Jason back to bed and comes back. Now he's sleeping peacefully. Once I'm fully opened; the midwife nudges me and tells me that we are going to proceed to the delivery. It's 6.30am. They calmly tell me how to push with each contraction and breathe through them. I have to push three or four times at each contraction, everything is in the breathing, I don't have any pain, but I still feel what's happening and it's an amazing experience. I don't have any stress and can peacefully focus on breathing and pushing, photographing every second in my memory. The only problem is that I can't feel or move my legs, like I'm disabled, so when one of my legs falls on one side, they have to move it for me.

I'm a bit disappointed that John doesn't want to film the delivery, so halfway through, they show me what is happening with a small mirror and I can see the hair on my baby's head coming out. They even tell me to touch it. It's beautiful. At 7.56am, I deliver a beautiful baby. John's got tears in his eyes and again, when they place our baby on my bare chest, John looks at me and says "Look, it's a girl." I can't believe it's real. All that time, I was right, we were right, we knew it would be a beautiful baby girl and here she is, covered in vernix and so calm. It's been so easy. The entire thing was such a breeze, she is such a miracle. I've got what I wanted, my gorgeous girl. John and I agree to call her Rose—the only name we found anyway—a beautiful name for our beautiful daughter.

I ask them not to cut the cord straight away so they wait nearly fifteen minutes before asking John to do it. Rose was so peaceful, resting on my chest, sleeping, like nothing happened, like she was still inside me. She stays there for another two and half hours. I'm so happy to be able to keep her against me. Then they weight her and give her vitamin K and hepatitis C vaccine. She weighs two kilos eight hundred and sixty grams for fifty centimetres and thirty-four centimetres of head circumference, born at thirty-six weeks and three days, as expected. It was weird to know the date of the birth in advance, but I'm so glad she's healthy, needs neither oxygen nor help to breathe and doesn't have to go to the NICU. I can keep her with me and she's a girl. Thank God. After about forty minutes, she even starts breastfeeding. I realise how much I missed out on with Jason's birth. I wish I could have had that with him too. Now, John brings Jason in to meet his sister.

"Jason, here's your little sister," says John, approaching Jason slowly to my chest.

"Her name is Rose," I say, gently putting his hand on her.

"Ose," replies Jason, intrigued, touching her hand gently, then her face.

"It's your little sister. You need to take care of her, so be gentle with her; she's only a baby," John explains to our son.

And we all laugh and contemplate the beauty of this magical family moment; John and me, our boy and our girl, the four of us, our family, now finally complete.

On her first day, I have to wake Rose up to feed her because she's too tired and still quite small but she gets better after a couple of days. Unfortunately, she's got jaundice, still under the limit to use the UV lamp, but we have to stay at the hospital until it's finished. I can't wait to bring her back home and I'm missing Jason. He's coming with John every night after day-care pickup. He's curious, a bit bored too and keen to have his mummy back. He's a bit scared to touch his sister like she's a little animal in his eyes. I want all of us to be together at home and I hope Rose will be good to leave very soon, especially since I have my PET scan on Friday.

Falling asleep at night, I have the beautiful faces of Jason and Rose in mind. Rose is blond with blue eyes, like me. I'm so happy I got what I wanted. It's really a miracle and I hope I will get what I want most of all—my life, for a very long time. They will give me the strength to fight this cancer, for every day I have. I finally have the family I've always wanted, nothing will take that away from me, not even cancer. I feel so lucky to have met John. What a coincidence it was; fate for sure.

With time, I come to the conclusion that it was such a miracle that I met John. If my sister hadn't met her half Australian first love, she would never have wanted to go to Australia; she would never have talked to me about it. If I didn't leave my class preparing for business school, I would never have gone to this big orientation event, never studied with La Trobe Bendigo, a partner of my school. Then, Australia wouldn't have been part of my dreams for so long. If I didn't lose my job, broke up with my boyfriend and got depressed back home, I would never have decided to realise my dreams. If I hadn't found the strength within me to go against everyone and follow my heart, I would never have come to Australia. Our relationship is the results of so many elements that, if they had been slightly changed, would have changed the course of our lives and we might have never met. We were born twenty thousand kilometres apart and finally united by a spiral of coincidences. It was like all the elements, good or bad in my life had resulted in our wedding. We were meant to be together.

On Friday, we are out of the hospital and finally I can bring my baby home with me. She lost hundred and sixty grams the first two days but stayed stable since then. She's taking ages to feed, at least an hour, but I'm used to it, like brother like sister. The jaundice is still there but feeding her every three hours should help. I don't want to go through the craziness of trying the breast, then expressing and bottle feeding. Anyway, I won't breastfeed too long because I will have to take my cancer treatment soon and I can't breastfeed with it. So if she struggles after ten minutes on my breast, I'll bottle-feed her. Jason was distressed by my absence and woke up every night so I can't wait to start our new routine at four and have my boys back.

At 11.30 am, I arrive at the nuclear centre in Darlinghurst. John leaves me there; the kids can't stay because of the radioactivity. The doctor calls my name and I follow him in a small room where he asks me the routine questions for a PET scan, tests my blood sugar, weighs me, and places a cannula on top on my right hand. Then he asks me to leave my clothes, put on a gown, and wait in another room. There, I lie on a bed, underneath a warm blanket, while a nurse gives me a contrast to drink. It tastes metallic. She comes back with a syringe and the isotope to inject, placed in a protective metallic system. She places herself behind a thick metallic board and proceeds to the injection. It looks dangerous and I'm a bit scared of all this radioactivity being transferred into my body but I've got no choice; I need to know what I'm up against. I drink three glasses of contrast, twenty minutes apart.

While lying there, I've got all the time to think about what's happening to me, how the nightmare started, the lump, the delivery, my beautiful Rose. I hope I'm not at stage IV, that this experimental treatment will work, that I can care for Jason and Rose without issues, keeping my strength and remaining positive. My children are such a blessing, they are so beautiful and amazing, so fragile and so young.

After an hour lying down, it's my turn. I follow the nurse into another room, where sits a very big cylindrical machine. I lie down where she tells me to and she places some kind of fabric around my arms for them not to move. Then, she lives me alone. Once the door is closed, they start the machine. My eyes are closed and I can feel the machine going backward into the big cylinder. It's noisy and I must stay still. It lasts forty minutes, going back and forth slowly. They are reading my body, soon I'll know. Once the machine stops, I can get changed and they remove my cannula. The results are printed on a CD fifteen minutes later and I can leave. I won't be able to breastfeed for the next six hours and I can't see my babies for at least four hours. I decide to walk through Darlinghurst to get to the Kings Cross train station. On my way, I see an old church and I enter. There's no one else. I pray and beg for my life. I light a candle and leave a note in the book of prayers. I hope someone heard me. My heart is broken by sadness and fear. I'm so scared of what the results can be. When I finally get home, I am so glad to hold my baby again, laugh with Jason and kiss my husband. They are all my life, I love them so much.

We spend the weekend enjoying our new life at four. It feels so good to have the family I've always dreamt of; I can't believe I got what I wanted, I'm so spoiled. Since I arrived in Australia five years ago, I've been so spoiled. I obtained every single thing I wanted. I wanted to find the One, I found him. I wanted to stay in Australia, I got to stay. I wanted a good marketing position, I got it. I wanted a boy, I got a boy. I wanted a girl with my eyes and my hair, I got it too. I've been so blessed, so lucky. I want to survive this and live now, I hope I'll get that too…I don't want to be greedy. But I really need it; not for me, for my family.

On Monday, we finally get our answer: we know at which stage of melanoma I am. We have another appointment with my oncologist at the centre for Melanoma in North Sydney. John and I are sitting in front of her, holding hands. Baby Rose in the pram next to us and Jason is at day-care. After welcoming Rose and praising her beauty, she becomes serious.

"So we've got the PET scan results…and we're not where we expected to be, unfortunately."

"So…do you mean I'm at stage four?"

"Unfortunately, yes. The PET scan shows metastasis in both your armpits, pelvic bones, spine, tailbone, and collarbone. You're at stage four, I'm sorry. The cancer is very aggressive and spreading rapidly."

I turn towards John, desperate and try to hold my tears. Our worst nightmare is now real. I knew it somehow; I could feel it in my bones, literally. That was the reason why I was so sore after the delivery. I didn't break my tailbone, it was bloody melanoma. Now I know why my back was sore and somewhere I feel lucky that my brain is still intact. John and I are devastated though. Our world is falling apart all over again. It's the worst-case scenario and it's for me. I can't bear the thought of losing my babies, I'm looking at my new-born in the pram and I burst into tears. I let a relieving gasp out, coming from my guts, excruciating; the one I held onto all weekend. I will just have to fight this shit. I'm terrified.

At least we know now. We can start treatment as soon as possible. After letting the tears out of my system uncontrollably, with John's arms around me, the doctor gives me tissues as she's probably used to. I wipe my eyes and try to compose myself.

"So now what are my options? What kind of treatment is available?" I don't want to ask about prognosis, which will only make me feel worse. I need to kill this thing before it kills me.

"You just missed out on an immunotherapy clinical trial but at your stage, there are two treatments on Pharmaceutical Benefits Scheme (PBS) partially refunded by Medicare. The standard treatment for a BRAF mutant patient like you is the combination of Trametinib and Dabrafenib. The same treatment you could have had on the clinical trial for stage III I talked to you about last time. It will shrink the tumours and hopefully we will be able to get you onto another immunotherapy trial as soon as one comes up because usually patients develop a resistance to this treatment after nine months. The other option is immunotherapy with Keytruda. It boosts your immune system to kill the cancer. Only fifty per cent of patients respond though but some of them are now clear of the disease. Unfortunately, you can't get it straight away unless you pay for it, because Medicare will refund it only if the first treatment doesn't work anymore.

"Really?"

"I know, unfortunately that's how it is."

"How much costs Keytruda?"

"It's very expensive, about eight thousand dollars just for one infusion, you need to add the hospital costs so for one injection you're looking at about seventeen thousand dollars. You'll need an infusion every three weeks and we don't know how long you're going to need them for, if it works on you."

"Okay then, I guess I don't have much choice in the matter. I will take the targeted therapy."

"At least, you start the treatment today. Like I said, this treatment works on ninety per cent of patients, shrinking by at least fifty per cent the tumours, the statistics are very good compared to the immunotherapy, Keytruda, working on only one patient out of two. So hopefully you should see your tumours shrinking quickly. As soon as there is an immunotherapy trial available, I'll let you know and we'll try to get you in as immunotherapy works better if it's taken in the early days."

"Okay, I hope there's going to be a clinical trial soon."

"I know it's disappointing to be at that stage but at the same time we now have two standard treatments, which wasn't the case five years ago. Research progresses very fast, and somehow it's a good time to have melanoma!" She said with half a smile

"Well, I guess I have to gain some time so I can still be there when they find a cure!" I look at my daughter.

"You have a beautiful baby girl..."

"I'm so worried not to be there for her..." I struggle articulate, a bowl of pain forming in my throat

"Listen..." She says looking at me in the eye, "we're going to do our best to save you, it's going to be fine."

"Really?"

"I'll try my best, I promise." She smiles.

And that's all I had to hear. I will hold on that sentence forever, as if it's the promise I will survive. It's hard to believe; the odds are against me, but I have to believe it. I will start my treatment tonight.

11

I spend my time thinking about my life, all the things I've done so far. I realise how much I've accomplished in only five years: skydiving, flying by myself to Australia, backpacking, picking in the middle of brown snakes, going on a road trip, surfing, getting married, snorkelling on the Great Barrier Reef, bungee jumping the highest jump in the south hemisphere, being pregnant three times, losing a baby, having a wonderful little boy, having a gorgeous baby girl...Having terminal cancer. With the birth of my children, I also discover that being at home is being with my family, the people I love the most. Wherever they are, they are my home.

I have to write a bucket list again. All my dreams came true and now my life is at stake, but I still have dreams, new ones. I have to do something about it. I'm in some kind of a rush. I feel pressured for time. The most beautiful dreams may not be possible but I will try my best to accomplish most of them and be as close as possible to the impossible ones. Yet, the best will be to have conversations with my kids, to hear my daughter's voice. I will fight for them, I will be strong; I have no other choice but survive. I think about John and I wish that my love story is strong enough to do miracles, that our love will save me, so we can stay together. Because I love him so much, even through the bad times, even when we argue; he's making me happy, I love his smile and his sense of humour and he is, with our children, the best things that ever happened to me. I remember how he left everything for me and proposed to me.

***

It was the end of April 2011 and it was time for me to make the big decision. I was already six months into my Working Holiday Visa and I wanted to stay in Australia. The only way to renew my visa for another year was to go picking for three months. It was part of my plan from the start, but now that John was in the equation, I didn't want to leave him for so long. On the last Thursday of the month, he came home after my shift and I had to talk to him about my decision. We were sitting at the kitchen table.

"John, you know I really would like to stay in Australia, and for that, I need to renew my visa, as mine will expire in six months at the end of October."

"Yes, I know..."

"So I decided to find some picking. I will have to go away for three months at least. I must find some picking somewhere in Australia, where I can work for three months so I can renew my visa without spending too much time away from you...because if I find a job for one month somewhere then need to go somewhere else for another month and then again for a third time, it will take me too long and I may not be able to stay. So I thought that the best would be to find a region where there is enough picking for three months and find a farmer who can guarantee me a job for that long...making sure that he will sign the paperwork for the Australian Department of Immigration too."

"Wow, it sounds so complicated to renew this visa," he said surprised.

"Well, you got to do what you got to do. And I really want to stay here, especially since I've met you..."

"Yes, I'd like you to stay here too..."

"You know the more I think about it, I can't help but feel sad that I will be away from you for that long...I mean three months don't seem much but I will miss you so much."

"I will miss you too my angel," he said sadly.

"But I really need to go, it's the only chance I've got. I am so scared being away from you though." I burst into tears.

"You're going to be fine." He took me in his arms and comforted me.

"But what if you forget me? Or you find someone else; I don't want to lose you." I was now crying big tears.

"I would never do that. I love you. I won't forget you, you're my angel. Life is so much better with you...You could find somebody else, look how beautiful you are." He said with a smile, his eyes humid with tears.

"No. I don't want to. I want to be with you. Three months seem so long without you. I don't know what to do. I don't want to leave without you."

"What do you want me to do?"

"I don't know. I'm lost. I love you so much but at the same time I have to go, otherwise I won't be able to be with you more than six months and it's been so good between us, I really want to give us a chance, but three or four months far away from you seems like forever. I really don't want to leave you."

"Then...I'll come with you." He said with a smile.

"Really?" I said surprised but happy.

"Yes, really. I want to be with you too, so why not?"

"But what about your work?"

"I will have to find a job wherever you'll go. I don't think it should be too hard."

"Oh my God. That's fantastic. Oh I love you, you're the best. I can't believe you're doing that for me." I was so excited.

After this comforting conversation, I advised both my jobs that my last day was the thirteenth of May and that was it. I spent the next two weeks trying to figure out which part of Australia was the best for picking and started packing my bags. I called Harvest Australia for some information and it didn't look good: there was nothing in the West for the moment and if there was any picking, there were so many backpackers there that I would probably arrive too late, and Queensland was just recovering from the summer flooding. I didn't want to bring John with me in a trap, even if he thought that an Aussie like him would find a job anywhere. I was hoping I could sort something out quickly.

My regular customers at the pub were aware of my departure and they all offered to help me out. That's so Australian, always helping each other out; I loved it. So after a few days, one of them gave me the details of a farmer, Lucas, who was cultivating mandarins in a small town near Bundaberg in Queensland; he could offer me a job packing. I just had to call him once I was there. Awesome. Bundaberg it was. I was a bit scared of this big jump into the adventure and the unknown because it was also a big step forward for the three-month-old relationship we had. John and I had also decided that we would probably live together after these three months, as he would be replaced by another roommate and I wouldn't have a place either. Everything seemed to go very fast and my head was spinning.

My disastrous past love stories didn't help me and I started to doubt. John was about to give most of his stuff to his best mate, Matt, and try to sell the rest to get some cash to help me out, as I was the one paying for everything since his surgery. Still, he was leaving everything behind him to follow me on this crazy adventure, with nothing for sure once we would be there. I was just hoping we wouldn't break up because we wanted to move too fast. I hoped for a great trip together; hopefully, we could both find a job and come back to Sydney happier than ever.

It was already a week we were on the road since we decided to make it a road trip rather just go straight to Bundaberg in order to enjoy some time off together. We left Sydney behind us, our accommodations, all his stuff except for a bag of clothes and my luggage as well. He left his labourer position and I left my waitress and barmaid jobs. We took the road together for our big adventure, leaving our past behind and just taking our short story with us, ready for the next chapter of our life together. I couldn't believe he did that for me, he left his life behind for me. Nobody ever did that for me before. The pressure was on though. I couldn't screw it up. I was really hoping that Lucas the farmer could help out, I needed it.

We spent our first week travelling across New South Wales and Queensland, and sleeping in caravan parks, in the small tent we purchased for the occasion. I loved camping but John wasn't a fan really, always saying "I work my arse off all year; it's not to do it rough once on holidays." But I made it my mission to convince him. On our way to Queensland, we stopped by Hat Head, Trial Bay Gaol (an old jail), then we travelled along the coastal beaches: South West Rock, Macksville, Coffs Harbour, and the Big Banana. I found it so funny that in Australia, they have all these big things. The big mango was in Bowen, regularly stolen for some reason. The big pineapple, the big prawn, the big potato, you name it. We were trying to achieve as many "big" things as possible since that day. We had a great time in a very nice holiday park in Corindi and I was awake to take some beautiful pictures of the sun rising on the ocean. Life was easy; it was the first time we spent that much time together, our first holidays really. John always listened to a classic rock radio in the car and I could now recognise some of the classic Australian hits. It was like I was back in time, between the old music, the camping and the way Australians lived outside the big cities. It was so different from home.

Then, we went through Grafton, Woodburn, Ballina, Murwillumbah and the beautiful Natural Bridge National Park. Lucky we had my Lonely Planet book, so we didn't miss the beauty of this park. It was mid-afternoon when we arrived there and we decided to go for a romantic walk to the waterfall. We discovered a majestic waterfall in a cave full of glow worms. I had never seen anything like it before. It was like a milky way on the rock ceiling of the cave surrounding the waterfall. As it started to get darker outside, we walked back to the car at night, through the dense rainforest, following the glow worms now everywhere along the footpath. That was the most magical moment I ever witnessed; we were both amazed by the surreal view the surroundings offered to our mesmerised eyes. We drove off to find a camping spot in Burleigh Heads, on the Gold Coast.

The next morning, we got coffee from a French café before having a walk on the beautiful beach of Surfer Paradise. It was so nice to be together, to discover all these beautiful views of Australia by his side. He could now see everything through my eyes too. I guess it's so different where you don't come from the country you're visiting…from the shops, the architecture, the habits, the pubs, the people, the fashion, the music, even the brands and products you buy are different, without mentioning the deadly spiders or the snakes. We left again to go across Brisbane and had lunch in Caboolture. Then, we headed north to Noosa and spent the night at Noosa River Caravan Park. On the way, we started to argue because we didn't find a place to stay yet and it was getting late, caravan parks were closing soon and we were tired. John could be so stubborn sometimes and he gave me the silent treatment instead of trying to solve the issue.

I hated us being apart. I hated us being in bad terms. So when I realised that there was the surfer league club next to the park, I told John we should go for a drink and try to relax instead of butting heads. Before entering the Club for karaoke night I asked him for a smile and a hug to bury the battle axe. And we had so much fun singing our song *"Through your arms around me."* I was terrible but tried again with a Pink song and we finished our night singing together "*With or without you*" from U2, one of my favourite songs. John hated karaoke but he sang for crazy me. I didn't care as I had no shame at being a terrible singer and enjoyed the night laughing with my love.

After a few drinks, we were a bit tipsy and we walked along the beach to go back to our little tent. Somehow, we started noticing each other's faults; but instead of pulling us apart, it brought us closer. He told me that I questioned things too much and he complained too much for my liking. But being on the road wasn't easy, especially when I was paying for everything. He was the one driving all the time and we didn't speak the same language. It was hard enough for a man and a woman of the same mother tongue to understand each other, so you can imagine how bad it could get at times when, on top of that, the Martian and the Venusian don't speak the same language. But love arranges everything and we didn't want to split anyway; understanding each other was also part of the love story.

I was now driving and it wasn't easy considering I was on the wrong side of the road and everything was opposite to what I was used to back home. So I was happy when we left Noosa and its hundred roundabouts. His car, a little black Daihatsu Sherade pimped with an imported Japanese engine, started to have some issues and we had to get it checked by the nearest mechanist…in Gympie, a very small town in the middle of nowhere. We left the car at the garage and while the guys were checking it, we went to the local pub, the Freeman Hotel. I noticed that in Australia, even in the smallest cities with only one road, there was always a pub. The heart of the community I guessed. John and I put our two dollars in the slot machine and we were made the better of sixty dollars when we left after a couple of beers. Back at the garage, the mechanics told us that the car had nothing wrong; they just added a bit more water and cleaned up the spark plugs. John insisted on giving them a ten dollar note each for the help and we were back on the road. I couldn't help but thinking how nice he was, even with people he didn't know, always so generous and positive about everything. I learnt that from him, what is to be really generous, without thinking of what you could get in return, pure generosity…and how to be genuinely honest too. Karma, that's how he justified his actions in life; good Karma was better than money and he was definitely right.

We went through Maryborough and its classic old Queenslanders and reached Hervey Bay in the evening. We stopped at a tourist park on the beach for the night. We had a lovely walk on the pontoon, watching the fishermen, the sun going down in beautiful orange and pink colours, melting in the ocean. After a good night sleep, we had a coffee on the beach and discovered the Marina and Shelly Beach before heading to our final destination: Bundaberg. It was John's thirty-third birthday and I wanted to celebrate it properly. We found a little cabin for the night, so he could be more comfortable, sleeping in a proper bed rather than a tent for his birthday. We had a couple of beers at the local pub—nearly half the price of what it cost in Sydney—and bought a couple of steaks, some veggies, and his favourite chocolate ice cream so I could cook a nice birthday dinner, a nice change from the backpacker Chinese noodles rule. I offered him some Quicksilver clothes that I had purchased for the occasion back in Sydney and showed him how we were wearing lingerie in my country. We had a great night.

The next morning, we went for a walk in Bargara, had some fried chicken thighs we bought in a local chicken shop, and spent the day on the beach, taking pictures and playing, until the beautiful sunset. We went back to the cabin and organised an appointment over the phone for the next day at 8.30am with Lucas, the farmer. The next morning, we were on the road to the farm. It was close to Gin Gin but we nearly got lost trying to get there, anxious we would be out of fuel before finding the farm. John showed me how much he could swear, which I wasn't used to, and Lucas wasn't in the walls when we got there twenty minutes after our appointment time. I talked to Lynn, the manager, and she confirmed that there would probably be some work for us this week; she would get back to me the next morning. We drove around Gin Gin to find a caravan park to stay overnight. There was no way I was sleeping in the scary Gin Gin Caravan Park. Not only because I wasn't sure we could get out of there—the car had to be parked in a very muddy spot—but also because there were lots of drinking box wine around us and it was only morning. It looked like people were living there full time, doing nothing else but drinking and swearing. We asked a refund at reception and left as quickly as possible. After driving further out, we found a beautiful caravan park on Lake Monduran. We were the only customers, camping on a green landscape, in the middle of a massive park, in communion with the wild. It was quiet, beautiful, and so relaxing, especially compared to the crazy place we just left.

It was now two days and we had no signs of Lynn or Lucas. I started to panic. I called Harvest jobs, the government phone line for picking, and they advised me to go through a backpacker hostel as they were the ones providing picking jobs in the area. The only problem was that we had to pay nearly two hundred dollars a week each to sleep with ten other backpackers and John didn't want to sleep in a hostel or do any picking because he was Australian and could earn his life better than that. Also he didn't understand why we had to live that way when we could rent a full house for ourselves for less than that. I understood; I was a backpacker, real estate agents didn't lease anything to us and farmers knew we had to do picking to renew our visas, so they exploited us. I didn't know what to do. I was a backpacker but he wasn't. I had to renew my visa; he didn't. I had to do some picking when he could get his good job back. I understood the hostel concept, even if they were screwing up backpackers in need…abusing the system. We were from two different worlds and our love story was threatened by a stupid visa.

John and I were at the local pub in Bundaberg, trying to figure out what to do.

"So what options are available for you to be able to stay in Australia with me?" He asked.

"Well, I can renew my working holiday visa with picking or packing for three months, and then, I'll be able to stay for another year and work but only for six months at a time for the same employer, and probably only in hospitality because no company would hire a backpacker to do marketing and for only six months. Then, I'll still have to go back home as I can't stay more than two years here, unless we do a de facto visa or a partner visa if we get married."

"Okay, that's a bit harsh. Well, one thing for sure, I'm not staying here without a job, and there's no way I live in a hostel full of backpackers."

"I know…well there's still the option of you coming home with me," I said with a smile.

"Hmm, I'll pass. I love my country and you're the one who came here. And it will be hard if I don't speak French."

"Yes, I know, and you're right. I left my country for a reason, it's definitely better to be in Australia."

"What about a de facto visa. Can't we do that?"

"Well, the problem is that you can't do it unless it's already a year we've been together and it's been only three months."

"Stupid rules...well, maybe we should think about getting married then..."

"Wow, that's intense. You know how I feel about marriage. For me, it's not something you do lightly. If I marry you it's because you're my soul mate, and not for a visa. And it's only been three months. I love you, but I don't want to rush into anything...It's getting late; we should go back to the Caravan Park before dark."

I didn't want to go home. I didn't want to sacrifice my relationship with John. For once I had this kind of love; I was finally happy in my life. On the way back to the park, we knew one thing for sure: there was no way I would stay picking here without him. There was no way we would spend one day apart. Once at the Caravan Park, we walked to Lake Monduran and were watching the eagles flying high in the sky, still trying to find a solution.

"So you're saying that without picking, there is no way to renew your visa?" John was trying to understand the immigration laws.

"Yes, pretty much. I could do construction too," I said with half a smile.

"Or, we could do a de facto visa?"

"Only after a year of being together, so it will be too late, as I cannot stay more than a year in the country. I would be an illegal immigrant..."

"You would be my illegal immigrant then. That's such a stupid law."

"I know but it's the law...unless I do picking and I renew my visa first. But just thinking of you going back to Sydney and leaving me here, it breaks my heart."

"I know, but I can't find a job here. It's crazy, I asked everywhere in the city, they are not looking for labourers, I can't believe it. I never had trouble getting a job before." He was actually upset, unused to being told he wasn't needed.

"I'm sorry I made you come all the way here for nothing. You left everything for me and now we both end up with nothing. Well,

I guess I could find some picking and live out of a backpack for the next three months, but I can't picture myself being here without you; I don't know what to do."

"I know. Maybe the best is simply to go back to Sydney. I would get my job back and put some money aside so I could propose later and we could get married before your visa expires."

"What? What did you just say? You're proposing to me?"

"Look, with a working holiday visa you can't find the job you really want anyway and I really think you're the One for me. We could get married, so I could keep you here forever."

"But you know I don't take marriage lightly. It's a lifetime commitment..."

"I know, me neither. I never really thought I would get married one day actually. I never imagined I would meet someone like you, especially a French girl," he laughed.

"I mean I love you, but you know if I get married, it's forever. It's not because of a visa, it's because I want to spend the rest of my life with you. It's very serious."

"I've never been more serious. I love you." He kissed me.

"I love you too John, but I need to think about it, I don't want to rush anything."

"Look, take your time. It's up to you, we will do whatever you want."

And that's how John proposed, watching the sunset on the beautiful Lake Monduran. Not so romantic, but again, he showed me how different he was compared to the other men I had in my past. He would do anything for me; he wanted to stay by my side forever and definitely wanted to keep me in his wonderful country. I had fallen in love with him and his country but not his family. That was the only thing that stopped me to say yes straight away that night.

The next morning, John and I didn't talk about it. I was still thinking about the situation and he left me alone with my thoughts. I was anxious, writing in my diary, taking pictures, sunbathing, all without talking about it. I had to choose what I wanted to do...and it was driving me crazy. I wondered if I would be able to stay here for him, so far away from my family, my sister, without anything sure. We had no money except for the five thousand dollars I had saved and we had no jobs. He could probably get his job back as it was only ten days we were gone and it wouldn't take me long to find a job either, even if it wasn't in marketing. Then, if I wasn't able to stay, I would have to go back home in a few months and I felt sad thinking about not being with him anymore, going back in my old depressing life, leaving the happy one here. I couldn't go backward; there was no way I would let this happen.

We left Lake Monduran the next day. Our decision was made; we would go back to Sydney. He called his mum and we could take the bedroom downstairs at their place for thirty dollars rent a week. It took us only two days to drive back to the big city and when we went to his best mate to get all his stuff back—he left everything to his place for storage—Derek told him that it was his now; he didn't want to give John anything back. I couldn't believe that. John had really lost everything with my stupid trip. So, back at his old place, his brother took his old bedroom and we didn't have a bed to sleep on. I broke down in tears, thinking that it was my entire fault, I felt awful. We even asked the Police for help, but they said that because John gave his stuff to his mate, it was his word against his mate's and they couldn't do anything. I was outraged.

From that day, John didn't have friends anymore. "They always let you down" was his motto. We were lucky to have our camping air bed to sleep on. We were living in a bedroom with no furniture and we had to take the outside stairs to access the rest of the house where his mum and brother were living. On top of that, I realised how weird his family was. I knew from before that they weren't a very close family, different from what I was used to in so many ways. For example, back home, we all ate together and chatted around the dining table, sharing conversations and emotions. They ate separately, one in each bedroom and his mum in the lounge room. She was also sticking tags everywhere around the house, reminders of what to do or not to do...instead of speaking out loud? On top of the heavy tension at home, I was now two hours away by train from the city and I found it difficult to find a job in the area, even if John was driving me everywhere around for job interviews when possible.

12

Back in Sydney, I was hopeless, feeling down, in a position even worse than ever before. Love was my only saving grace; we were more in love than ever. John told me that he couldn't guarantee me anything regarding the proposal, but that he thought I was the one for sure. He had never loved anyone the way he loved me and he rarely pronounced these words in the past. He said that if we had to get married to stay together, it would be rushing things a bit but he would do it because he really thought I was the one, the love of his life. It would be easier once I would be a permanent resident. But I didn't want to get married for a visa; I didn't want people to think that we were getting married for a visa. I knew how it was; I was the first one to point a finger to my sister's first husband, an illegal immigrant in France who got papers as soon as he married my sister Lali and later treated her like crap. I didn't want people to think of me that way.

I loved John and if I married him, it would be because I really thought he was the man of my life, the best man I ever met. He was affectionate, funny, generous, genuine and hardworking, and on top of all, a real gentleman. We watched movies together at night, curled up in the couch. He prepared my coffee every morning and the sex had never been so good. Okay, money was missing in the equation but he worked hard and knew how to prioritise. The most important thing was there: we were in love and we shared the same values. It was hard for me to lose my independence as he was now the only one working. Also, I was in the middle of his divided family and not so sure about what the future held. I figured it was very hard for me not to be in control. I had to control the situation to avoid feeling lost or vulnerable. One thing was for sure, I was trying to learn to let go. I was also trying to stay positive. I printed out a bunch of resumes, determined to find a job. I was also trying to find a job in marketing. In life, nothing was easy; I just had to deal with it, like I always had.

Thinking of marriage was scary and exciting at the same time. But the signs had been there since our first date with all these brides and grooms following us on every single date. We were talking more and more about it and we even figured out that we would need a babysitter for our kids—a boy and a girl, we agreed—because his family wouldn't be very helpful. My parents and sister were very supportive, even if she was a bit reluctant to start with because of her first marriage experience. And even if we would get married in Australia, we could give them another beautiful wedding back home, at the church. They didn't know John, but after all the guys I had in my life, my dad was convinced that if I'd picked this one to be my husband, he would be the one for sure. The most important was to be together and to love each other, nothing else mattered.

In mid-June, I got a sales job working for a gold buyer in shopping centres. It was weird, boring, and definitely annoying, as I had to go in shopping centres around the city by train, but it was a job. Things couldn't be better between John and I and we were about to move into a better flat. His mum continued to stress me out; she was always whinging for anything and asking John for the money he owed her for the rent and all the bills she paid for him after his surgery. I paid her back with my savings and was glad to leave her house. I didn't think she liked me much; she was against this wedding too, thinking it was too early and didn't understand the visa situation either, probably thinking I was using her son. Anyway, we were about to be on our own, living the couple's life and preparing for our wedding.

After two weeks, I quit my job; the travel time was driving me insane and I barely had the time to see John since I worked on weekends too. It was better for me to find a job in my field, marketing, and I would take the time I need to find one. Meanwhile, I was playing the perfect housewife—Cooking meals, cleaning, washing clothes, applying for marketing jobs online, and exercising. It was nice to start exercising daily again between my housewife duties, but I was desperate to find an office job. Employers were reluctant to give me one because of my visa. I couldn't work more than six months for the same boss and that was definitely a deal breaker. It was nice of John to take care of us, without questioning it. He didn't care, he just wanted me happy. He knew how to make me feel better when I was down, and even if the routine started to settle in, we were falling in love deeper every day. He wanted to offer me a beautiful engagement ring and was trying hard to save money. We were thinking of how our life would be once married; we wanted to have kids, buy a house, and imagined how it would be if we could build it from scratch. Big windows, lots of them, a large bathroom, so we could still have our showers together, one bedroom for our son and one for our daughter, a pool, a large lounge room, a home cinema and a massive screen to watch movies, with recliners and drink holders. It was nice to dream out loud together, laughing about it because we still had to by ourselves a proper bed since we were still sleeping on our camping air bed.

By the end of August, I had a marketing job. I was a Marketing Executive for a company selling conferences and workshops to professionals. I was doing a lot of social media promotion, emailing, and definitely improving my English and my digital skills. I was working hard but I was happy to finally be able to work in my field of study. They accepted my application because I was engaged. John was proud of me and we were now living the way a married couple lived. I had the routine I thought I'd never wanted: working, train, sleep…and I loved it. John had started helping me with the chores as I couldn't do them all by myself anymore; I was leaving home early and coming back late, it was a three hours return to my work in St. Leonards.

Also, I prepared everything for the wedding. I found my custom-made dress for less than two hundred dollars on a Chinese website and it took only a month to make, bought my shoes, and booked the date with the Registry of Birth, Deaths, and Marriages in Parramatta. We didn't have either the time or the money to find a celebrant and get married on the beach. We chose the first of October for our wedding day. It was Labour Day and we could have a long weekend every year to celebrate our anniversary. Also, we just bought the rings. John chose a bridal set for me and I picked a nice white gold wedding band for him. I was still waiting for a proper proposal though…I also planned a pamper day for myself the day before the wedding with a full body massage and a manicure-pedicure. I wished I could have done that with my sister but unfortunately she wouldn't be there. I would have to get married without my family. John told me we could get married with only two witnesses, but I wanted to celebrate that day, and I thought it was nice to have his family with us. After all, they would be mine afterward too and we would go to France to get married with mine later when we could afford it.

I was so happy but scared at the same time because it was the beginning of a new life in Australia, forever far away from my family. His family was absent and didn't really care for us, except maybe his dad and his girlfriend, whereas I was very close to my family; we loved each other so much and were very affectionate. I had trouble picturing never seeing them again, not the way I used to anyway. But I loved John and I remembered why I left France, to create my own life, and I knew this could have happened. Lucky it did, I found the One, even if it meant I had to live without my family, I would create my own here. It would be tough for me, but less for my kids because they would have their parents here. I knew I was doing the right thing, but I couldn't help thinking about my parents. Dad never told me he had a MALT lymphoma, a cancer diagnosed in January when he had stomach surgery for ulcer. He just told me about the ulcer! Mum was still coping with her health too, my twin just had her first baby, a little girl named Amélie, and my grandma was losing her mind and moved in a nursing home…I though they needed me, but I was missing them, lots! And my friends too. All my backpacking friends were gone, back to their country…I was the last man standing! And I was missing my friends too, I may not have many but there were still there for me, despite the distance. It was a big move and I started to get cold feet! And his family wasn't what I could call family.

I announced the wedding to my family and friends by email and Facebook and everyone was really happy for me, for us, even if they didn't know John. He told his family the same way but didn't get any reply. That's when we decided not do much after the ceremony. So I arranged to just open a tab where we met, at The Point Hotel, in the nice function room upstairs which had an eight-metre fish tank bar. We would have some drinks to welcome everyone and that would be enough. We were broke anyway and the most important thing was to get married and start our life together. John was already thinking of having kids with me very soon.

A week before the wedding, John officially proposed. Better late than never. He did propose to me before that but without the ring… it was quite funny actually. The first time was when we were playing Fable III, a video game on Play Station, and even if I'd never played video games, he insisted that I played with him and I knew why when he used his knight character to propose to my lady character. We even had the wedding at the castle, followed by the honeymoon night. The second time around, he proposed at the Royal National Park, while we were on a row boat and we nearly went overboard when he tried to go down one knee. And the third time was at home, when we were about to watch a movie and he proposed with a box open containing a Magnum Ego ice cream. So, yes he did propose many times since August, but never with my engagement ring, which had arrived only ten days before the wedding. He surprised me by inviting me to a great seafood restaurant on Sydney Harbour. He booked a table with a view of the Opera House and the Sydney Harbour Bridge; it was beautiful and our seafood platter was scrumptious. Before the dessert, he went down one knee with the box opened on a beautiful diamond ring and proposed. I waited so long for that moment.

He said something along those lines: "Lucie, you're so beautiful, nothing is more important than you in my eyes. I don't think I could ever live without you, you're my everything. Would you marry me?" And I felt like in the movies. It was nearly weird hearing these words in English: "would you marry me?" I was ecstatic. It was the most beautiful things someone ever said to me. Of course, I said "Yes." I was happy and flattered, people were looking at us and I helped him stand back up for a tender kiss. It was a wonderful night, definitely the best one I had ever lived so far.

On September 30, 2011, a day before our first wedding, everything was ready: the shoes, the beautiful dress I ordered, and the rings. I was getting nervous and deep down, I was ecstatic. The big day had come. After all these years looking for the One, I was finally making my dream come true. My family wouldn't be there and there wouldn't be any cake or photographer because we were broke and I figured that the most important thing was that John and I were both there to celebrate our love. Nothing else mattered, not the cake, not the people, not the photos, not the venue. I was glad I had booked my pampering session because I definitely needed to unwind and the massages and manicure-pedicure brought me to a peaceful stage. Everything was ready, including me, for the blissful day.

I woke up at 8 am to an empty flat, as I told John to sleep at his dad's. I spent the last night of our single life apart to keep with tradition. I was super excited and I couldn't be happier. I was getting married today. I was quickly getting a shower and put on some makeup. I had an appointment with the hairdresser down our street so he could do my hair for the big day. I was about to leave when the intercom rang. I wasn't expecting anyone that early in the morning. I opened the door and discovered with surprise a big bunch of flowers. It was the first time in my life I was offered a delivery of flowers. They were from my parents; I nearly cried they wouldn't be here but I was so thankful they were sending me some love. I took the phone to call them straight away. With eight hours difference, it was very late at night there but my dad answered and was glad to hear that I received the flowers he booked for me. Yes, they made a mistake in the French spelling on the card he added but the thought was beautiful and I thanked him and Mum for this great surprise. I didn't have any bouquet so I told them that they could be with me through the flowers if they gave me the permission to create a bridal bouquet with the amazing creation. Once they agreed, I took the flowers out of the foam, placed them in a round bouquet, and attached the lot with the ribbons of all the bouquets John had offered me so far and that I kept for memories. It was beautiful and I had a smile of satisfaction looking at my creation. Now, I would have my parents with me.

The sun was out, the hairdresser did a great job with my hair placing it in a braided bun, finished by a crown of pearls made of the same necklace I was wearing. I added some pearl earrings and bracelet. I just had to pass on my dress and I was ready to go. I felt like a princess, between the pampering on the previous day and all the preparation I was undergoing! After all, it was my day. Yes. When I came back from the hairdresser, Ellen, John's dad's girlfriend, came with a bottle of champagne and we celebrated with a glass before putting on the gorgeous gown. I loved this dress. I put some music on and with Ellen's enthusiasm, the bubbles, the lovely hairstyle, my gorgeous French manicure and the flowers, I felt a perfume of happiness in the air. I really felt like a princess, with my sleeveless corset; tightened by a long ribbon at the back, embellished by pearls at the front. My waist was accented as the tight top went down my hips to a beautiful asymmetrical gown made of lace and silk finished by a short train. I couldn't wait to be with my fiancé, my future husband.

He sent me a text message saying that it was more than fifteen hours without me and he was lost already; so sweet. I put on a white fur shawl, fingerless white gloves, and my stilettos to finalise my look. After telling me how stunning I looked in this attire, Stan and Ellen helped me go downstairs and into the car. After a forty-five minute drive, we parked at the Registry Office of Death, Birth, and Marriages of Parramatta. I chose the only Registry in Sydney with a garden as I wanted to get married outside.

John saw me through the glass windows of the building but I didn't see him. I entered the building and saw his family: his uncle Georgio, his wife Becky, and their two sons, his mum Concella, and his brother Jacob, Ellen's brother Andy... but no sign of John. After kissing and passing by everyone, I finally saw him. He was sitting at the back of the waiting room. He was so sexy in his black costume, with his black tie and a fresh haircut. He stood up, kissed me quickly and told me I was beautiful. We were excited, awkwardly shy, and a bit lost. We waited for everyone to arrive for about fifteen minutes which felt like forever. The sunny sky was slowly getting covered by clouds but we still wanted to proceed in the garden. I was a bit disappointed when I realised that our guests would have to stand up and that they would unfold a plastic table covered with just a white cloth for us to sign the official papers. But never mind, nothing would take the smile from my face on our big day. Still, it was nice to feel the fresh air and somehow be close to nature. The wedding was short but very emotional for us.

After the celebrant made sure we were both free to get married, John and I held each other's hands, face to face, and exchanged our vows. My John was serious and I could see in his eyes how important this moment was for him too. He was so cute when he said "I do." Then, it was my turn; my English was a bit lacking with the emotions flooding within me and the smile clenching my jaws. But I managed to follow the celebrant's lead. My voice was weak but my heart was filled with love and my eyes full of affection, facing the man of my life. I finally pronounced the words "yes, I do" with my most beautiful smile. In fact, my lips were frozen in a massive smile all day as I was happy every step of the way. Finally, John and I, desperately waiting for it, had been given the go with, "I declare you husband and wife, you can now kiss the bride," and we kissed passionately and had a long cuddle; his loving arms felt so comfortable and reassuring.

The whole time, it was like it was just the two of us and the celebrant, no one else, no witnesses, no family, just us immersed in each other's eyes, face to face, hands in hands, wrapped in our loving bubble. So when the kiss came, it was the same; we were two people crazy in love, kissing madly after a day apart and such a long wait. I felt so blessed; we had never been happier and we were now husband and wife. The exchange of the rings was a big moment too, very symbolic. Everything went so fast, like in a dream, the most beautiful one. We signed the official paperwork, still shaking with emotions, and everybody congratulated us. We took some pictures and invited everyone to join us at The Point Hotel, where the function room awaited. His mum and Jacob, his uncle Paolo, and girlfriend Laura couldn't stay but the rest of our family and friends came over for some drinks. We arrived at the pub. My former bosses welcomed us with big applause and the rest of the pub followed. Everyone there was congratulating us and we enjoyed drinks and laughter in the upstairs function room for the rest of the day. For sure, when I started to work there back in December 2010, I didn't know that one day I would meet my husband there and later, come in my wedding dress, hand in hand with my husband to celebrate. Around 8 pm, we left the hotel to start our honeymoon at the Harbour View Hotel, in a beautiful suite of the thirteenth floor. That was John's surprise for me: a beautiful room for our first night as a married couple. I didn't eat all day and with all the drinks I had I was tipsy and needed to eat. John had to stop me otherwise I would have been getting the takeaway pizza we had, still wearing my wedding dress. What a day it was. We had so much fun, we were in love, and even if it was raining now, it was all sunshine in our hearts.

The next morning, we were both hungover and my hubby grabbed us some coffee and a bacon and egg muffin for me. Nothing beats bacon and egg for hangovers. I called my parents to let them know how it went. It was only 8 am and my dad was surprised to receive my call, but happy to hear that I was now a married woman. I hung up the phone when John came back with the yummy breakfast. We were so happy that morning, waking up for the first time as husband and wife.

Andy came to pick us up around 10 am. We had enough time to get a shower and pack away all our stuff lying all over the floor. We went home quickly to swap our bag of summer clothes for warmer ones as the weather would be rainy up the coast. We left an hour later for Avoca Bay where we spent our short honeymoon—three days of romance, love, and relaxation. We enjoyed a sumptuous suite with a spa bath, and we were welcomed with champagne and chocolate-coated strawberries. Terrigal was beautiful and we appreciated doing nothing but relaxing, walking hand in hand along the beach, laughing, and kissing. We went to a seafood restaurant, a French one, took lots of pictures, and had lots of fun doing nothing, thinking about nothing, living in the moment. It was too short, but it was so nice to be together. We didn't have any holidays since our road trip and this time, we were married. After so many emotions, it was hard to go back to work, especially since I decided to quit smoking on that day. John and I wanted babies and there was no way I would fall pregnant being a smoker.

I spent the rest of October finalising the three-hundred-page document required for my partner visa application and giving up three thousand dollars for it. My parents came home for the Christmas holidays and met John, my husband, for the first time. It was quite tough to be on top of each other for three weeks, frenetically visiting a new place every day. Sydney CBD, Taronga zoo, the Rocks markets, Queen Victoria Building. We didn't stop but I loved spending time with them and guiding them in my new country. We played the tourist guides and Mum and Dad loved Australia.

They also appreciated John very much and while Mum was trying to communicate by signs and facial mimics with him—she didn't speak English, but laughed at his jokes anyway—Dad would help him do the Christmas cake or fight with him to pay the restaurant first. We decorated the Christmas tree and enjoyed quality family time together. We spent the week before Christmas visiting Sydney, Christmas day at the beach and left for Cairns, the Great Barrier

Reef, John's dream destination, and Fitzroy Island the week after. It was a first proper holiday with John and a sort of second honeymoon for us, especially in Fitzroy Island. I figured that the less there was to do, the better holiday it would be since we couldn't do anything else but relaxing. It was the first time in my life that I felt like my parents really appreciated my choice of man. We discovered the tropical weather, the beauty of secluded beaches, colourful fish, and the magical reef.

I had to leave my job before Christmas because I couldn't work more than six months for the same employer; my partner visa was granted but I was still under the working conditions of my working holiday. So I enjoyed my holidays but I was also thinking that I would have to start looking for a new job as soon as we were back in Sydney. But first, once home, after hard goodbyes to my tourist parents, we spent the weekend watching movies and spooning on the couch.

In February, we moved to a bigger flat, with two bedrooms, storage, and a garage. It was in Bexley, closer to the M5 motorway, and more central to John's work. I was one of these desperate housewives, cooking and cleaning, taking care of my hubby...again. This time, I enjoyed it a bit more as I had an entire flat to move into. It wasn't renovated but spacious and I was glad to unpack the few boxes we had to make it our home. The rent was cheap and we could save money to buy a house later; our next big project with starting our family. And once my working conditions changed and my partner visa approved, I found a Marketing Executive position in a company five kilometres away. Patience always paid off. We couldn't be happier. We started together broke and we were slowly getting a better life, definitely stronger and happier together. My first work assignment was to go to the annual sales meeting the first week of June, in Fiji. I was over the moon. Life was finally smiling at me. What more could I ask for? Maybe a baby.

We were adjusting to our married life, to the role each of us had to play in our household and the daily routine. Even if we were both working hard, we still tried to compromise and had a couple of romantic weekends together visiting Jervis Bay and its beautiful white sand beaches and Canberra to see Uncle Tino. We also enjoyed renovating second-hand furniture found in council clean-ups—my favourite hobby—or watching movies on the couch. Since we were both working, we could afford to live a bit more and it was nice to feel like we were moving forward. Like any married couple, we had some tough times trying to find our way, but we were happy and the arguments helped us know each other better, to compromise, and to get closer. Though different, we complemented each other. The most important thing was that we shared the same idea of married life and wanted the same things for our future, a happy and close family. In August we were able to buy a second-hand car, bigger, for a potential baby and he offered me the Harbour Bridge Climb for my thirty-first birthday. We also planned a road trip around New Zealand for our next Christmas holidays. We spent our first wedding anniversary in the beautiful Southern Highlands region and fell in love with it.

New Zealand was amazing and, thanks to John, I fought one of my biggest fears and bungee jumped in Queenstown, at the Nevis Bungee, the highest jump in the southern hemisphere with one hundred and thirty-four metres. Another tick off my bucket list. We were delighted by the geothermal park and its colourful grounds and rocks. We soaked in the hot lakes, spreading some smelly mud all over us. We celebrated Christmas in Rotorua with some barbecued ribs, discovered the fascinating underground caves filled with glow worms, drove along the dangerous roads of the South Island, saw lots of sheep and the greenest landscapes. We missed out on our helicopter flight because of the weather and struggled to find a caravan spot for New Year's Eve at Lake Wanaka and ended in Harrow Town, a small village near Queenstown. We finally had a great time at the local pub, met new people, had lots of fun and after the crazy bungee jump, went south to discover the wonderful Doubtful Sound and the Cadbury factory. We finished our trip in Christchurch, sadly unchanged since the 2010 earthquake. I twisted my ankle and fainted on the last day on our way to the airport, and was unable to walk for six weeks. We had an amazing time and if John wasn't too keen about doing a road trip in a caravan for three weeks at first, we had heaps of fun, especially since we planned to make children our next adventure.

13

This Christmas will be Rose's first but maybe my last. The season is supposed to be such a happy time, but it's a very difficult one for someone on death row. I feel like I'm a bomb ready to explode, I just don't know when it's going to happen. I'm a control freak and living in such uncertainty is overwhelming and stressful. So I try to act on the few things I can still control. I research a lot online about melanoma, trying to get as much information as possible on all the treatments available and potential future progress. It's scary. All these people with cancer dying around me, all these blogs of desperate people…like me. I've actually been advised by my oncologist not to follow these people, as she said that sometimes it's better to stay in denial. She's probably right. When I stop looking and try to focus on positive statistics and hopeful stories, I feel a bit better. Yet, I'm not ignoring the darkness of my situation and work on accepting the morbid potential outcome. I start a list of things to do before it's too late, before my life is over. Some of them are already a work in progress:

- *Give a hug to my big sister (we don't really talk to each other since my mum's stroke)*
- *Get married at the church, with my family and have a wedding cake.*
- *Baptise Rose*
- *Go on a "proper" honeymoon*
- *Exercise again and lose at least 10 Kg of my pregnancies weight*
- *Show my country to my kids and introduce them to all my family and friends*
- *Meet my nephews and see my kids playing with them*
- *Go to Uluru*
- *Get my paperwork in order*
- *Plan my funerals*

- *Get surfing lessons*
- *Eat at the restaurant of the Opera House I've seen the first day I visited Sydney*
- *Live in a house with a pool*
- *Go to New York, see the Empire State building, Central Park & Statue of Liberty*
- *Cover up my old tattoo*
- *Go on a cruise*
- *Travel around the world*
- *Discover Kakadu National Park*
- *Visit San Francisco, Las Vegas, the Great Canyon, and Niagara Falls*
- *Go to Vietnam, Thailand, Bali, & New Caledonia*
- *Write a book*
- *See my kids getting married*
- *Become a grandma*

It's a lot. And I'm not sure I can do it all, but I will try my best for sure. I start to organise the most important ones and those easily achievable. But first I help my parents prepare their visit; they are finally coming for a few months. Luckily, the flat underneath ours is available and I hope we can get it before anyone else. It will be so convenient to have them so close to us and for all of us to keep some intimacy as they will stay for quite a while this time. After insisting for a couple of weeks requesting their support and help in these difficult times, I think they are in complete denial of my terminal condition and not ready to accept that I may die anytime soon. I tell them that I can get the flat if they decide to come over and the practical stuff being apparently the only obstacle for their visit, they decide to come the last week of November and I rent the flat for them.

Before their arrival, I prepare everything. I'm excited and want them to really feel at home since they'll be here for a while. I treat the flat for pests and get all furniture necessary to fill up the two-bedroom accommodation (thanks to the generosity of Stéphanie's in-laws who were getting rid of their guest house furniture, perfect timing.). I'm exhausted from the side effects of my treatment and the sleepless nights nursing Rose but I'm very happy to have my parents by my side soon. They will stay for at least three months, and then we will have to renew their tourist visa.

The night they arrive, we hug and kiss strongly, all very happy to see each other again, despite the circumstances. The kids are already in bed but my parents want to see their grandchildren sleeping and find them beautiful. They're relieved to be here, closer to me and thankful for the flat arrangements. They're in such denial though. I have to show them my pet scan for them to acknowledge the damage. But even looking at all the black spots in my body, where the tumours are, I'm not sure they understand that their daughter may die soon. I can't blame them, I don't want to hurt them either, but I need a real support and they have to understand the situation. Also, if shit hits the fan, I don't want them to be shocked, but prepared. It's not a holiday trip this time; I need their help with the babies and their emotional support. I helped them so much when I was younger; unfortunately, this time, it's my turn. I'm now the one who needs help. I'm not the kind of person who asks for help but for the sake of my kids I have to and it scares me to tears.

It's the second week of December, Rose has a forty-degree fever and is shaking uncontrollably; she freaks me out so much that I bring her to the Emergency Department of our local hospital straight away. Apparently, she didn't cope well with the immunisation she had today but to be sure, the nurses take her blood, a urine sample and try to perform a lumbar puncture to rule out meningitis. It's awful to see her crying and screaming like a little animal while they attempt four times to put a big needle in her little spine. It's horrible to feel so hopeless in helping my own daughter. I ask for another nurse to try, or maybe a doctor, because this one is shaking so much that she will miss another time for sure. I can't stand what I see, I can't even believe this nurse hasn't given up yet to ask for help. It feels like an eternity and it's excruciating for me too. I'm trying to comfort my poor little girl, only six weeks old, screaming and crying in pain. They finally get the sample and we are admitted to the children's ward at four in the morning. Thank God, I have a bed and not one of those crappy folding bed seats you usually get.

I start feeling the side effects of my treatment. What timing. I really don't need that right now. They put a cannula on Rose, give her a drip of antibiotics and it's 5.30am when I finally go to bed. I'm shivery, extremely cold, exhausted, and nauseous. It's not the first time and I know what to do, but the eight blankets they give me don't help. I take some painkillers, hoping for my fever to drop. It's the only thing I can do unfortunately. By 9 am, I've only slept for an hour and Rose is awake.

So far, I had these side effects nearly every ten days—high fever, shivers, joint pain, feeling incredibly cold, and pretty much like having the worst flu ever, every week or so. When it happens, the only thing I can do is to take painkillers and wait until it's over. Then I have to stop the treatment for a couple of days. I've stopped it so often that I wonder if it's still working. But when I call Amanda, my nurse, she explains that the treatment may actually work even better after a break because it would sort of shock my body once I'll take it again. I'm hoping so anyway. One night I had another side effect. I was itchy everywhere, scratching myself to the point of bleeding. It was horrible and I had to take antihistamines to get over it. Otherwise, the only annoying thing about this treatment is that I have to take it an hour before and two hours after any food. So I take the tablets when I wake up and can't have my coffee for another hour. Being a mum, it's hard not to get my caffeine first thing in the morning. But my life depends on that treatment, so I deal with it. Amanda tells me to stay off my tablets for a couple of days as my white blood cells are low too. I have been very tired all day, waking up just to feed Rose and calm her down when her fever picks up. She's doing good, feeding well and still so pretty. My parents are coming over for a couple of hours so I can rest a bit and John comes in the afternoon to bring us some fresh clothes. I only see him for a few minutes as he lets me sleep until quarter to five. He snoozes a bit too; he's tired as it was a short night for him too. He left the emergency department at 1 am and woke up to start working four hours later. After visiting me, he has to pick up Jason at day-care. I'm missing him, the nice him; he's been very short with me lately, taking everything I say the wrong way. I wish he could be nice and caring, holding me tight in his arms, kissing me softly. But he always seems preoccupied, under pressure, stressed, and overtired. He's always on his phone, with his Facebook group, his remote control cars, forgetting what's really important—his family and spending quality time with us. I don't want him to learn that the hard way, like I did.

Rose is fine, no meningitis, just a bad reaction to the vaccine, probably due to a cold she's starting to get. I want to get quickly out of this children ward that I know way too well. I'm so used to come here for Jason that everyone knows us. Waiting to be discharged, I'm watching TV and this very touching documentary about people who experienced after-death or spirits encounters. One of them tells about a young lady who can see or hear her Nana in difficult times. Her grandma passed away but she had a very strong relationship with her while alive. Her nephew was born at twenty-five weeks and unfortunately didn't survive long after birth. She explained that her Nana was there to take him when it was time. This story gave me hope that at least, if I don't make it, I may still be able to see my kids growing and somehow be there for them and my hubby.

Before I left France, I was in sort of constant bad luck and actually thought that someone had put a spell on me. Anyway, I was desperate to recover my luck and went to see one of my work colleague's friend, clairvoyant in her spare time, a first for me. I remember she told me that I would live very far away. She also told me that my grandma, recently passed away at the time, was with us and that she was watching over me, like a guardian angel. I was close to my grandma; she'd been a second mum for me since my mum's stroke, so I got very emotional but I was also happy to know she was by my side. She told me that I could speak out loud and ask her help because she could hear me. This documentary on TV reminded me of this. Since then, I've asked my Grandma Lucienne to help me with my cancer. I've prayed with her and asked for her help to stay on Earth, with my family, my hubby, my kids, and also my parents and my twin. I've told her how I'm sure I would be an awesome angel but I'm an even better mum, down on Earth. I have to stay here, whatever it takes. And I'm sure she's listening.

I remember my grandma so well; her smell, her cheeky grin, her kindness and all her stories. Since my mum's stroke, her mother Lucienne, was visiting her every afternoon at home, she was feeling so guilty about the situation. She used to repeat herself saying how this should have happened to her instead of her daughter and that it wasn't fair. Mum used to spend her time brooding over her sad situation but we wanted her to have a hobby again, to do something with all her spare time. With my grandma's help, we managed to convince her to water paint again, with her left hand this time. After a slow start and lots of opposition, it was good to see Mum enjoying something again. Of course, it was hard and she got frustrated many times, but overall, she learnt to be more patient. It was therapeutic for her, giving her the motivation to get better. She impresses me now with what she manages to paint and you wouldn't believe she was right-handed before.

Yet, writing and talking are still a struggle. "Mamie" Lucienne, as I used to call her, became my confidant for the following years. I could nearly tell her everything. We learnt to know each other better, talking about our personal stories and she used to love giving me advice on men and relationships. She was a modern woman for her time; born on February 2, 1922—obviously, her favourite number was two—she'd been through the Second World War and told me so many stories about it. At the end of the war, after years of waiting for the return of her love, trapped in a German forced labour, she married my grandpa Emile. She used to tell me how she organised her wedding, paying for her shoes with food tickets, how she started working at sixteen years old as a secretary in insurance, how everyone used to love her handwriting, the joy of being the mum of four beautiful daughters, but also how my grandpa made bad business decisions as a real estate developer and how they ended up living at her parents with their four kids. My grandpa died when I was four years old, so I've got no memories of him, just a black and white picture of him in his forties. He was a good-looking man, blond with blue eyes and loved to paint. Lucienne told me that he cheated on her with one of her girlfriends and the best way to get rid of the mistress was to bring them together more often. So she organised all these lunches with the two of them and my grandpa got so irritated that he asked her to stop inviting her. They never saw the bestie again. They never divorced but Emile left their home for a while, to be with a sugar mummy who let him paint as much as he wanted. He came back to my grandma at some point and even if she probably still loved him, she never forgave him but let him sleep in the kids' bedroom where he died of a heart attack in his fifties.

My grandma witnessed the beginning of the mass consumption society, discovering life with a car, TV, and fridge. Before that invention, they were going to a special place to get ice in order to keep the food for a few days. She used to go to the river to wash their clothes and dirty diapers by hand. She was from a different time, without technology for people. After the war, everything became accessible and she told me how revolutionary it was; I was fascinated by her stories. She was a very good storyteller and I could picture everything like I was there; it was magical. I loved her so much. She definitely taught me a thing or two about men, but the best lesson she ever gave me was that women should never chase a man. Only men should struggle to get the one they want, not us. That was probably the mistake I was constantly making, one story after another...Until the day I decided to follow her advice, with John, my husband now. Without my grandma by our side for the rough beginning of our new "normal" with mum, I'm not sure I would have cope that well. Every time I had to tell someone about my mum, I used to fall in tears and it took me a few years to get over this tragic event. The day I lost my grandma, I felt like my world was falling into bits, leaving a big hole growing inside me.

★★★

It was 2004 when I had my most devastating loss. I was twenty-two years old, studying in Montpellier and in a long-distance relationship with Enzo. I met him at twenty and we stayed together for eight months of ups and downs until he cheated on me for the fourth time. After some time apart, I decided to give our relationship another chance. I really thought we were back together for good. The day I found out I was wrong was particularly cruel by virtue of the timing.

On the first Friday of February, I woke up suddenly at 7 am and felt the urge to go back to Nice. I called Enzo and told him that I had to go home. After a day of unexplained dreadful feelings—a sense that something wasn't quite right—I picked him up after class and we arrived in Nice at night. Lali, who was living in Paris at the time, was spending the week at my parents' house but nobody was home when I opened the door. I called her, anxious. She answered in a state of tears and told me the devastating news—Grandma Lucienne had passed away that morning around 7 am. My entire body was shaken by shivers and I couldn't talk anymore. I was shocked. I drove there, very fast, trying to see through the tears. I couldn't digest it. It was too sudden, too soon, too painful. I cried uncontrollably like I'd just lost my mother. I was inconsolable. When I arrived there, my dad had placed her in her bed, after the doctor confirmed her death. They found her in her shower; she must have fallen over, probably while taking her shower that morning. They told me that she didn't want to have another pacemaker when hers had to be replaced. I knew she was tired after a full life and that she wanted to go but I didn't know I'd lose her so early. I still needed her. I still wanted her in my life. I was in her bedroom, desperate and in tears, looking at her lying in her bed like if she was asleep. She looked so calm and rested. A small lamp on her bedside table was lighting the room. I couldn't stop crying and I took her in my arms, kissing her cold cheek, desperate to feel her moving again. She was so cold. I was too late, I didn't have a chance to say goodbye.

That weekend, I spent my time comforting my mum and my sister, helping dad prepare everything for the funerals, and crying. I couldn't help it, I was in such pain I could feel the bowl of sorrows forming deep in my stomach and trying to go back up through sobs and tears. I didn't have much time for Enzo but he was very understanding, and after four days I knew why. Despite standing beside me throughout my grandmother's funeral, I discovered he'd been cheating on me with his ex, the one who had so coldly dumped him prior to our relationship. She had come back into his life… and he chose her over me.

I lost two very important people that day and I couldn't stop crying for the next two hours driving back to my lonely student flat. I didn't give Enzo any possibility of repairing our relationship; it was just over. He wasn't there for me in this painful time. I figured out that I was the one giving the most to this relationship. It was like rowing the boat alone, because I was the only one helping the relationship move forward; we were going around in circles. A relationship can't be successful without a team effort.

I cried for the next six months; it was so hard to deal with grieving my "Mamie" by myself. I had my friends but I didn't want to be sad with them. I needed them to help me forget. I was crying every night for what seemed forever. The next months were tough for me but since that day, I feel like she's always been by my side, because even if the worst situations, I've always had some sort of luck.

★★★

It's nearly Christmas and my wishes this year aren't materialistic at all. As you get older, your wishes get more intangible and even harder to obtain. I have only one wish, to get cured and survive; living a long healthy happy life with my children and my love. Hopefully it will come true; hopefully, my grandma and guardian angel will help me go through this too. I take my beautiful daughter home this afternoon and I enjoy my evening with my son, my daughter, my husband, and my parents like it's the last one. I see every detail of their faces, their smiles, like the time is slowing down for me to contemplate the beauty of the moment. I am now living mindfully, every single day. *"We only live once."*

14

I have started to see a psychiatrist for my condition. I don't feel depressed and I definitely don't want to die. But I'm anxious, I can't stop thinking and my brain has been messing with me. The doctor teaches me the basics of mindfulness and meditation and if it doesn't save me, it's saving my soul from the darkness of cancer. The medical side of cancer may be painful to live with, but the emotional roller coaster of it is even worse. One of the most important things I'm learning is that just because my brain wants to talk doesn't mean I have to listen. I can just say "Oh, interesting" and move on. I don't have to hold on to every thought and analyse them all. I can just acknowledge them and let them be as ignoring them worsens the problem. I can't let my brain and my thoughts bully me. What a relief. I start to meditate daily, breathing, scanning my body, visualising it as healthy, with no tumours, no dark spot anywhere and finding peace in bringing my mind back to meditation when it's trying to take me elsewhere. My anxiety decreases and I can deal with my emotions with more ease. The mind is so powerful that I prefer to have it on my side, strengthen me in positive thoughts, rather than against me, bringing me down in my darkest and deepest negative thoughts. Living mindfully also helps me to appreciate every detail of everything. My psychiatrist also told me that it's normal for me to go through the five stages of grieving my own life: denial, anger, bargaining, depression, and acceptance but I'm not sure I've been through any of them so far, except maybe denial.

Christmas is around the corner and I'm glad my parents are with us for Rose's first Christmas, like they were also here for Jason's first Christmas. They already came three times in Australia in four years: for the kids' first Christmas and my first Christmas as a married woman. I'm thankful to have them; they love me and they show it.

Mum can barely walk. Her right arm hasn't moved much in twenty years and she doesn't understand a word of English. Dad is pushing her in her cheap and now quite dangerous wheelchair and he recently developed lymphoma, so he's still dealing with doctors. Even still, they travelled across the world six times for me and my young family, staying at least three weeks, and this time nearly five months, for us. They are giving me the support I need.

Jason grew so much in a year and they've met our beautiful Rose. They were straight away under her spell. They take her in their flat when I feel too tired to nurse her at night and Dad wakes up to feed her; it's a big effort for him because he loves his sleep. But Rose is easier than Jason; she feeds in ten minutes now and goes back to sleep straight away. And it's also easier to put her to bed, no rocking or patting necessary. She is the best baby ever, such a relief with my exhaustion, exactly what we needed. If she was as difficult as Jason used to be, it would have been a lot more difficult to cope with this cancer. I'm telling you, there's a God. Also, Mum and Dad keep her while I go to my doctor's appointments; she's better off playing at home than being trapped in the car for hours and visiting the Melanoma Medical Centre clinics.

I'm glad we're celebrating Christmas again together and we don't work too hard on the menu this time. We love our traditional Christmas Eve, so we still have a wonderful meal: French fat liver, of course, and smoked salmon for the entrée. Then John's dad brings a beautiful lamb shoulder and a roasted pork leg with beans and potatoes on the side. We also have a delicious cheese platter and we make a great chocolate "*log*" for dessert. As usually, Stan and Ellen, her brother and her dad are with us too. We light candles and place a big table in the middle of our flat for everyone to be able to feast around. It's great, but again, looking at everyone smiling and having a nice time, I can't help but think it could be my last Christmas and an intense sadness overtakes my body.

My parents, my kids, my husband… they all seem so normal, probably not thinking about it because obviously, it's not their last Christmas. They don't feel the urge to live the moment, they don't have to. I feel lucky somehow to live that way as I'm even more thankful to have them around me on Christmas Eve, appreciating every second of them. Every detail is here; I can see everything and capture the magic of the moment as if I was outside of my body, looking at the scenery. It's beautiful and I love it. But when everyone leaves and I find myself alone with my husband, sitting in front of the Christmas tree, I can't help telling him how I really feel.

"What if it's my last Christmas, John? I can't stand this idea. I barely know Rose and Jason is still so young. They won't remember me." I burst into tears, reaching for the comfort of his arms.

"Don't say stupid things like that, it won't be your last Christmas." He tries to reassure me.

"How can you be so sure? How do you manage to remain so calm and confident all the time?" I reply, sobbing.

"Because I know it. You will have many more Christmases. Remember, you have no choice."

"I know. I am so sorry, love. I'm so sorry to put you in such a bad place. I wish to be there to help you with the kids. It will be so hard for you otherwise."

"You will. I still don't know what I'd say to them otherwise." He's now sobbing with me.

"Oh John. It's so scary and if I'm not there anymore, they won't remember their mummy. They won't have any memory of me."

"I'm sure you'll be there. You will live a long life. Stay positive."

"How do you know?"

"Don't say that. I know because I made a deal," he says with confidence.

"What? What are you talking about?" I ask surprised.

"Yes, that's right; I told whoever is in charge up there that he had to swap my life with yours. He let you live and I take your place; if one of us has to go, it will be me."

"You're silly." A smile breaks out on my crying face. "It doesn't work like that. And I don't want you to say stupid things like that. Your life is as important as mine and the kids need you as much as they need me. And I love you. I want you to live. You can't just trick the system like that. Stop asking for that, please."

"No, I won't. It's a balance thing. If one life needs to go, it has to be mine. The kids need you more than they need me and I want you to live."

"I want you to live too. No one is going to die then. Please stop doing that," I beg.

"Okay, don't worry; you're going to annoy the crap out of me forever." He tries to laugh.

"I hope I will."

"You will. I'm sure you will," he says holding me tight in his arms.

The kids have been spoiled by Santa and Jason loves having presents. He starts to understand what Christmas is about as every time we see a nativity scene, I talk about Jesus, Mary, and Joseph. Every time he sees one, he asks where Jesus is. I tell him that he could ask anything to Jesus and if he wanted it very deeply in his heart, Jesus would help him. Deep down, I'm praying that he will save me. He needs to help me recover, help me get better, help me get cured. I have to survive for my kids and my husband; he can't call me back now because it's terrible timing. He has to wait at least until the kids are in school, so it will be a little easier on John. Even though, deep down, I want him to wait until my kids have kids themselves.

We celebrate New Year's Eve at home, watching the amazing fireworks of Sydney on the big screen, sipping a small glass of Champagne, cheering and kissing at the end of the countdown. I've got a PET scan on the fifth of January, then a CT scan and oncologist appointment on the sixth. We can't wait to know how the medicine is working or if it is. To my delight, it is. One of my tumours can't be seen anymore and the two big ones I have in each armpit have significantly reduced in size; the rest are inactive. Having tumours with no activity is good because it means the cancer is under control and it's like you don't have cancer; if all tumours disappeared, it would be even better. Finally, I'm not eligible for the clinical trial they wanted me to start because I've already started a treatment and this particular one is for people who never had treatment. I couldn't have waited with no treatment; I'd be dead by now.

But the news isn't too bad at all. More clinical trials will come up towards March or April and we are hoping I can start one of them. Meanwhile, I have to tick the boxes off my bucket list. So I go for two surf lessons within the next two weeks. I haven't touched a board since shortly after arriving in Sydney and I really want to be able to take a wave without falling once. And I make it happen. It's exhausting doing the washing machine again, but now that I learn about the rips on a beginner board, it's easier. It's awesome to feel so free and revitalised again. I have a wonderful time both mornings and it's great to do something for myself for once. I love it and I leave Cronulla Beach with a big smile on my face and a happy mood both times.

I also start exercising again in order to be in slightly better shape. After nearly two years of pregnancies, I'm keen to regain my body shape and getting my energy and self-confidence back. I have gained nearly twelve kilos with Rose and I have to lose the weight. I can't stand myself anymore. I'm feeling heavy and uncomfortable in my skin, which doesn't help my fight against the black beast. One thing is sure, it's hard. Exercising is demanding and losing weight while on steroids is tough. But I need the drugs to limit the side effects of my treatment so I can stay on it longer. Breastfeeding would have helped a little, like it did after Jason's birth. I never got big with Jason though. I didn't have the chance to because he was in a rush to see me. I'm stuck at twelve kilos over what I was before falling pregnant.

I found a great venue for Rose's baptism and the renewal of our vows. It's a gorgeous little cottage in Peakhurst, with beautiful gardens full of roses and flowers and a charming fountain. I've ordered my dress custom made in China again; it's a light pink sleeveless one this time, with a gorgeous ruffle organza gown. It's beautiful. I just have to order the cake, prepare the music, and send the invites. Then, it will be sorted. Finally, I will have a proper reception for our wedding. Our wedding five years ago was beautiful but I missed my family and I'm happy to be able to make it up for it, especially since we never managed to have the wedding in France. I'm so glad to finally have my parents and my twin sister by my side to marry my love.

John and I didn't go far for our first honeymoon, so I think it will be awesome to have a few days on an island before renewing our vows. I am going to book us a few days on Hamilton Island. The wedding being on Valentine's Day weekend, it's way too expensive to fly that week, so we will go before. It will be our first holiday alone since we went to Europe after the loss of our first baby, two and half years ago. We weren't really alone and it seemed like forever ago—a tropical island by ourselves, no babies, four days and three nights of cruises, cocktails by the pool, relaxation, and snorkelling on the reef. I can't wait to conquer my husband again and have some desperately needed quality time together. It will be short but without the kids, time will feel longer for sure.

Also, as Mum and Dad will be here with us until the end of April, I decide to tick another item off my bucket list: Uluru. My sister will help with the kids while we are in Hamilton Island, but for Uluru, she won't be here anymore and my parents will have to manage alone. Since Jason will go to day-care during the day, I plan to leave on a Monday and come back on a Friday afternoon so they just have to deal with him on mornings and evenings. Rose, still quite young, will be super easy to take care of during the day. I'm ecstatic. We will enjoy a helicopter flight over Uluru and Kata Tjuta and rent a car to go to the rocks and back to the resort. I also plan for a romantic dinner by the stars for our last night.

I'm trying to make the most out of the time I've got left. I saw it written in black and white that I have twenty-four months to live since my diagnosis in October, so technically I have twenty months left. Since I'm not working and we only rely on John's wages, it's getting tough to pay the rent, day-care, food, electricity, doctors, and medicine. Also, I start to wonder if I did well organising the wedding and holidays when money is running out…But these ticks are things to look forward to and help me feel better. Also, the hardest part of dying is to realise how big the gap is between what I've done in my life and what I want to achieve before the end of it. Once I've done most of it, I will feel more peaceful. I know I can't make all my wishes happen. For example, owning our house is impossible since the prices in Sydney are ridiculously expensive and I'm not working anymore. But I can realise most of them, or at least die trying.

Twenty months, that's nothing. What an awful feeling to see your life expectancy on a piece of paper. I didn't want to know but I know now. I call my nurse who tries to comfort me saying that it's the odds but it can be different. I have to fight and nowadays with new treatments and clinical trials, things can change. They have to…I will defy the odds; I have to survive longer, for my babies.

Rose is helping me as much as she can since she's now sleeping twelve hours straight at night. She's always so happy and smiley, she gives me all the positive waves I need for a good start of the day. Lucky for my sister too, as she's just landed from Paris and will take care of her nephews tomorrow. John and I are leaving for Hamilton

Island. I'm so happy to be able to take her in my arms, my beautiful twin sister, my rock, my anchor.

We have a quite an emotional reunion because of the circumstances and she falls in tears when we talk about prognosis and treatments. I saw my oncologist the morning before my sister's arrival and she's happy with my results. I'm responding very well to the treatment and she won't rush me into any clinical trial as she'd rather make sure that the one I'll go for will have the best chance to work on me; once started, I may not be able to go back on my actual treatment.

Lali is glad to meet her niece and nephew for the first time and finds them very cute. She's looking forward to spending some time with them. I explain to Jason and Rose who she is and that Mummy and Daddy will be away for a few days. I'm not sure Jason understands and he's very clingy before we take off. Lali is a mum of three kids and I'm sure she will take care of my babies like they were hers. I hope Jason won't drive her mad with his tantrums—terrible twos— and I can't wait to enjoy more time with her once we'll be back. She grew her hair and it's the same length as mine now, so we look so much alike that Jason and Rose think she's me. I explain to my sister their routine and how to handle them for the next five days and we are off.

John and I have a magical time on the tropical island. I was hoping for a relaxing, romantic, and bonding quality time with my dear husband and I'm not disappointed. We are back in Sydney on Saturday morning, perfect timing to be able to spend quality time with my babies. Apparently, since we left, Jason and Rose really thought Lali was me, it's only when we come back that Jason realises he's been tricked. He called her "Mama" all week long and when I come back, he looks to each of our faces, back and forth, confused, not knowing who is who and then runs toward me crying "Mama" as if I betrayed him. I have missed the kids a lot. I was right, four days without kids seemed to last two weeks. It was great to relax and enjoy some dating time with John, even if it was hard to avoid the baby talk. But it was nice; we had heaps of time for ourselves.

We arrived on Tuesday and enjoyed an afternoon soaking and drinking cocktails at the pool bar. We watched the sunset on a catamaran and savour a nice dinner in a Mexican restaurant on the marina. The next morning, we went on a cruise to Whitehaven beach, one of the most beautiful beaches of Australia; it was amazing. It was very hot and the sand was burning our feet, but swimming in the light blue ocean and admiring the panorama was extraordinary, even if we had to wear a complete stinger suit because of jellyfishes. We also had a scary close encounter with a wild giant dragon lizard. We had another afternoon relaxing by the pool bar—definitely our favourite—and went to the Tavern pub for a chicken parmigiana for dinner. Our reef combo composed by a seaplane flight over Heart Reef and snorkelling on the reef was cancelled for the next day so I had to check what else we could do to get a similar experience. There was no way we wouldn't see Heart Reef. I arranged to go on an all-day cruise on Bait Reef with helicopter flight option over Heart Reef. We just had to rush to get the flight in as it must be booked on-board only. We spent the afternoon like teenagers, playing a weird bowling game called Kegels, with nine pins placed in a diamond shape and bowls with only two holes, which definitely killed our arms and fingers, but we had so much fun. We snoozed in our bedroom before getting ready for the Denison Star Dinner cruise at 5.30pm at the marina. This was such an awesome dining experience. It was one of the best nights we had in a very long time. John and I were closer together again. We watched the sunset drinking a beer, sitting side by side, John's arm around my shoulders, we had a delicious three-course tasting dinner that we shared, describing their taste like food experts on a mission. Then we finished the date night looking at the stars, in each other's arms, kissing.

On our last day, we had to wake up early to depart for a fantastic cruise on the Great Barrier Reef. After cruising to the reef, we flew twenty minutes over Hardy Reef, Bait Reef, and Heart Reef, which is very small, only sixteen metres long. I was in the co-pilot seat and enjoyed the amazing views of the ocean. The waters were so clear that we could see the asperities of the reefs, observing a continent of corals. After a quick lunch, we spent two hours snorkelling hand in hand, watching the colourful coral and all sorts of fishes. It was beautiful. No turtles this time; we were lucky to swim with them when we went on a reef cruise outside Cairns years ago. But so much more fish this time. At the end of the day, we were exhausted and savour some Greek specialties with a few beers for our last dinner at the Mantra Bay Restaurant on the marina; it was the last night before having the kids again and we enjoyed every minute of it. It was great to have some time for ourselves but I'm glad to be with my babies again. I missed them and my sister too.

We had trouble avoiding the cancer talk during our holiday and during one emotional night, I told him I wanted to tick another two items off my bucket list: pass my citizenship and move from our flat to a house. We need more space with two babies and it's stressful to put them to bed in the same bedroom. Also, a little backyard would be awesome for them to play, especially if my health worsens. I wouldn't have to keep them trapped inside or go out to the park, we could stay in our own backyard. On top of that, there's no way in hell that I will die in this claustrophobic unit. But our budget is tight so it will be difficult to find a house in our Rockdale area around the five hundred dollar mark a week, but we'll try. I want to get out of here, I'm suffocating.

With only John's wages, it's tough to pay everything and we have to take from our small savings every month. I hope we can get a bit of help from Centrelink and I'm wondering if I shouldn't try to work from home, create some kind of work myself or something else in order to make money. I'm selling every unnecessary item we have on Gumtree to make a few bucks but it's not enough and I find it very hard to go from being the breadwinner to making nothing. I feel guilty again. Maybe I should learn how to sew and design handbags, selling them on Etsy? That would be quite cool, not so sure I would get much out of it though. I bought a Desigual bag seventy per cent off at Sydney Airport on our way to Hamilton Island, and I was thinking about it. If you fall in love with a handbag, you have to buy it. That was my justification. I'm living like there's no tomorrow so I'm pleasing myself a bit, after all these years of sacrifice for a house we will finally never buy.

At first, it was the opposite; I was wondering if I should buy anything, it would be a waste if I die. John would have to get rid of everything…or I would, just before I go. I thought that I shouldn't waste money on me anymore since I wouldn't last long. It was better to keep it for the kids, for John, in case I wasn't there anymore; they needed it more than my dead body. I was even thinking of emptying my closet, getting rid of the shoes I never wore…but then, I thought that hopefully I will still be around and it wasn't that time yet. I could still do that later. For now, I had to enjoy, think positive: I will live a long life and that handbag will die of being used before me. I love it and it's the first thing I bought for myself in over two years so it put a monster smile on my face while making my dress look heaps better.

When we come back from Hamilton Island, my parents leave for three days in the Blue Mountains, our Christmas present for them. They are helping us so much I wanted to thank them with some relaxing time off. Also, the only time they went there was with us and it was pouring in rain; lucky this time the weather was very sunny. Meanwhile, Lali and I prepare the final details of the baptism-wedding coming that weekend. I show her the venue and she finds it beautiful. I'm so glad she can be there this time. I laugh with her when I realise that she got engaged at the same time as I did and I had the time to get married twice, had two kids and baptised them both when she is still to fix a date for her wedding.

I'm so happy to spend some quality time with my twin. I haven't seen her since our trip to France and I'm missing her badly. I feel complete with her around, like something is missing when she's not close to me. With Skype and Viber, emails and phone, things are better than twenty years ago for sure, but having her physically with me is so much better; I can talk to her at any time. We have breakfast, lunch, and dinner together, I don't have to report anything, she's witnessing life at the same time, she's with us and with my kids too. She laughs with me and comes with me to my doctor appointments. We visit around together, have fish and chips on Watson's Bay after a nice walk on the beach; we go body boarding in Cronulla, lazing in Manly, shopping in the city and talk like we left each other yesterday. It's refreshing, uplifting and energising to have her by my side. On top of that, she's an awesome help. She prepares my coffee in the morning after waking up with the kids while I continue to sleep for a bit. She dresses them up and plays with them and they love her naturally, like if she was me. Jason still calls her mummy as he struggles to figure out why I doubled up. It's only in the last few days that he starts calling her "Tata," aunty in French. With all her help, I manage to rest and we can enjoy our days out, while my parents take care of Rose and Jason is at day-care.

We go to Kiama markets with John on our last Sunday so she can see outside the big city as well. It would be so nice if she was living here with her kids and partner David; we could see each other more often and raise our children together. But David is in the French administration and doesn't speak very good English. She's in payroll and laws are so different here. On top of that, she had surgery at eighteen to remove her entire thyroid to avoid cancer and was taking a daily treatment since, entirely financed by the French medical system and couldn't get that here. But I miss her badly. I never missed my family as much as since I was diagnosed with cancer; I guess it put things into perspective. It's a lonely journey and having them all here feels so good. I'm afraid to lose them again. I want to see how it is without them because I'd like to know if I can handle our new routine at four...They help me so much; I wonder if I will manage without their support. I hope I will cope without damaging my health; I have to limit stress and rest as much as I can but without them, I'm afraid it will be very difficult.

The wedding goes well, except that John's brother, who was supposed to be our witness and Rose's godfather, comes in shorts. I'm shocked and hurt. Couldn't he make any effort, really? I'm so upset that I forget my flowers at home. I have to go back, halfway to the church, and Lali runs back upstairs to get the flowers for me because my gown and I are all squeezed in the front seat. When I arrive at the church, I start panicking and I can barely breathe. I decide to have Jordan for witness since he's John's stepbrother and he's wearing a costume. It's so different from the first time. It's weird being so shaky for a second time. I know my husband this time and I love him even more; my family is there too. There's some kind of pressure, since I also know why I'm doing that. I want to marry him in the presence of my family, even before my diagnosis, but this time around when the priest will say "in health or in sickness." it will definitely make more sense.

I have trouble walking down the aisle, with my shoes catching in my gown, but this time I have my Dad by my side, all proud of his beautiful daughter. I'm glad to arrive face to face with John. He's smiling looking at my pink dress, knowing how much I love pink. When we have to exchange the rings, he surprises me with another one. I gave him back my original ring so he could give it to me during the ceremony and he did the same, but when the priest asks him to get my ring and pass it onto my finger, he takes his wallet out of his pocket. I'm thinking *"what is he doing?"* Then I see the simple band I wanted. Yes, I got a beautiful bridal set five years ago, two thin bands of diamonds, one with a bigger diamond for the engagement ring, but it was hard to wear on a daily basis as I had to take it off to wash my hands, go for a swim, do anything really and I wanted to be able to wear my wedding band every day and every night, like my parents are doing with theirs; my dad can't even remove his. So I wanted a simple band to never have to take it off. I'm nearly in tears when I see the surprise ring. He got me once more and passes it to my finger with a big smile, satisfied of the surprise effect. I love him so much; he still manages to surprise me after five years, three pregnancies, two kids, and one cancer. He's still in love with me, still keen on pleasing me. I wrote our prayers for the wedding and my sister is in charge to read them out loud. It's a very emotional moment for me, hearing them out loud, in front of all our loved ones and God; "officially" asking to be cured so I can help my family and be there for my children. I'm so hoping that my prayers will be heard and answered.

Jason starts to be unsettled and wants to join us at the altar; Stéphanie can't keep him preoccupied any longer. So after renewing our vows, Jason offers me the flower he found in the garden outside and comes with us to celebrate Rose's baptism. All of a sudden, the tension comes down and the atmosphere feels so much more relaxed for me. We did it again. We got married with God and my family as witnesses. Rose is beautiful in her little white fancy dress and, like Jason a year ago, doesn't cry when the priest sprinkles the holy water over her forehead. All goes very well, except for Jacob and his shorts...Grrr! Rose looks like an angel and she behaves like one too. I'm so happy she's now part of the Christian Church and so glad we have such a special day, surrounded by our loved ones. We all leave the church listening to one of my favourite songs *"somewhere over the rainbow"* song by Bob Marley, who died of melanoma the year I was born. I'm happy. It wasn't as emotional as the first wedding but still filled with love. John and I know each other so well now, yet, he still surprised me. It felt so quick too. Also, it was hard to focus on the ceremony with Jason and Rose; Jason was really unsettled at some points, but overall it went even better than what I expected.

After a few group pictures outside the church, we all drive to the venue in Peakhurst and everyone is pleased to discover the charming cottage, surrounded by the garden full of flowers. I planned an afternoon tea with delicious savoury and sweet bites. After we thank everyone for coming, my sister gives a great speech about how happy she is for us and how special I am to her. John and I cut the cake with lots of fun and dance on our song, *Throw your arms around me*, from Hunters and Collectors, since we couldn't on our first wedding day. I'm so happy to have my sister, my parents and my friends there: Stéphanie and her boyfriend, Agatha, her partner Nils and son Taylor, Mary, hubby Barney and daughter Lillian, Lise and Rod with their son Tristan. This time around I'm not alone; I'm with my loved ones too.

My friend Judy couldn't come as she's celebrating Valentine's Day with her hubby on a getaway. But somehow, since I had cancer, she let me down. Most people don't know how to deal with it and unfortunately, with cancer, you lose a lot of "friends." I think they try to avoid a future pain, don't want to see you die; maybe it's wrecking their happy environment or just because it's hard to take something good out of a friendship with a potential dead person. It's a lonely journey and I can understand them because even my parents, my hubby and my sister have trouble understanding what I'm going through.

I'm glad the reception is a success, I'm proud and happy to be married to my gentleman again and baptising Rose on the same day was the icing on the cake. I feel blessed to share my life with such a wonderful man. He could be grumpy and lazy sometimes but deep down he's such a sweetheart and a generous soul. I'm so lucky to have given birth to two beautiful children with him; they are my little miracles. Jason did everything early; he's now twenty-one months old and he's got all his teeth, he's running and playing soccer like a champ and is starting to go to the potty. Rose is also a little miracle because for my third pregnancy, and after a premature baby, she was born healthy and safe after I was diagnosed with thyroid issues and a stage four melanoma. She's beautiful with her big blue eyes and doing so well.

I always get what I want so far and I feel very spoiled and blessed, living the Aussie dream with my Prince Charming. My grandma is probably watching over me. I just have to be cured to believe in fairy tales. I'm so scared to die; sometimes I find myself crying at night. I don't want to die. I want to survive. I love my children and my hubby so much. But I've been blessed with three miracles already, my hubby that I met by a miracle coincidence, my son, and my daughter. I must have a fourth one though: my survival, if it's not too much to ask. It has to happen. I need it to sustain the first three ones. After the wedding, the next tick on my list is to find a new place to live with my young family, preferably a house with a garden. I want a fresh start; our flat was supposed to be temporary when we moved in four years ago.

15

Every three weeks I have to go for a CT scan and see my oncologist. I will do a PET scan every two months or earlier if necessary. The PET provides the activity rating while the CT localises the tumours. It's mid-March and it's that time again. I've got the results of my last CT and it shows neither amelioration, nor worsening. The tumour in the left armpit has grown slightly and of course I'm worrying. My oncologist tells me it's stable, which gives me more time anyway. She still wants to wait until I have no other option but to go into a clinical trial as my treatment is keeping me stable for now. If it's not working anymore, my next option is infusions of Keytruda, the new immunotherapy that seems to do miracles. But it works only for one person out of two.

Time is running out quickly and with it, my hopes. That's the scariest part. I can see around me, through social media and Internet, through the melanoma community, that when patients are told that their treatment doesn't work anymore, and they don't have any options left, they die very fast. Usually, three to four months and that's it. From life to death, there isn't much time. I'm thinking about my kids again. Always them. I'm always thinking of them, they are my reason to live, I want to be there for them and I want to stay alive with every cell in my body. Living in uncertainty is very challenging for the control freak I am. But meditation teaches me that the sky is always blue behind the clouds and the storms. The dark times never stay forever. It will be nice again at some point if we remember that.

I have side effects all week, fevers and all the crap, and also weird sensations in my legs. I can barely move them; they are heavy and painful. So, my oncologist advises another PET scan. I hate these scans. They take me all day. I can't have a coffee or anything for breakfast because I have to fast for six hours beforehand. But I'm

glad to do it so I know where I'm at; information is my only ally.
It's crucial.

On a positive note, John and I went to an acclaimed restaurant
of the Opera House. I wanted to go there since my second day in
Sydney when I visited the Opera House and looked through the glass
windows. I saw this beautiful restaurant and imagined how amazing
it would be to get a table there, the food was probably delicious and
it would certainly feel so special looking at the stars through the
glass ceiling. Well, we had a wonderful time. Another tick on my
list. It was such a special moment for us. Uncle Georgio offered us
a hundred-dollar voucher for any restaurant and I managed to book
the past week for a table on Friday 11th of March at 7.30pm, our only
option, otherwise every Saturday night was full until the end of the
following month. That the kind of wait you get for a famous fine
dining experience. We knew we'd still had to pay a lot more on top
of it but we only live once. John was wearing his wedding costume
and city shoes for the occasion and looked handsome. I was wearing
a lovely black dress—the only one I could still fit—and we were two
beautiful people about to enter the fancy restaurant.

The waiter welcomed us and asked if we came here for a special
occasion –as probably many people are since it's about two hundred
dollars per head. I didn't know what to answer and John and I looked
at each other, lost for a moment, wondering what to say, until the
waiter prompted "just celebrating life?" And this answer was just
perfect for us. We replied with a big "That's it." Happy to be placed
at our table, without having to mention that my life was at stake and
we were trying to tick off my entire bucket list. The three-course
dinner was delicious, we enjoyed describing every sensation, the taste
of each element composing the plate and how the mix of flavours
was astonishing. There wasn't much in the plate but our palates had
a fantastic time.

The place was gorgeous; the glass ceiling was reflecting all the
little lamps lighting the room and it looked like a sky full of stars. But
the best part was to get to spend a wonderful time with the love of
my life. He had left his phone and talked to me nicely, smiling and
looking at me like back in our dating time. We were sitting on the
booth and while I was sipping on a fruity rose, John was savouring a
boutique beer. We were chatting and enjoying each other company

before the start of our dinner. He was romantic and funny, very sexy in his suit and I felt like five years ago, before our parenting time, when we were dating. That was the best part of it: I felt like he really cared for me and loved me. He seemed genuinely happy being with me and looked at me like nothing else mattered, like he used to.

I remembered that I fell in love with the way his eyes delved into mine. I missed it and I had it back that night. It was the most precious gift ever. I appreciated every second of that magic night, the beautiful dinner, each of the three dishes and sharing our delicious desserts. John picked the best one, as usual. And to conclude beautifully our date, we received a glass of champagne from our waiter. In fact, he asked us to sit face to face when some VIP arrived, not long after we'd been seated, and sat a girl in the booth right next to us. Since we'd clearly been asked to move to accommodate the other party, the staff felt sorry for us, and even if we didn't really care, we appreciated the nice gesture. The service was definitely the best I ever had. And we loved sipping on the bubbles before leaving the restaurant for a romantic walk on the harbour. We contemplated the night views of the city, like tourists, newly in love and had the surprise to see fireworks above the Opera. It was such an amazing finish for the magical date with dear hubby.

The week after, I get good news from my PET scan: the tumours are less active, even if they grew slightly, it's not concerning. On my way back from the scan I go to St. Mary's Cathedral. Last time I was there with John, a couple of month ago, I lit a candle, praying for my health and my family, without the coin donation required because I didn't have any change. So I give back what I owed and added enough to light another candle. It's also confession time and I wait for the priest to receive me. It takes quite some time, so I take a seat and start thinking about my recent behaviour. I realise that I have been quite self-absorbed lately. John mentioned it at the restaurant, telling me that his dad didn't understand some of my ways because he didn't get how difficult it was for me to deal with all this crap. I'm not sure I like the woman I'm becoming.

My life is never going to be the same anymore. Cancer has changed it forever. Not that I'm not used to change; I feel like my life was full of life-changing events, but this time it's different. This time, it's not only life around me that is changing, it's also life within me and that's the scariest part of it. I'm not the person I used to be anymore and I will try my best to become someone that I love again. I tell the priest how bad I feel, how I've been awful at times with my parents and my husband, even though they tried to help me. They are a precious help, a good support and instead of being thankful and loving I'm getting upset and unsatisfied. As if they owe me something. But that's it. That time is over now.

I will change; I will open my eyes and turn towards others instead of always feeling sorry for myself. It's not just about me. Okay I have cancer and that sucks big time but I can't let cancer define me. I'm other things too, and my family has to live too. They are not responsible for my disease; no one is. I must stop cancer from bringing me down and defining me. I'm not just a person with cancer, I'm so much more. Also, when the priest receives me, he gives me a very good analogy about Jesus during his own journey to death, carrying his cross. He didn't complain, he wasn't upset, he kept loving and caring for us, he never gave up. I realise that no matter how long we have to live, the most important is to love and care for those around us. Also, as my psychiatrist told me before, to find peace, I need to live by your values. It's the only way to be at peace with my own self. So, from now on, I will try not to complain anymore, and live not like I don't have cancer because it's impossible and denial doesn't help, but like I'm not defined by my terminal condition. I have to be happy again, as much as I used to be. And love sex with my hubby as well. As it seems to have been ages since we had some intimate moments. It's hard to find the energy, the time with two kids and my parents in the middle. But cancer isn't sexy for me either and kind of kills the mood. I will plan it if I have too then. This stop at the church makes me feel better; hopefully one day I will be able to thank God for saving my life and curing me. I think about my beautiful kids; Rose is crying a lot lately, teething, and I can have full conversations with Jason now. I'm so blessed to have such a beautiful family; I will stop fearing, I will take my head out of the sand, put my shit together and look at all the beauty surrounding me. Because life is beautiful.

On Sunday, March 20th, it's my first Melanoma fundraiser, a yearly march organised by the Melanoma Medical Centre, and I have to speak for the occasion. So, I tell my story, the quick version of it, in front of the crowd of patients, relatives affected by melanoma, and my family. I don't give too many details but this speech has an important echo in my dad's mind. I think it's what he had to hear and see to realise that all this shit is real. When I leave the stage to return to his side, he gives me a big hug. He releases a loud sigh and falls in tears, crying in my arms, like the day we buried his sister, who passed away from breast cancer. I tell him that I will be fine. I will give my best fight and I will win, I have to. He's just hoping I'm right. He's desperate to see me better. I'm happy my mum is not here. It started early and it would have been difficult with her wheelchair anyway. She is worrying too much already; I don't want her to suffer because of me.

I cut the ribbon before we start the march. It is emotional for us, John, dad and I, and all the others around us, affected by melanoma. But we're walking through this journey like we're doing it now, one step at a time, with our kids by our side, smiling and playing, unaware of the sad situation, enjoying their life to the fullest, bringing back a smile on our faces, one day at a time.

At the beginning of April, I feel better, knowing that my health is stable. I'm not as depressed or sad. Dealing with uncertainty and not knowing what will happen next is very challenging for me. The loss of control is overwhelming. So I have to do even more in order to stay as in control as I can. And somehow, I'd never imagined that preparing everything for the worse would help me as much as it does. If shit hits the fan, I may have only a couple of month left and definitely not enough time to sort out all the paperwork and leave behind what I want for the kids. Plus I don't want to have to do this. If I have two months left, I'd like to enjoy and appreciate every second with my kids and my hubby, my sister and my parents, not doing stupid paperwork and organising my funerals. I must be ready, just in case I die. Because just thinking about the paperwork to complete, people to contact, and my funerals to organise, it's already overwhelming and stressful. So, getting rid of this now will take that off my mind and help me think that I will have all the time in the world for what will count then: my family. One of the first things I do is buying birthday cards for my kids; as soon as I see one that I like in a shop, I get it. I will write twenty one of them, for both my children. I will take the time to write letters for each birthday and place the letter in the card, for each of their birthdays, until they will be twenty-one. Then, they will be big enough to survive without mummy's wishes and advice. Hopefully, I will get rid of each letter for every birthday and write on the actual card instead. But, just in case, they are covered for the next twenty years.

I start to think about what has to be done just before I die. It seems like an awful thought but it's actually good to overcome this. It comforts me; I'm in charge. I will trick the Murphy law. I don't know if you've noticed, but it's always when you take your umbrella that it's not raining and when you get a life insurance that you don't need it. Well, I had a life insurance for a month, everything was sweet: half a million dollar in case I die, I'd get two hundred thousand dollars for trauma and two years income protection. But I cancelled it four months before being diagnosed just because a home loan broker told me it was better to go through my Super for tax purposes. So I cancelled my insurance thinking there shouldn't be any issues to get the other one but finally my Super was using a sub-contractor and they were so painful to deal with that I gave up after three months. They wanted a letter from my thyroid specialist for the issues I had during my pregnancy and the specialist wouldn't write the letter if they didn't send her a letter explaining what they required. Nobody was willing to do what had to be done and I was over it. That's how I missed out. I've been so upset about this. That killed me for the first couple of months and I still keep a bitter taste. The money would have helped us so much...but like John always says, I had to move on and I did.

I don't want my husband to struggle with paperwork and funerals when the time comes. He will have enough on his plate; dealing with grief and two very young kids. It will be hard enough for him, especially since he hates paperwork. I'm the one in charge of everything at home: kids doctors, day-care, clothes purchases, his company invoices, payslips, super, budgets, accounts, our bills, rent, real estate issues, food shopping, cleaning, cooking, washing, event planning, holidays, everyone's doctor appointments and all the internet accounts. He won't know a thing. So since the beginning of the month, I look into how to do a will, what paperwork to put together in an *"Emergency"* box and how to prepare my funerals.

I've created three boxes. One for Jason, containing all his birth memories, including the diary I wrote every day at the NICU for him, a box with all the birthday cards, all his paintings and drawings and a photo album of him growing up. I've prepared one for Rose too, with the same content. And finally, I created the important box for John that I called the *"Emergency"* box. It contains everything important: the internet password for all the websites we use, my personal accounts and emails with their passwords, our passports, identification documents, French paperwork, superannuation details, leaflets about widower help and funeral documents. I actually advise anyone to do this box, as if your home is on fire, you just have to take that to save everything. I need to add a letter for John, explaining everything and also how I would like him to dispatch my jewellery to our children. Preparing all this relaxes me as I'm feeling more in control of the situation. The *"good"* thing about cancer is that you can be prepared to die. Even pre-paying and arranging the details of my funerals is good in a way because if I die in fifty years, I won't have to pay for the inflation and any tax increase; it will be paid already. And, well, if I have to pass away soon, my hubby will just have to pass one phone call and the funerals company will follow my plan. I have planned two appointments with two different funeral companies and will go for the cheapest; I won't be there to enjoy the party, so it's pointless to spend money on a swish coffin when we could use it for our kids' studies. Especially since I want to be cremated. A cheap pine one will burn faster anyway, and it's more environmentally friendly.

This cancer is a wakeup call for life and finally for a lot of things. I figure that work is the least important thing for me now whereas I've always put my career first in the past. I've always tried to boost it for money and intellectual challenge. Now, I revised my priorities and my family is my number one, on top of my very short list. Anyway, I have the job I've always wanted, deep inside me, the best career in the world—I'm the mum of a beautiful boy and a gorgeous girl. I'd like to spend more time with them. I really hope that if I'm finally part of a clinical trial, the side effects and the treatment will allow me to do so. I could keep them two days a week and they would continue to go to day-care three days while I go to doctors and scans appointments, do the chores at home or rest a bit. Maybe I could start having a hobby too. I've never had one, except for salsa and running when I was at Business School. I'm missing doing something nice for myself; taking care of my children feels great but it's very tiring as they're growing up.

My parents are about to leave. I will miss them a lot, and the kids will too. They are so happy to wake up with them around, play and speak French with them. I just hope they will get used to their absence quickly as I don't want them to be sad for too long. I can't imagine how it would be if I was gone forever. That idea is breaking my heart so badly; I really don't want to be responsible for the suffering of my children. I don't want to make them sad...Grieving their mum at such a young age. I'm supposed to be the nurturing, loving and caring mother, the one avoiding their pain and suffering. That would be devastating for me. It's on the back of my head again, coming back like a wave, uncontrollably popping in my mind. But again, I fight back fiercely. I will get better; I will destroy this stupid cancer.

When I have my last PET scan results—yes, it's that time already—I don't have any active tumours in my spine anymore. Just the ones in my armpits are still active, stable in size but less active than before. It's fantastic news. Overall, the pills I'm taking are improving my health. The cancer is not gone but I'm getting better. I'm getting more time. On the downside, the average patient will develop resistance to the treatment after eight months, and I'm already five months in. My oncologist reassures me saying that unlike most of her peers, she won't wait for my treatment not to work anymore to put me onto a trial, and the one we are thinking of is opening in three to four weeks. It's taking longer than expected due to administrative paperwork and if it opens earlier, she will see me straight away. I can't wait to see what's on offer and what kind of immunotherapy it is. I have read a lot about all sorts of immunotherapy treatments and trials and I'm ready to see what I will be up to. These therapies seem to be the future for cancer treatment and giving fantastic results for those who respond. Keytruda was on trial four years ago and with advances in research, hopefully the actual trials will do even better.

16

Holiday time. Now to enjoy some quality time with my husband and discover the wonders of the Red Centre, finally. I'm a bit skeptical of leaving my dad in charge of my babies, as he will have to take care of them and for my mum too. I trust him but he's definitely not as nurturing, understanding, and patient as my sister. I ask them to call me daily to let me know how things are going and after giving big cuddles and lots of kisses to Jason and Rose, we leave for the airport. I'm missing my kids already.

Before leaving Sydney, I had to cut my long hair. It was down to the middle of my back but with the kids, I always put it in a ponytail. I was desperate to lose the pregnancy weight sticking to me and steroids were no help in the matter. My hair was annoying the crap out of me. I felt like it covered my face and was suffocated me. I had to make drastic changes to my appearance if I wanted to get my positive mood back, so I cut it all. Time for changes. I've got a concave haircut, very short at the back, following my jawline and to the length of my chin at the front. Like back when I was twenty-two, a student in my Business School, ready to succeed and make the most of it. Change is always good. This one will give me back my motivation.

Next step: fighting this cancer to death. Not mine, its. Sorry, this quick parenthesis was important to mention, as really, hair sets your mind. Any changes in the way you look always make a big change in your state of mind. I've regained my energy by losing my long hair. I can fly now. I'm ready to take off...to Uluru. It's such a long time I wanted to see the sacred rock and I'm glad John and I will see it together.

While we are flying over Australia, I'm looking out the window, overall this space with nothing, no humans, no cables, no cities, nothing but colours: yellows, reds, and sometimes a bit of green. I feel so blessed to see the desert with my own eyes, all this nothingness is fascinating. It looks like there's nothing to watch really, but there are so many colours, shapes, and details to it. I can't wait to see the Aussie Far West…or Far Centre.

We land in a tiny airport and take a bus to our resort, the only resort and pretty much a small town in itself. The prices are very high and the service very poor, but who cares, we are in my dream. The day after our arrival, we have to wake up early to take the bus at 5 am direction King Canyon. We admire the sun rising on the desert while driving for hours across the outback. It takes us nearly three hours to arrive at Kings Creek Station where we have a frugal breakfast. We jump back in the bus and half an hour later we are at the bottom of the Canyon. After climbing about five hundred steps to arrive at the top of the Canyon, we walk along the edge for six kilometres; the landscape is splendid. The weather is with us; not too hot with a slight breeze of air. The colours of the rocks made of different concentration of iron, provide a beautiful contrast with the green and the black of the vegetation.

I feel so privileged to be there that I stop for a second to contemplate the landscape and can't help the tears coming up my eyes. I'm still alive and I'm here, with my love, in front of one the most breath-taking part of the world. I can still walk, climb and admire. I'm thankful to be able to share this special moment with my best friend and lover. We walk down the canyon to the Garden of Eden where a water hole appears between the red walls. We spend some time taking pictures and feeling the strength of nature in such a quiet place. A small stream is giving birth to the massive water hole and I'm wondering where it comes from as it looks so deserted. We climb back up, through a very steep sort of ladder. We walk along the cliff and finish the canyon ring where we started three hours earlier. It's amazing to see these rocks, shaped like piles of stones, apparently the result of the sand being moved by the waves billions of years ago. The high of the cliffs, the trees growing between massive rocks, the vegetation, and the water in such a deserted landscape are demonstrations of the force of nature. In such an inspirational and powerful environment, I'm feeling small, vulnerable, like a speck of dust in an ocean of sand. My life on Earth is meaningless. I'm nothing. Or maybe just another thing dying on Earth, coming in and getting out in not even a fraction of second in the planet's life. After such a big day, a warm shower, and a quick bite, we're falling asleep in no time, exhausted.

On Wednesday, after a sleep-in, we walk to the centre of the resort to get our pre-booked car rental. They upgrade us as they only have four-wheel-drive SUV. Awesome. We drive to Uluru straight away and walk around a small part of its base for two kilometres. We discover that every part of the sacred rock has a meaningful function for the Aboriginals. The stone is red and smoother than at the canyon. It looks that there are still some sediment deposits but more like a knife painting. It's massive, enormous, impressive. I'm very emotional again now that I'm finally here; I can see Uluru with my own eyes, after such a long wait. Another dream comes true. We enjoy a nice picnic with the flies before a shorter walk to a water hole. Yep. The flies are everywhere and so annoying. We came after the high season but they are still a lot of them, always around your face, your eyes and your mouth. It's the only thing I don't like here. We follow a thin stream to find a sacred hole, still filled with water, so we're pretty lucky. Again, the bright red contrasts with the green of trees, grass and the blue of the sky is magic. We immortalise the moment with a selfie and drive back to the resort for a quick shower. We are ready for our helicopter flight at 4pm. John is the co-pilot this time and I'm seating at the back. The view from the sky reveals some kind of patterns: stains of high big trees surrounded by smaller bushes and circled by even smaller ones, like in the local aboriginal paintings. They are views from the top of Uluru. And in this immensity of red land and small circles of bushes, Uluru and Kata Tjuta rise above the ground. It's fascinating. Uluru looks like slices of red stones stacked side by side. Kata Tjuta is very different, more like a formation of thirty-four domes, made of some red cement and pebbles. After this breath-taking trip in the air, we savour a relaxing dinner at the Pioneer Bar, the pub of Resort town washing down a wood-fire pizza with a refreshing beer. Again, in bed early-ish as the walks, the heat and the flies took the most out of us.

The next day, we drive to Kata Tjuta. My feet are killing me with the blisters I've got from the Canyon walk, so I have to do the long trek in the rock formation wearing my flip-flops. I've got no choice; the back of my right heel is too painful to handle a shoe.

John shows his support by doing the same. We get a weird look every time we come across by someone. The view at the top of the Valley of winds is stunning. We're sitting here for a while, between two gigantic domes, like in the heart of the Valley, looking deeply into the horizon, appreciating every detail of the scene. From here, we can see other domes, further away, after a big drop into a luxuriant green valley, and the big blue sky. The entire scenery is framed by a very high wall of red dome on each side. John smokes a cigarette while I'm taking pictures and it's time to go back to the car for a quick bite —there's no way I'm eating outside again with all these flies, even in front of Uluru, they are too annoying. We finish the day on another side of Kata Tjuta, with a short walk between two long red domes, along with a string of water forming small water holes, until a lookout in the middle of a luxuriant bush. Both Uluru and Kata Tjuta are magical but I've got a preference for the second one, more intriguing I guess. It's still early when we head back to the Resort, so we stop by the camel farm. I didn't know there were half a million camels in Australia, more than anywhere else in the world; they catch them and use them for travel, tourism and also sell them overseas. A good looking one can go for millions of dollars.

After a warm shower, we finish packing and get ready for our last dinner. We take a bus to arrive in the sand dunes where a cold beverage is awaiting. An Aboriginal dance starts while we admire the sunset over Kata Tjuta. It's in the dark that we walk down the dune towards a nicely set outdoor restaurant, made of round tables lighted by candles. Unfortunately, the clouds are covering the sky and it's a night without stars but we still enjoy the stories about the stars and the local tribes. We are dining with an older couple from Bendigo, two mums from Sydney and a young couple from Japan who doesn't understand a word of what we are saying, poor things. We all get to know each other and after a bit too much of alcohol we are back to our hotel room.

The next morning, I have a ten-minute ride on a camel named Norseman, a good looking one; I can't possibly die without riding a camel. It's pretty cool too. Well, I've only done it once, with Lali when we were kids and a circus came to the village where we used to spend our summers. We raced against each other for five minutes, without saddle though. It was fun. This time is more a slow walk on a camel Cade and John is my official photographer. Then, it's time to catch the plane back to Sydney. It was so short. It feels like it was a lot of walking but an amazing experience and we leave the outback dazzled. We're happy to have enjoyed another few days just the two of us, but it feels like we already need another one, just to recover from the physical effort of this one. But nope, nothing more, it's the last one for us, until maybe never, since my parents are leaving at the end of the week and we don't have any more babysitters. But I can't wait to see my kids again, hold them tight in my arms, and kiss them. I miss them so much. I'm glad to be back at home with my babies, but I can't help feeling sad; it's the end of the romance and I don't know when we will be able to be just the two of us ever again. On top of that, we will be by ourselves, with no help at all. I'm a bit scared but happy to start our new little routine, just the four of us, as a family.

17

It's Wednesday, May 4. I have an appointment with my oncologist and she tells me that I could start a clinical trial with Keytruda combined with a genetically modified herpes virus. We don't know if I will actually receive the virus or a placebo in my injections. I'm excited but scared. It will be painful to get these injections. I will have to take care of my wounds with caution and the kids won't be able to approach me or the sensitive parts of my body. This modified virus is supposed to indicate to my immune system the location of the tumours and get it to fight them. It will fight the virus where it is, so the tumours at the same time. A clever trick. And even if I don't receive the virus, I will still get Keytruda either way. And if it doesn't work—which we'll know six months later—I can go back to my current targeted therapy. So I stop my actual treatment straight away in order to start the washout period and flush my body for the next twenty-eight days, a compulsory step before starting this trial. Keytruda seems to do miracles on two-thirds of patients and I hope I can get clear of cancer thanks to it myself. My spine is free of tumours now, or at least they are inactive, as any scar will always be seen in the bones. This trial can be the next step towards my complete recovery. And if not, it can give me more time with my loved ones and more time for new treatments to come.

But I'm ready. I finished planning and I started pre-paying my funerals. Just in case. It was painful and awkward but I did it. I even managed to laugh about it. John and I are wondering where he could spread my ashes, what kind of urn he will get me in, since it's the only thing I left for him to sort out. I've planned a small ceremony at the crematorium close to one of my favourite places in Sydney, La Perouse. It's nice to think that I will be close to the beach and it's a place we use to go so often. A nice, familiar place, peaceful and close to my heart, where we walked on the beach after we knew we had to say goodbye to our first baby, where I had my first ice cream dipped in chocolate and peanuts, where Jason had his first steps in the sand and where my sister enjoyed spending time too. I chose the cheapest pine coffin I could get, no point wasting money in something that would get burnt down. John will just have a call to make and it will all be sorted for him. Also, he will have to pick my flowers but that's all. He will be able to take care of the kids and start grieving without being annoyed by all the crap. It's awful to think of how my little ones will cope on that day. They won't realise what's happening; they'll wonder where I am and John won't know what to tell them. But we aren't there yet and hopefully I will trick my fate. I'm going to be so ready to die, that nothing will happen anytime soon.

I started writing Rose and Jason's birthday cards and finished the *"Emergency"* box with a long letter for John. He will have everything he needs in case I'm not there anymore to help him out. I also started the photo book including Rose's birth. It's such a nice feeling to know that all the things I can control are done.

My biggest fear is that I won't be able to help them out if I die, that the day my oncologist will say, "That's it, I'm sorry. There are no more options available; you should start palliative care." I will feel overwhelmed with all the death preparative stuff. At least, now, I won't have to waste my precious time in the end to do all this. It's already done and I'm glad it is. If cancer wants to kill me, I'm ready, everything is sorted and my papers are in order. I can focus on surviving now, enjoy my time with my babies and my hubby, do the things I love, without worrying about the *"what if?"*

After two weeks without treatment, the doctors attempt a biopsy on my biggest tumour and realise that it's too far deep to reach, even with the longest needle they've got. These technical issues won't allow me to go ahead with this clinical trial but they think about another one, opening in July. Anyway, I didn't like the risks of this trial for my children, so hopefully, fate is on my side and I hope it's for a better. The other trial doesn't test Keytruda but it's still an immunotherapy. I don't know what it is yet, but I hope it's the one that will cure me. When you have cancer, you're always hoping for a cure. You want to be saved from your death sentence. The hardest part of having an incurable cancer is that you're not living, you're surviving. Otherwise, I would still go to work and live as usual, unaware of my potential death, I wouldn't think about the things I want to do *if* or *before* I die or people I want to see, maybe for a last time. That's the hardest bit of it; uncertainty and close mortality. I know my time will come soon, I just don't know when exactly, and it's killing me but I'm already dying anyway. Yet, it's better to laugh than cry and I find my sarcastic dark sense of humour getting sharper as my time goes by. My parents and John think that I'm going a bit too far in the morbid jokes sometimes but I try to find some fun in the tragedy of things. Also, knowing that your life is at jeopardy helps you live to the fullest and that's priceless. I just wish I have done that without being scared of dying, just for the fun of it.

Jason is celebrating his second birthday already. He's such an awesome little dude now; talking heaps, active and smart. He plays a lot and understands what's going on and that it's his birthday too. He's looking in every single bag to see if there's a present for him. He also surprises me by grabbing a chicken kebab on the table and eating it on the stick, like us. He's growing so fast. When I help him blow his candle, I wish I will be able to see the wonderful man he will become. Rose is now rolling madly, sitting by herself and crawling. She wants to stand up all the time and loves her food; at seven months, she is nearly the size of a year old baby. I'm so lucky to have these two in my life; they are definitely worth fighting for.

On another side, John and I are slowly drifting apart. Five years and counting down the track and there are no signs of romance anymore. My parents are gone and we have no help at all. Between his labouring job and the kids, my cancer, and the financial pressure, it's hectic and we don't have any quality time together anymore. For most married couples, cancer brings them closer and finds the best in each other. It doesn't seem to be working that way for us. Two kids under three killed the romance. My husband wants to be one of these manly men and he doesn't understand that nowadays men need to help as much as they can with the households. He doesn't want to think that one day I may be gone and that he will have to do everything in the house and care for the kids, on top of his job. As long as he's got me he thinks he just has to go to work to fulfil his duty. I can do all the rest of it, also because I'm not working either. I'm sick of it.

I'm sick of not having any smiles and kisses in the morning. I miss the young couple days and the man I fell in love with. He used to always be happy and willing to please me. Now it's all about his stupid remote control cars and Xbox games. I married a teenager without all the good stuff of a teenager including the unconditional love. I want us to be different, to behave differently towards each other but I feel like every time I'm trying to make things better it's a one-way road, always coming from me. He doesn't want to change. Like his stupid habit of smoking. How convenient is that. Especially when he smokes in his garage to avoid being with us… don't tell me it takes half an hour to have a cigarette. I used to smoke, I know it doesn't.

Sometimes we see only the bad side of things, so I try to focus on the good ones. But lately, I don't see many. He's always tired and grumpy, yelling and swearing. I hate our relationship. I hate his attitude. But I still don't hate him. I'm just not quite sure how long I'm going to last pretending I can deal with this shit. I want the rest of my life to be happy even if that means without him, struggling with this fucking cancer. I may not have many years in front of me and I want him to realise that; I'd like him to cherish the time we have together, show me more affection. I need more support. I'm just upset I don't get enough. I'm seeing red because I'm very scared of wasting our time not loving each other enough. I love him but I don't find much echo to it. I want more of him, more of his soft side. I'm not a soldier. I'm strong, but I'm very emotional and sensitive too, and the roller coaster of emotions I've been through lately starts to drain me and kill us slowly. I just need him to be present for me and loving.

For the past five years, it's been the same when we argue; while I'm confrontational, trying to understand the reasons behind our conflicts, he just switches off and leaves. I find a coward in him when he does that; a quitter. Can't he fight for us? Can't he do his best for us? Hang on; he says he's trying to do his best. I can't believe it. Is it all he can do, really? Is it the best of my man? Do I have too many expectations as he always tells me? I don't think so. I think he's just lazy. We are so different, even more than I thought. I'm outgoing, social, and driven when he likes his solitude, doesn't trust people and is content with his job. I love the outdoors when he prefers to stay at home. I'm confrontational; he gives me the silent treatment. I'm affectionate and talkative; he's undemonstrative but at least he listens, most of the time.

At first, all these differences didn't matter because we worked through them and found ways to make the most out of them. But with years and babies, they start to matter, especially when his family isn't supportive and mine is too far away to help us out. With less time to communicate, less time to compromise, less time to understand or find excuses for each other, and more obstacles to overcome, it's destroying us. The day after the argument is always supposed to be a better day; he usually doesn't want to talk about it anymore. And since he doesn't want to talk about our conflicts, we don't solve our issues. Unfortunately doing so, things built up inside me and got toxic. We usually forget everything after I manage to extract some kind of apologies from him, but he usually says that he's not good enough, which definitely isn't my point. I've never seen someone more stubborn when it comes to apologising; he just doesn't want to say *"sorry."* But we will get over it because at the end of the day we still love each other. Isn't it all that matters?

Looking at him, I feel like he's just observing his life, watching it pass by, not being a real actor of it. It's disheartening and at times, I even think he could be depressed, overwhelmed by the situation, but denying it. I don't need a zombie robot that doesn't care about anything. I want my gentleman back. I also notice it's only a month we came back from holidays, and I feel like we need more time off already. The reality is that we need time off from cancer. Even if it doesn't kill me, it's killing our relationship because it's such a crazy ride of ups, downs, bends and U-turns; one day great, the next in tears, sometimes with no apparent reasons. This cancer and the babies, on top of a lack of family and friends' support, our augments, him being silent and me confrontational, is the perfect mix for auto-destruction. But we are trying to understand each other needs and I think I need to see my friends and my country again, homesickness doesn't add up well to the equation.

Living like you're going to die the next day is way too emotional for me. I can only do that for so long. I have to find some sort of routine and normal way to live my life to stay sane. I'm trying to live one day after another, without thinking too much of the *"if I die."* I try to enjoy every day with my young family. I'm not sure I will go back to work, even if I was cured one day as I don't earn enough to justify my entire salary going into the payment of day-care and

I will be happy to have my children home with me full time. But for now I'm sick, I can't physically cope with them and I have to go to doctors and scans appointments. But I want to have them with me two to three days a week on top of the weekends. I try to make decisions based on what I really want and what we can afford, not because I have cancer. That way, whether I will get better or not, I won't have any regret.

I'm officially a pensioner, though young. I'm in a sort of retirement, not working and trying to enjoy the few years I may have left, like an old person but with young babies and definitely no one to share my spare time with. I don't have any activities to go to. The fitness clubs don't have any classes during the day and I don't see myself going to the club for a bingo in the afternoon. I'm desperate to find some kind of hobby. I've never had one, except for fitness and I'm cruelly missing one now. I remember how my elitist teacher from my business preparatory class used to tell us how important it was in job interviews to talk about our passions and how we all had to learn how to talk smartly about them, finding ways to promote ourselves through them. I didn't have any back then and I still struggle to find one.

I was always into sports but never kept one longer than two years. I was drawing a lot as a kid but when my big sister told me I didn't have any talent, I stopped. Then I learnt to dance salsa and later, my favourite hobby was to go out and get the guys I wanted. I have to find something else. If it's not a hobby, at least I'll find my next project. I must have something to look forward to in order to save me from insanity. I love travelling, that's my favourite hobby if it can be considered as one. I'm missing my sister. I'd love my kids to meet their cousins and I'd like to see my family and friends a last time. I have to find a way to bring us all to France. It would be such an awesome experience, being in my hometown with my babies and my hubby, catching up with my friends, my sister, see their kids playing with mine while we chat. It's nearly three years. I haven't been back and, I don't know why, it seems to be the right amount of time for me to be homesick. The first time I went back home was also after my first three years in Australia. I need to breathe the French air; I miss the French cheeses and pastries and nice food in general. I just have to find a way to make such an expensive trip happen.

18

It's the fourth of July already. Rose starts day-care for three days a week, while I can go to my doctor appointments, scans, do the chores, or enjoy some me time. She's nearly nine months old and she's better playing with her brother at day-care than being trapped in the car with me. She starts to move a lot and she's getting very interactive. I'd like to find a better day-care because this one is a bit boring for them; except for painting, they aren't doing anything and the education isn't very good as they let Jason do whatever he wants. But it will stay as it is until we move into a house, then I will try to find a new one, close to home. I'm glad to see that Jason and Rose are playing a lot together now. He doesn't wrestle her anymore and he probably figured out she's also a human being. They love to play hide and seek together and Rose is so intrigued and attracted to her brother. She's eating very well and taking the spoon out of my hands to eat by herself. She's such a little woman already, getting her independence quickly and caring for all of us with her sweet and cuddly attitude. She's a real little Frenchy, loving bread and cheese. Jason starts to get a bit jealous and is asking for my arms a lot lately. She said *"Maman"* clearly two days ago. John and I looked at each other with a smile. It wasn't the usual babbling; it was a very neat *"Maman"* meaning "Mum" in French. And since, she doesn't stop.

John felt a bit left out but he thinks they're both mamas' kids. I'm sure very soon he will be fed up when they start asking after him all the time. But I'm a bit worried that Rose hasn't bonded much with him. I've been the one taking care of her since birth; he only gave her a bath a few times and never put her to bed at night or woke up once for her. He should do it more often; it's important for them to bond.

Also I can't wait for the kids to have their own bedroom; it's so tough to put them to bed. Jason makes bedtime painful, crying and all and I'm so scared to wake up Rose. We visited houses for rent but nothing seemed to be right for us—too expensive, not good enough—until we saw an ad for a lovely three-bedroom house in Sylvania. It's quite far from where we live; there's no train station around, but when we get there, we find it perfect. Old but big, three bedrooms, a bathroom with bath and shower—the kids can still have their bath together—a lovely backyard, a big family room, a formal lounge room, a large kitchen with potential for a dishwasher, and a garage converted into a workshop for John. Okay, we can't buy a house in crazy expensive Sydney but we can rent. We just have to wait for the landlord to get back to us. I hope we'll get it because it would be a great relief for me. Not only to have the kids in separate rooms, but the big rumpus could be a great playroom for them, surrounded by windows and I won't feel claustrophobic anymore, trapped in a coffin; I could live again there. I don't wait for their answer to start packing. We have accumulated so much stuff since the two bags we had to start our life together. I'm starting now to be ready in two weeks, the date they gave us for a potential move-in.

Having a few days a week for myself allows me to start organising our trip to France and I started a fundraiser to finance it. It would be amazing if we could go back home for Christmas. I love this time of the year and I miss a cold Christmas and the charming markets we have in France for the occasion. Also, I can't think of a better present than seeing my family again and introducing my babies to my aunties, my cousins, my nephews, my friends.

I just wish I could see them all for Christmas because I'm really scared it could be my last. I'm not the kind of person to ask for help, even less for money, but times are tough and it would mean the world to me to celebrate my first Christmas back home since I left. The only fundraiser I have ever done was for the Melanoma fundraiser back in December and it was quite a success, but this time, my workmates, my friends and my family are all in. They've been very generous and are glad to help us spend Christmas together. I'm moved by their kindness and I'm again astonished by how Australians are always so keen to help their community members. I asked for a Christmas miracle and they made it happen. We raise enough to buy four flight tickets to Paris in order to spend Christmas with my twin sister. I'm ecstatic for Jason and Rose to be able to meet their cousins and the rest of their family for the first time. We will spend a cold, hopefully white, Christmas in France. I will be so proud to introduce my young family to everyone. It feels so good, looking forward to such a tremendous event. I miss my roots, even if I was happy when I left, it represents my childhood and it's calling for me. I can't wait.

I can't go back without organising something with my best friends, Rachelle, Frieda and Anne. I met them in Business School, thirteen years earlier, and we never lost contact. Every time we catch up, it's like we've never stopped seeing each other. Yet, it's been seven years I haven't seen them and it feels like a lifetime. Rachelle is still single, but Frieda is married to Gustavo –an Italian who seduced her during one of their company's night event and I was there– and have a five years old son, Ernesto. Anne is married too, living in her hometown of Bordeaux with her hubby Joseph and their now two kids, Eugénie, four and a half, and Gaspard, ten months old. We decide to spend New Year's Eve together at Frieda's new house, hoping that its renovation will be finished by then. I can't be happier, it's going to be so awesome, for me, for the kids, and even for John as these guys are speaking very good English, not like the rest of the Frenchies we're going to catch up with during this three weeks trip. I'm so excited. It's such an amazing time to look forward to. Maybe we can even stop by Sainte Tulle, on our way to Montpellier to have a quick bite with my parents and family friends Julie and Julien; they've known me since birth and are family for me. But we will definitely spend one night in Montpellier at my Aunty Marguerite and Uncle Mathieu before spending the New Year's Eve weekend with the girls. I haven't seen them in ages. It's funny to notice that, back home, a two-hour drive was pretty much a day trip when you can drive the same amount of time here just for a return trip to your favourite coffee shop. When I was living in France, if I had the relationship with the distance that I've got now, I would have travelled so much more.

Also, looking at the numbers going higher on the fundraising page, one of my workmates suggests that I could squeeze my dream of going to New York in. At first, I think it's crazy, travelling to Europe with two kids under three will be hard enough with the jet lag and all...but then, I think "Why not? When will I get a chance to do it again? We only live once right?" So I check the prices with my travel agent and we find the cheapest round-the-world tickets. It will be a lot of stops and planes but we can see New York City for three days. It will be freezing too but it's one of my dreams too. It's such a long time I want to see New York, pretty much since mum told me she went there as a nanny of a very wealthy Portuguese family when she was a student. I was a child back then, but I still remember the black and white photo of my mum in front of the crazy high building and the feeling of freedom and happiness she had when she told me her story. It seemed that she had the time of her life there and I wanted to experience the same feeling. Under the snow could be even better. Christmas holidays too, just after New Year's Eve… And I will tick the box of travelling the world somehow as we will actually go around the planet: Sydney – Hong Kong – Frankfurt – Paris – Nice – Zurich – New York – Los Angeles – Sydney. Okay, it sounds crazy to do that with two babies, but we've got only one life right? I can't wait to live this big adventure with my babies and my hubby. I'm so thankful to all the people who are making these dreams possible.

My oncologist confirms that I can go on the trial opening very soon now, it will be two immunotherapies combined: Keytruda and another one, on tablet this time. I hope it will work for me…after all it can be the cure of tomorrow. If I'm on this trial, I will have to receive the infusion of Keytruda the day we leave and on the day we come back, so I book our flights accordingly. These infusions must be done every three weeks, so we can't stay too long in Paris, only three days in Nice, same in Montpellier and another couple back in Nice before leaving for three days in New York. It will be a lot of moving but we have no choices; I hope I won't be too exhausted as I'm already tired just thinking of this hectic holiday. I guess it's a small price to pay to go around the world and tick three items off my bucket list.

Another dream comes true on the twenty-second of July—we're moving into a house. We got the Sylvania house. I'm over the moon; everything is coming together for us. I can't be happier. I finish unpacking in two days; John thinks I'm crazy as I don't stop for a minute. But I hate living in boxes and I'm glad to have everything in order and see how nice the house is. How big it is too. We need more furniture. So I find a great deal on Gumtree, a nice bloke from Manly is getting rid of two beautiful brown leather lounges and coffee table for free on that exact weekend, as he's moving too and didn't find any buyer. Perfect timing.

John picks them up and they fit perfectly in front of the chimney, in our formal lounge room. I place our big family portrait canvas on top of the chimney and it becomes my favourite room. The kids have their massive playroom and they love it. I sleep so well here. I'm usually sleeping in the afternoon while Rose naps for two to three hours; she's definitely a great baby even though she now wakes up at night because she's teething. Jason is still very clingy, doesn't want to share me with his sister and is full of tantrums. But he's so good at putting himself to bed now, we just have to leave him with a light on and a book and he eventually falls asleep. It's so much better for all of us, not having to pat him forever. But between taking care of the kids and all the packing and unpacking, I'm exhausted and don't have much chance to do anything for myself since Rose started day-care. Lucky, John and I have an extra hour for some quality time together every night since we have now a dishwasher, my new favourite machine and such a relief. I'm so happy in this house; I don't want to go outside anymore. It's so bright with all these big windows everywhere. It's not our house, but it feels like home and that's all that matters.

To tick another box, I started a diet with prepared meals, giving me only twelve hundred calories a day and I'm exercising again. I had to lose the pregnancy weight to feel better in my skin and I did. Plus exercising gives me some energy back. I'm not training like the mad woman I used to be, but doing an hour of light cardio with abs and butt toning daily helps me feel better with myself. From sixty-three kilos to fifty-six now, in six weeks; I can fit in my clothes again, and that in itself is an amazing feeling. I am back into my size ten and threw out all the size fourteen clothes I bought after my pregnancy. I've got my young body back. I've never thought I could go back in my old jeans. I feel so much better. Everything seems possible now. I don't need anything else but a healthy body. I have the house, the lighter body, the trip to France to see my loved ones, and even New York. I just need no cancer and I can actually believe in miracles.

19

It's August 5, 2016 and I'm thirty-five today. It's my birthday. Should I say already? It seems like I've already lived a lifetime. I have accomplished so much. Since I've been diagnosed, I had lots of flashbacks of my life. My friends, parties, studies, boyfriends, family, moments which seemed insignificant at the time but that I can recall so vividly—Flashes, lots of them. Lots of "If I had done things differently," or "if I die." Lots of thinking. Apparently, when you're about to die, you see all the images of your life before your last breath. I feel like it's what's happening to me since I've been diagnosed. Memories. Where would I be if I had changed slightly some moments of my past? But I can't change the past, I can only live now. And it's okay that way because I wouldn't change a thing, even all the stupid mistakes I made in the past. Because they brought me where I am today and it is where I want to be, even though I never suspected I would live in another country, speak another language, be so far away from everything I know. And my past experiences, good or bad, made me the person I became. I don't want to be anywhere else, with nobody else than John. I love my husband, even if he can be annoying and grumpy at times, even if since day one I know he won't dress the way I like; he's the kindest, most generous and funny soul I know. The most genuine too. He gave me the most beautiful presents ever: two amazing kids. They are my pride and the best thing I have ever done in my life. They are my world.

Thirty-five years so far on this planet and maybe not many more. But I want at least another thirty-five years. I have terminal cancer and I'm the happiest woman on Earth, so deeply happy. But the happier I get, the more scared I become. Because the more I have, the more I have to lose, and I don't want to lose any of it. I've worked so hard for all of this, I've sacrificed so much. It's like it has just happened. I've had so many years of sadness and struggles; it feels like I've just started to be happy. I don't want this birthday to be the last one. Birthdays are like Christmases, they raise so many emotions. They make you think back on all the things you've achieved so far, the persons you love, the things you look forward to and where you are now. And I am happy where I am, just afraid to lose everything. I have to focus on the happiness and leave the terrorist cancer aside.

Ten days after my birthday, I stop my treatment. It's time to start a clinical trial. It's not the one it was supposed to be as it's not opened yet, but an open spot came up for another clinical trial and my oncologist offered it to me. I jumped on it. Firstly because who knows when the other trial will finally open, it's months I'm waiting for it, and secondly because this one gives me the opportunity to access a drug that is not yet approved. The clinical trial I was supposed to go on was composed by Keytruda—already approved and available to me if my actual treatment fails—and a protein called IDO which tells the immune system which cells to fight by revealing the cancer cells, usually hiding. I have one chance out of two to get the protein as it's a randomised trial. With this new trial, I can get anti-PDL1 which, in theory, should work as efficiently as Keytruda, an anti PD1, but is not yet approved, and a protein called CD137 which boosts the immune system by increasing the number of T-cells to fight the cancer. I will get the combination for sure as there is no randomisation for this one.

It will be intense, with an infusion of Anti PDL1 every two weeks and one of CD137 every four weeks. The infusion itself will last an hour and I will have to stay another couple of hours afterward to make sure I'm fine. I also have to come to the Melanoma Medical Centre every week for an entire day in order to go through some tests. This trial has been given to patients with other cancers too, with good results so far. Only seven patients are part of it in Australia, out of the twenty-eight melanoma patients in the world and eighteen other cancer patients. I feel very lucky and hope to be able to be part of it this time; it's my third attempt for a trial so far. I have to stop my treatment for twenty-eight days to flush my body again. We should be able to see the results from the trial within four months. I hope it will work because stopping my treatment for five months could be dangerous.

I can always go back to my treatment after if it doesn't. John tells me he would do the same and trusts my judgment anyway. He's so tired lately, without the help of my parents and with the lack of sleep, we are both burning out. The kids are draining all our energy. Rose is still waking up at night, four teeth coming out at the same time and she's been sick quite often since she started day-care. Jason is still very clingy and I don't know what's wrong with him. Sometimes I think he knows that my life is threatened and tries to stay with me as much as he can…I'm still on my diet and seven kilos down and I've revised my goal to fifty-four as this diet is driving me nuts. It's great but hard not to get my chocolate treats. If I have to die, I want to be able to indulge a bit too. I just have to be reasonable. Also, I've been a bit slack with cooking dinners for hubby and kids and it's getting costly to continue these diet meals anyway. I dropped all the pregnancy weight so it's all about maintenance now.

The day after, I have my first PET scan in four months. I think my cancer is still stable as I didn't feel anything wrong except for some side effects of my treatment. I see my oncologist the Monday after.

"Hi Lucie, how are you?" She asked when she enters the office.

"Good, thank you." I smiled, expecting to talk about the trial.

"So I have some good and bad news. The good news is that the PET scan revealed No Evidence of Disease (NED). It means that the tumours may still be present but they are not active."

"Wow, so that's great. I mean it's what every cancer patient wants to hear right?"

"Yes, that's fantastic. But the bad news is that you can't go on the trial."

"Oh yeah. It's the third time we try to put me on a trial too. How long can I stay like this for?"

"We don't know how long this situation can last, especially since you're not taking any treatment. So what we can do, if you agree, is that you'll stay off treatment for another three weeks and we'll see if the tumours are getting bigger. At the moment, there's only one tumour of three millimetres showing on the scan, but it's too small for the trial. I'm not sure three weeks will be long enough for the tumour to grow but I can't keep your place in the trial for longer than that. At least we can try."

"Okay. As long as it's not too dangerous for me." I replied a bit concerned.

"It's great news that you've responded so well to your treatment, but we've got to try immunotherapy because it works better early in the diagnosis."

"And if the trial doesn't work, I can still go back onto my combo treatment as we know it's working right?"

"That's exactly right."

"Do you think I could get resistant as it's been nine months since I started and you said that, on average, patients will become resistant after eight months?"

"Well, that's only a statistic. Also, you could be part of the ten to fifteen per cent of people who never become resistant."

"Do you think that losing the extra weight helped in any way my good results?" I asked, happy about my new healthy body.

"Maybe, being healthy and eating well may have helped in clearing the tumours. So don't worry; we'll do another scan in three weeks and see you after okay?"

"Okay."

"And remember, being NED is great news."

I'm happy to get rid of this cancer and a bit scared to bring it back for the purpose of these trials. I hope immunotherapy will work as good as my treatment, if not better; as if it works, the immune system will apparently recall how to fight, so I'll be able to stop the treatment at some point and still get the benefits from it. With days passing by, the great news is changing into anxiety; it's so hard for me to deal with the chance of this cancer coming back, anywhere. In the brain too, my biggest fear. But I also wonder if I could stay NED long enough to go back to a "normal" life. The uncertainty of what's going to happen and the question of what I should do with my life if I survive worry me. I love taking care of my kids, having more time for them and also for myself. I won't have that precious time if I go back to work.

Just thinking about working again with my previous boss is irritating me. He never asked if I was doing well, never donated for any of my fundraisers or even sent a text to see if I was coming back at any point, or if I was only alive. I don't really want to have to deal with him anymore. I don't want to waste my precious time with him. Because that's the thing when your life is at stake—you want to use your time mindfully, with worthy people. There is not enough time to waste anymore, every second count. Even queuing at the shop is annoying, wasting an hour in a traffic jam is excruciating. Time becomes the most valuable thing in your world. So you choose carefully what you want to do with it, even if you waste some of it doing a photo book or watching TV. I may have to look for another job, not too far from home as I don't want to spend hours driving when I can be with my kids. Also, I'm thinking of working for a company doing good for the planet or people, and maybe being part-time so I can stay with my kids one or two days a week, at least until they go to school. Anyway, I have to make sure I will stay stable for a while before jumping the gun. For now, I need to see if I can start a trial soon. The eternal question.

All this anxiety is weighing on me and soon John and I reach the breaking point. We need some time off so John planned for his brother to keep the kids for once, but Jacob cancelled at the last minute. It's was one drop too many in my already full shit vase. We need time together and we can't find any. Between the health, the questioning about work, money issues, and all the rest of it, I have had enough. I'm pissed off because his family is unreliable. I don't understand it. I was raised to be reliable; in my family, when we say something we do it. I can't stand it anymore. So that afternoon, I leave him with the kids after another argument. This time he's not the one who leaves, I am. How good it feels. I drive the car but I'm not sure where to go.

I could get a coffee to calm down...But instead, I decide to go to the movies to watch "Bad mums." I couldn't have found a better movie for the occasion. I laugh so hard and realise that I'm asking way too much of myself and can't go on like this. I have to take it easy and learn to let go. Be less perfectionist. It's already hard enough to cope with terminal cancer and two babies; being the perfect housewife will wait. I have to do less or at least less often and find more time for myself, and more time with John, even if we have to trust his dad for the babysitting, it will only be a couple of hours anyway. I have to be kind to myself. Overdoing is my way to stay away from too much thinking but I have to stop or it will kill me, or my marriage, or both.

It's time to enjoy my new body, my new home and try to relax. But for me, duties have always come first, pleasure only if you still have time for it. The thing is that nowadays, if you don't plan time for it, you will never have a chance to relax; there's always something to do. When I come back home, on time to help John feed the kids and prepare them for bed, I enter the house with a smile and thank my husband for the afternoon I had for myself. I pour a glass of wine and don't care if Jason doesn't eat. Dinners usually stress me out because Jason never wants to eat and as his weight gain has always been an issue, I never stop worrying about it. That night, I didn't force the issue, and it was easier.

I also figure that I have to socialise. Back home, I used to be such a social butterfly, and even if I was the same here with my backpacker friends, they were all long gone now. So I reach out to the melanoma community on social media and ask if there are any mums out there, close to my place, who would like to catch up sometimes. That's how I meet Kathy, another stage four melanoma patient, mum of three young teenagers.

It's the first week of October 2016, nearly a year after my diagnosis. We decide to go for a coffee at Carss Park, the park next door to my place. For our first meeting, we spend nearly four hours talking. It feels so good to meet another mum in the same condition, finally someone who gets me. Someone who can understand what I'm going through and who doesn't judge me but support me. I can be myself with her, with all my fears and my morbid sense of humour. She's going through the same bullshit and becomes a sort of melanoma sister. I also become friend with three other stage four mums on Facebook.

We spent the long weekend of our fifth wedding anniversary at home to potty train Jason. I keep him home another three days to make sure we are on the right track before putting him back at day-care. He's doing great with only one or two accidents since. I'm so proud of him; my baby is becoming a little boy. Rose is about to celebrate her first birthday and I can't help but feeling emotional again. When her big day comes, I prepare a great party for her. I clean the house all week and bake two cakes, one for day-care and one for the evening at home. She's super excited both times and rushes to eat the chocolate cakes. She's so happy to see the candle and hear me singing the Happy Birthday song for her; she even tries to grab the lollies I placed on top of the cake. Jason and I help her blow the candle while dad is filming the scene, it's perfect. She's perfect. She even manages to rip all the paper to open her presents. I can't believe she's one already.

I couldn't have asked for better babies, they are magnificent, smart, alert, expressive and affectionate. They are my pride, my everything. I love them more than myself; their life will always come before mine. If I had to go through cancer to have my beautiful Rose, then it was worth it. I love her and Jason with all my heart and soul. Before being a mum, I didn't know what unconditional love was but now I know: it's the most beautiful feeling anyone can ever experience, being so deeply linked to another human being. They are my blood, my guts, part of me. I always knew I wanted to be a mother since the days I was playing with my dolls. But I didn't know how good it would feel. It's so rewarding, inspiring, and surprising even if it can also be painful and difficult sometimes. Looking at my kids smiling and laughing, running towards me when I pick them up at day-care, feeling their little bodies against me when they give me a cuddle, hearing Jason telling me "Je t'aime maman" –I love you in French– are the most precious moments ever. I am so thankful to have met John, I love him so much and he gave me all this happiness and the chance to be a mum. I feel accomplished being a wife and a mother. I'm just hoping I'm good at it because I try my best. John, Jason, and Rose, the three persons I love the most on the planet, my family. I feel at home anywhere with these three. And I can't wait to be with all the other people I love, back in my country of birth and show off my precious offspring.

The PET scan from November shows that I'm still stable, no growth and no activity. So all my worries and the weird feeling in my left armpit and the pins and needles I had were probably just the normal weird stuff happening sometimes. It's very hard not to worry when you don't have any safety net without any treatment. I'm like climbing a cliff with no cord, just my arms, suspended on the edge and I can fall anytime. It's difficult to live like that and requires so much strength that I feel like I can barely breathe at times. It's tiring.

I'm angry at the system. I don't understand how governments can put millions into war equipment and weapons research when people still die of cancer. I don't understand that we still haven't found a cure when we are able to go to Mars. Yet, I'm thankful I'm still alive and in a good shape. I feel lucky when my oncologist tells me that it's very rare after three months of no treatment not to have any reoccurrence. So I'm happy to win more time and defy the odds, just anxious. I've always been an anxious kind. I got that from my mum and dad, both anxious and perfectionist people. But these days, I've really understood what anxiety is: difficulty sleeping, over-thinking, wondering, feeling tense all the time, being edgy and short. I hate it. But I'm trying hard to cope and meditation is the best thing I've done to live with it and make it bearable. Also, I think that being good with no treatment is pretty sweet and it won't happen often, so I have to enjoy while it last. I can pretend to be normal and healthy for now and that's priceless. I try to make the most out of it; exercising every day and enjoying life as much as I can, the glass is half full and I hope it will stay that way.

One good thing about the news is that I can increase the length of my stay in France. So I change my flight tickets for ten more days in Paris. We will leave Sydney on the 11th of December and stay in Paris until the 27th. We will have more time to recover from jet lag and more time with my sister and her kids. Mum and Dad will join us on the 17th; we will all be together in a flat close to my sister's place, her two-bedroom flat being already too tiny for the five of them. So we will all spend Christmas Eve together and Christmas day at my aunty Céline with her hubby and three kids.

I'm a bit concerned for Jason as he wakes up at night screaming like crazy and has stopped putting on weight again, so the paediatrician put him back on the reflux medicine. I think he's got sleep apnoea and she advised me to do a sleep study. We have to wait until March to see a sleep physician. His tonsils are very big, he's snoring at night, sweaty, most of the time he ends his nights in our bed. I can hear him stop breathing at times and he usually freaks out. Hopefully, he will be okay until then, but I'm upset we have to wait so long, again. Since he's eight months old he struggles to grow and Rose is as tall as him now. His weight chart looks like a staircase, up and flat and he's out of his curve again. I want my boy to thrive and me to stop worrying. I'm upset the doctors wait so long to treat him, just because we don't have any private health insurance. Why can't we remove these tonsils if they are the cause of his sleeping issues? Obviously, sleep can also be the reason why he's not growing properly, on top of the reflux. Poor thing, I feel guilty again, having given birth too early.

20

Before our trip to France, I get my last scans results and I'm still unbelievably stable. I'm scheduled to have another PET and CT scan when we will be back in Sydney. For now, it's holiday time. It's nearly a month I'm taking care of my babies by myself when we take off for Paris and I'm exhausted already. Being a full-time mum of a toddler and a baby is hard work. But I wanted to see if I was able to do it and I was desperate to spend more time with them. It was great the first week and getting harder and harder as time went by. I didn't have a minute to rest or just to wee by myself. HARD. But I enjoyed every minute of it. It will be better for them to be at day-care a day or two a week so I can do the chores on that day and have actual quality time with them the other days. We spent most of our time playing at home, at the park or shopping, the last being super painful with both of them.

It's been hard on our marriage too; John was swearing so much, I couldn't stand him anymore. It was hurting my ears. I would rather have him not helping than whining doing it. I was getting tired so I asked for more help from him at night. I found a great day-care for the kids to start full-time mid-January and John will take a week off after our big trip to recover from holiday. Sometimes, I just want a nice chat with him, drinking a beer at the pub or going for a coffee but it feels like we don't know how to spend quality time together anymore, we'd need an entire week to remember. Maybe I can ask my mum and dad to keep the kids home one night while we have some well-deserved time off in Paris together.

We arrive in Paris after three planes and two airport transfers. The one in Hong Kong was awesome; they had these little capsules on wheels to seat the kids, so we placed Jason and Rose in two of them and raced them in the extra-long corridor we had to go through to reach the train bringing us to the other side of a town size terminal. Jason loved the plane but slept very little, maybe seven hours out of thirty-five. He watched a lot of cartoons on the on-board entertainment screen though. Rose could only sleep attached to me in the baby carrier, so I spent all that time sitting with twelve kilos baby over me, and still, she was on and off in the three planes. We are all very tired of the trip and still recovering but we still enjoy a day in Paris three days after our arrival. We walk in one of my favourite streets: *Rue Mouffetard* and eat crepes for lunch. The kids love it. They actually love the French food, I don't have to worry at all for Jason. I've never seen him eating like that.

Then we go through the Pantheon to reach the Luxembourg gardens. The immense park has a big playground for the kids and we spend a couple of hours playing there. Then, we take the bus to return home and, like on the way in, Jason loves it. He's looking at the people walking on the streets and make friends with some old people sitting next to him. It's their first time on a bus as we always take the car in Sydney. It was their first time on the plane too, so lots of excitement for Jason in a few days. Since we arrived in France, we indulge ourselves with baguette with jam or *"pain au chocolat"* and croissants for breakfast every morning. Every time I come back, I forget how good the food is; everything tastes so much better and food shopping for fruits, veggies, cheeses and breads is so much cheaper than in Sydney. Also I wish we had as much frozen choice in Australia as we have here! Everybody works late so they have lots of ready to cook meals, sauces, dishes, mix of veggies to pan, crepes, all sorts of fishes; pretty much everything and anything is available frozen and at a cheap price tag too. Awesome for the working mum and time-poor families. We even have a retail shop specialising in frozen food. The traceability of any kind of food is also a legal requirement so we always know where the product we eat comes from, definitely something I would like to have in Sydney too. I'd say Australia is great for a lot of things but behind for some of them, like food legislation and medical care accessibility for kids. A kid shouldn't be a public or private patient; he should always be taken care of as fast as possible, whatever his parent's wealth.

After five days, the kids just start to recover from jet-lag, so lucky we arrived earlier; I don't think it would have been good if we were in the middle of the Christmas festivities. I'm so glad to be here for the twins' birthday; they are two years old already. My sister came over a few nights with my four-year-old niece Amélie but it's the first time for the five cousins to be together. Rose is walking around happy while Jason looks like a tiny prawn compared to the twins. They are seven months younger than him and so big and strong. I want Jason to grow and catch up on the size and weight quickly; otherwise, he's talking a lot and very alert for his age. It's a bit crowded and hectic in the small lounge room but it's great to finally see them all playing together, after all this time, my sister and I get what we've always wanted. Rose is very calm and Jason, even if excited, behaves without any fuss; they seem like angels compared to their cousins. I feel for my poor sister; she's taking care of her kids by herself most of the nights, her partner coming back home long after bedtime. They are struggling in their cramped flat and I feel lucky to have a house with plenty of space. We spend ten days with them, playing at my sister's place in Villejuif, a suburb outside Paris.

John is tired and not used to being with our children full time. He's very short and edgy. I can't wait to have some quality time with him and getting some help from my parents. My head has been spinning since we landed and I'm overtired. The flat my dad found for us isn't very kid friendly with stairs and floor tiles and Jason and Rose hurt themselves all the time. We have to pay attention constantly, which is even more exhausting. But it gets worse when Mum and Dad finally arrive because no one gets any privacy, everyone living on top of each other. So we try to be out and about as often as possible in order to breathe. It's very cold and just dressing up both children with all their layer of clothes takes us an hour, but it's nice to go around Paris or at my sister's. I was missing France, the food, and the familiar feeling of knowing the products and the brands, the streets, speaking French all the time and having French TV too.

It's weird. I've had some trouble re-adapting myself for the first week and then it's like I've never left. I'm a bit overwhelmed by the situation, the planning of Christmas and living again with my parents. They are definitely getting old; not just physically, in their head too. Mum can't stand the kids screaming and crying. They both have their little habits and it's hard for all of us to live together that way. We still enjoy some tourist time together and go to the Christmas markets on *Champs Elysées*. The kids play in the magic forest and I'm glad to see the Christmas decorations on the beautiful avenue. Later in the afternoon, my parents go back home while we walk to the *Galleries Lafayette* and *Le Printemps* in order to admire the animated windows they create every year for Christmas. The shop windows are decorated with paper artworks, handmade and articulated bears and penguins, wheels, castles and more. Jason and Rose enjoy looking at the displays, listening to the music and staring at all the lights. A few days later, we see "the big tower" as Jason likes to call the Eiffel Tower. Once my parents leave and the kids are asleep, John and I have a nice romantic walk along the Seine. It's good to feel the Christmas spirit in the cold air.

We celebrate Christmas Eve at Lali's with her partner's family and it starts an endless flow of reunions. We see about sixty of my favourite people in the same week. Christmas day is awesome at my aunty Céline's, in Arcueil, another suburb around Paris. There are twenty-three people in all, good food and wine, lots of kids playing together, and lots of chatting about everything, and Australia too. It's been over fifteen years since I've seen my cousins, since my grandma Lucienne passed away and it feels like I saw them the previous week. It's such a warm feeling.

The next day is our last in Paris. So when we come back from my aunty's, I decide to finish packing so we can leave early in the morning to enjoy the last day in Paris. That afternoon, I have one of the best moments I ever had with my daughter. I'm overwhelmed by Christmas and my emotions, arguing with my parents about my big sister, because Dad forgot to give my kids their presents from her. It's the first time she's ever acknowledged them. He knows how our relationship is broken; she has barely talked to me since I was fifteen and I used to try hard for us to be sisters but she couldn't care less... Until I had cancer. Even then she thought it was hypocritical to talk to each other again because of that but I didn't care, I wanted my big sister back. And Dad knew.

On Christmas Eve, he took all the presents and gave them to Lali and her kids but he forgot those Sandra had for my kids. And I was so disappointed, so sad for my kids even more than for me because they didn't receive anything from her. I'm in tears, still on the floor trying to play with my daughter. And then a small miracle happens. She crawls towards me, takes me in her arms and gives me her first kiss. That's so sweet. I'm shocked and stunned by the empathy she shows for only a few months old. I smile, looking at her in the eye, my hands around her shoulders and I kiss her back, saying "thank you, you're beautiful, I love you so much my Rose. Thank you." I'm stunned she can understand how sad I am and finds the way to make me feel better. This moment of peace is what I need to stop and calm down, noticing how my babies can be affected by my mood swings. I'm very lucky to have them by my side in this awful journey; they are the light at the end of the tunnel, my positive thoughts and the source of my strength and resilience. I believe in the power of love and my love for my children will save me. I will defy the odds for them, nothing is impossible for me to stay here for them.

After the argument, we decided to find a hotel for Nice, instead of my parents' place. Not really because of our argument—my Dad could really have forgotten—but also because, after living on top of each other, out of our routines, in a not-at-all kid friendly tiny space, we lack intimacy and help with the kids. I asked for a break hoping they wouldn't take it personally. They had been sick too and it was better for all of us to be apart for the next three days; they could recover without giving the germs to our children and we would be back again together for our last week in France. We all needed some time off. Family is great but when you're not at home, it's tough after two weeks stuck all together in a shoe box. The most important was to spend quality time together, not quantity.

Overall, Paris was nice, but not as good as when we went there three years earlier. With the cold, two babies and a pram, it was hard to move around and enjoy some romance.

On the 27th, we fly to Nice. It's a very painful day for us. Not only because the security check is a nightmare, without prams, holding the kids in my arms, all the baby food checked more carefully than for the three international flights we've taken so far, but also because the crew placed Jason by himself in the aircraft during check-in, so we have to be moved around for John to be able to sit with him, our hand luggage not fitting in the overhead lockers. Then, after an hour delayed landing, we have to wait nearly two hours queuing for our car rental. The only good thing is that we've been upgraded, otherwise our luggage and baby seats wouldn't fit in the car. When we arrive in the city, we manage to park after two hours driving around the block, and walk back to the hotel through the pedestrian street of the city centre. We deserve a break and we stop for a bite and four margaritas each to relax from this hectic day. It's nice to be seated outside, looking at people passing by and finally have a relaxing hour. We even meet one of my friends as she's passing by with her mates. The happy hours are definitely worth it and we are merrier when we leave to check in our hotel.

We spend our first morning going to Old Nice, my favourite area. John is already better as it's warmer and he can wear only his T-shirt. I think that's what I missed the most, the micro-climate of my hometown and its three hundred days of sun a year. After a quick walk through the *Cours Saleya* market, we go for lunch on *Place de la République*, in a restaurant where five of my school friends are waiting for us with partners and kids. We have an awesome time and stay all afternoon talking about everything and anything, again, like we left each other the month before and not six years ago. We even talk about cancer; with them, it's easy and honest, non-judgemental or pitiful. It's nice to be able to discuss with no dramatization, no taboo, no precautions, being myself, and they are genuinely concerned without overdoing it. It's a nice refreshing change and I appreciate their friendship. I realise how much I miss them, laughing with them, talking to them, each and every one of them, with their own character and own way of interacting with me. I'm also happy to meet their kids for the first time and show off mine.

It's like we're back in our school days. We didn't change much physically, but now most of us have kids and it's funny to see us as parents. After a nice long lunch, we walk back to the hotel through the nice long pedestrian alley the city built a couple of years ago. It's such a beautiful city centre now, with gardens, playgrounds, and a large fountain made of enlightened water sprays coming from the ground and reflecting everything like we are walking on a lake. It's been a wonderful day and John and I are happy again. The hotel room is spacious and cosy and the blinds help us with a long sleep-in. The kids don't wake up before ten in the morning.

The next morning, we are on Laundromat duty for three hours, just before joining my cousin Léon, his daughter Lilly, and my cousin Sophie on *Place Masséna*, in the city centre, two minutes away from our hotel. We have some *niçoises* specialties in the Old Nice for lunch and go for a coffee before catching up with my big sister Sandra, her hubby Rémi, and eleven-year-old niece Morgan. It's weird to see my sister. She didn't bother meeting us last time we were in France and it's been seven years I haven't seen her, and double as many years we didn't have a proper chat together.

Morgan is so choked to see us. Sandra didn't tell her they would join us as she wanted to surprise her. Well done, Morgan is nearly in tears. She is as tall as me now and so grown up. She is excited to play with the kids and we all walk to the playground. Sandra doesn't talk to me, but spends her time playing with Jason and talking to John. Rose is sticking to me and doesn't want a bar of my family. I'm glad my sister came, even if we don't chat. After years not talking, it's awkward for me too, and even if I want to, I don't know what to say either. I'm just happy to take her in my arms and somehow make peace. I can die peacefully. My niece is very happy to chat with me and loves her cousins. Lilly, whose mum is English, doesn't really speak with her Aussie cousins; she can understand them but talking is another story. I wish Rose and Jason can speak fluently French one day, so they can all stay in touch. It will be hard for them to grow without their family, without cousins. It's very cold for once and we have to leave before the sun goes down.

We leave Nice the next day for Montpellier. We stop by Sainte Tulle to have lunch with Julie and Julien, our family friends and godparents of my big sister. They are glad to meet the kids and happy to see me. The cancer talk, again, is like with the rest of the family, a bit guarded, but still, it's nice to be able to talk freely about it and like the rest of my friends, they are hoping I will stay clear forever. It's weird that I feel upset every time someone says that. Like if they are quickly dismissing the fact that my condition is terminal and that this thing will probably catch me one day for good. It's not that I am not glad if they are right, but more a feeling that they try to comfort or protect themselves that way; thinking they are protecting me too, when for me, it's a sort of deny I don't appreciate at all. I'm still struggling to accept the various ways people have to deal with cancer or cope with the cancer talk.

We arrive at my auntie's in Montpellier in the evening. Marguerite, Mathieu, and my cousin Adrien welcome us at home and it's good to see them again. I studied in this city and used to see them often back then. I feel at home again. Marguerite is the youngest of my mum's sisters and she and Mathieu are very down to Earth. It's good to see all these people who've been part of my life growing up. I tell them how I'm glad to see them after catching up with their son and brother Olivier back in Paris. By now, I've pretty much seen my entire family: my parents, my two sisters, my two aunties, their husbands, all my cousins except for Christian, all their kids. I will see my last uncle Jocelyn back in Nice in a couple of days. Sometimes, these reunions make me feel uncomfortable; I look at all these people that I love, doing their thing, and I think it may be the last time I see them...I'm trying to enjoy every second of it, capturing their faces and their smiles in my head.

The next morning, we go for a walk with Marguerite and Adrien in the historic city centre and I'm happy to show John and the kids where I've lived for two years. I was missing all these historic old towns back in Sydney...and I admire the old streets paved with stones and the sandstone medieval buildings. We have a last yummy meal with them before leaving for Cabrières, a small village in the countryside, where we will spend New Year's Eve with my best friends from Business School.

After a quick stop at the shops to get some food and drinks, we drive to the Bed and Breakfast and arrive at 4.15pm. The entire villa is just for us. My friends are already there and how good it feels to see them and jump into their arms. Rachelle, thirty-eight years old tall brunette, Anne and Frieda, both blonds with blue eyes, are also here, with their husbands, Anne with baby Gaspard, now ten months old with crazy blue eyes, daughter Eugénie, a four-and-a-half-year-old with curly hair, and small doggy Chance, a white terrier with seven allergies out of the eleven known in dogs. He was Rose's best friend for the weekend; she loves dogs and this one is going to be all hers. It's awesome to be with the girls again. And so much better for John to be able to participate in our conversations as my friends speak English fluently.

We drink, laugh, talk, cook, enjoy together and it's so good to be with them again. Friendship is when you realise than even ten years later we are still the same, hubbies and kids added to the picture, but we remain the same crazy ones. We are back together, in this little house, on top of a hill, in the middle of the French countryside, a bedroom for each of our families, a common kitchen to share our meals and celebrate life and the New Year together. The champagne is flooding on the first night and we wish for a great and healthy 2017. We immortalise the moment with selfies and chat until late. I'm so happy to have my friends by my side again. The next day, after another Raclette, we walk through the village of Villeneuvette, down south after a fifteen minutes' drive.

Jason and Rose are excited to hold Chance's leash and nearly fighting over it. I'm talking to each of my friends and it warms my heart. It feels so good to walk in the countryside, the kids running around us, talking about life, our families, and work, like if we were all living in the same town, since forever. I love them so much and I miss them. I wish we could live together, in the same country if not in the same city. That night we have a big laugh on a business project we could have together in Australia, how it would be cool to work together again. And we have the cancer talk as well. But, it's easy with them, hopeful, honest and concerned, no false hope and no fake wishes, just a raw and genuine conversation. With them, I can joke around my death, I can be sarcastic and they help me laugh about it, and that's a real friendship to me. They are my friends and I love them more than they could ever imagine. They offer me a lovely silver bracelet with an angel on it. Saying that it will be a reminder of them being my guardian angel; the most beautiful present I've received from anyone other than my hubby. They move me. They're so good to me.

On our last day, we all leave after breakfast. It's hard to say our goodbyes as I'm not sure I will ever see them again and I'm extremely saddened by the situation. We had such a fantastic time together in this house, living together for a couple of days, such a short time but such an amazing one. As I'm raising funds for my second Melanoma fundraiser and because people were very generous to help me with this trip, it's been quite difficult to raise any dollar for that fundraiser, so I'm selling black bracelet labelled with *"hope for melanoma"* for the cause. Before leaving, they don't hesitate one second to buy one each and I'm falling in tears. It's coming out of nowhere. It's so tough to say goodbye to these three amazing souls. They have given me so much love and attention for the past two days, after all these years apart. They are my friends and I don't have them back in Sydney. I'm missing them; I'm missing my family, my sister, and my parents. I've seen so many of the people I love in a week, it's been overwhelming. And I know why: because I have terminal cancer and because I love them. I don't have much time to visit the country but I take the time to enjoy the company of my friends and my family, around lunches and dinners, in four different parts of France. There are so many people to see but so little time…and it may be the last time. That's my worse fear.

They don't wait to hold me tight in their arms and comfort me. I'm so happy and thankful for that special time we've shared together but also so sad to leave them, not being able to see them more often, share my life with them, be by their side, closer. They tell me that I'm living too far away and they are so damn right. I'm in Sydney by myself, with no real friends. I've got a good life in our little house and good melanoma specialists, my hubby making a decent living, but I feel like a hole is growing deep inside me. A lack of true and deep friendships like theirs, bringing me down one day after another. It is so difficult to make friends in Sydney; everyone's got their friends already, usually from their childhood, and they don't need more or don't have time for more. My friends feel for me, they know I'm strong and a good fighter; they don't know how I'm coping but they know I will do great. They are thinking about me and sending me good vibes every day and I'm grateful to have such beautiful friends; crazy, funny, smart, caring and loving ones. I'm so lucky to be surrounded by so many wonderful people. I just wish I could bring them all back in my luggage.

We come back to Nice and settle in at my parents'. We are all glad to be back together and my parents welcome us, recovered from their terrible cold. We spend the third day of the year in Italy. It's great to have lunch on the sunny terrace of a nice pizzeria in San Remo, an hour away from my hometown. I'm excited to show John how great it is to escape the country just for a day. We do some shopping too and walk around the small town centre. The same evening, my parents are happy to keep the kids while John and I enjoy a dinner with my childhood friends. And we have so much fun. Some of them didn't make it for lunch last time but came this time and after a fantastic evening at the restaurant, we go for some drinks in the Old Nice; talking, drinking, laughing, joking, and relaxing, all night until 3.30am. We don't want to stop the party but all the pubs are now closed. I'm tipsy but John is drunk after many shots taken straight with my friends Didier and Hector. It's the third time in nearly six years I see him like that and when for the first two he was funny. This time, he falls in tears in front of the entrance of my parents' building.

"I'm so sorry. I try so hard to make you happy and I feel like it's never good enough. I don't know what to do anymore," he mumbles.

"Oh John, I'm sorry you feel that way. I don't want you to cry. You make me happy, it's just that I feel overwhelmed doing everything at home and with the kids. Taking care of them full time is so hard. I never have a minute for myself as I'm taking care of everyone else."

"But I try to help you with the kids too. I'm doing my best really, but I'm never good enough."

"You are good enough. That's why I know that you can do even better. And it's not so much about the chores and the kids. What would really make me feel better is to see you happier and less grumpy in general. Since we left Sydney, it seems that you always find something to whinge about instead of looking at all the little things that make the trip worthy for me. For once, it's just for me. There's a reason behind that trip: I may never be able to come back here again. I may never see my loved ones ever again. I'm sorry you feel that way but please, if you want to make me happy, try to enjoy this trip with us."

"But you're always all over me, asking me to do things and I try so hard."

"I know love, but the kids are very demanding and I need your help. I can't take care of them by myself. I also try to enjoy some time with my friends and family. I don't have them back home. I may never see them again and I'd like you to appreciate the moment instead of being on your phone all the time. I don't want you to learn the hard way like I did. Life is short, witness it." I give him a kiss and hug him.

"But I'm not always on my phone..."

"Babe, you go for a smoke every twenty minutes and you're on your phone the whole time. If I knew it would be the case, I would have bought the French sim card for my phone, not yours."

"Oh come on. Anyway, no one speaks English and it's hard for me here." He is getting upset.

"Look, you're drunk and it's very late. We should go to sleep. I don't want us to argue again. Thank you for your efforts Love, I appreciate it. But please, just try to be happy and a bit more present for us, that's all." I say opening the door.

We just don't have the same perspective on things anymore; a death sentence is tearing us apart. Not because I'm dying, but because I'm appreciating life so much, all the little things and it's painful to see him unhappy; I can't find him any excuses anymore. He's alive; he must enjoy mindfully. He doesn't know how long it will last. He should trust me on this one. Instead, it's like he's mocking me, wasting his time on his phone, instead of being present with his family. He doesn't get that it's not because you are here that you are actually here, actively present in the moment. He spends the next day hungover. I sleep three hours and take care of the kids all day. That evening, my dad organises a dinner with a couple of their friends and my uncle Jocelyn. They all know me since I'm born and are close to me. Yet, they avoid the cancer subject, even my uncle who lost his wife, my dad's sister, to breast cancer. My friends talked to me about it, the raw shit of the disease, the treatments, how to deal with your own death and the uncertainty of the future; I've never felt uncomfortable with my friends. I'm uncomfortable now. They're talking to me about insignificant stuff, avoiding awkwardly the subject. Maybe they think I've got enough talking about it? But I take it like they're avoiding the subject. At the end, I sell them my bracelet to raise funds for the Melanoma fundraiser. Too bad they have to talk about it. Just a little though, trying to stay positive, a little too much, revealing more fear and deny than providing help and comfort. Again to tell me that of course I will survive. I'm pissed off but feel for them at the same time because it's probably hard to deal with it. On our last day in Nice, we visit the biggest Park in town, Park Phoenix: a park with beautiful fauna and flora where the four of us have lots of fun together.

It's already time to leave France and kiss my parents goodbye. It's the 6th of January and we have another plane to take. This time it's to New York, with a quick transfer in Zurich. Fifteen hours flying and it goes pretty well. The kids are so tired of all these visits, people, and movements; they sleep pretty much all the way, and so do we. The previous night we had a hard time figuring out how we would go from the airport to our hotel but we finally found a chauffeur service; the driver comes with a massive black van and I feel like we are a VIP band, except that we've got six luggage and one stroller instead of instruments. Jason and Rose are awake for a little while, since we left the plane and Jason ran around like crazy while waiting to pass the border; it was hard to catch him. It's night time and we've prolonged the day by an extra six hours with the time difference, so we are all overtired. But I'm excited already. I can't wait to see the Big Apple.

We put the kids in their seats and drive to Time Square, where the Sheraton hotel is located. Our driver is commenting on the itinerary and it's pretty cool to have some information about where to eat and what to do or avoid from a local. I get us some yummy hot dogs and Philly cheese dogs from one of these mobile snacks around the block while John is bringing the kids upstairs. Back in our tiny room, I undo the only luggage we have for the next few days in the drawers and cupboard. Lucky I've already packed the stuff we don't need here in the other bags because there's not much space to move around. We all crash into a deep sleep very quickly after.

The next day, when I wake up and I open the blinds, I discover a great view of the city centre and the building surrounding us. One of them is displaying the time and temperature and I'm shocked to read minus twelve degrees Celsius at 8am. I knew it would be cold but come on. I plan a big bag to put away all the jackets, beanies and scarves so we will finish dressing up downstairs, in the hotel lobby. The kids are already rugged up in four layers of clothing and when we add their beanies, jackets and hoodies on top, Rose can't bring her hands together. We put them in the pram and add blankets and rain cover over. After more than forty minutes of preparation, we are ready to face the freezing cold of New York. I want to take the ferry to the Statue of Liberty but as we walk outside, we feel some light moisture falling on our faces...it's snowflakes.

Change of plans, we are going to Central Park, as I've always wanted to see it under the snow. It's too bad we can't do the carriages with horses as there is definitely no room for a pram in it but we walk in the park. Jason is leading the way, standing on his seat, facing forward, his body only protected by the back of his seat. He doesn't want to wear his gloves or the blanket. His jacket is super warm but I'm afraid he's going to get cold. We discover all the beautiful landmarks: the rink, Alice wonderland sculpture, Bethesda fountain, the lake and the Mall. It's mesmerising; there are only a few crazy people jogging and us. There are no traces in the snow yet and old street lamps and bridges offer a stunning landscape. We can't see the building surrounding the park as we can barely see ten metres away now. The light snowflakes have quickly changed into a snowstorm and the wind is beating our faces. The walk pushing the pram gets harder as the snow is accumulating on the ground and we decide to leave the park after the Cleopatra needle, by an exit on 5th Avenue.

It's weird to be there, after all the movies and TV shows I've seen featuring New York, I'm here, walking in these streets. I'm realising another of my dreams, even if it means fighting the snow and the lowest temperatures I've ever experienced. We head to Columbus Circle, a massive shopping centre, in order to find refuge. The weather is now very painful to cope with and our cheeks and eyes are burning from the cold. Who can live in such weather conditions? The empty bag is quickly filled with all our layers of clothing and we enjoy a meal in the warmth. We have lunch in a sort of grocery store where we can buy any kind of food; prices are based on the weight. We also get a large coffee and I confirm what everyone told me before, coffee definitely sucks in the United States. After a walk in the galleries, the kids playing mannequins in the windows of the shops, we put back on all our layers of clothes and are back in the cold. We go to Nike Town, an entire building dedicated to the sport brand, six levels of apparel and shoes. Too bad for me, there's no discounts; I was hoping that after Christmas sales would be on, but I guess it's NYC and obviously with tourists sales are pointless. We still look around while Jason is perched on the mannequin's pods, dancing on the background music, for the amusement of the staff. We leave empty-handed and walk back to the hotel for a warm bath and another Philly cheese, I love it.

After all this snow, we are lucky to have a beautiful sunny sky the next morning. It's still freezing cold but at least we don't have to fight a storm and are glad to be able to walk around the street peacefully. On the right corner block of our hotel, there's a Wendy's diner where we enjoy a massive, and expensive, breakfast; blueberry pancakes for the babies and chocolate ones and coffee for us. I ask for a refill of my black coffee and I feel like we are in the movies. With the leftovers now in a doggy bag, we have enough to munch for the rest of the day. We walk down to Times Square, past Bryant Park and the Public Library to reach the Empire State Building. We nearly miss the entrance. Going through security check with a pram and both babies asleep in it is quite a challenge but we finally reach the top and admire the wonderful view.

The view is amazing, and freaking cold too. So much that I struggle to take photos touching my phone; my hands are freezing in seconds out of my gloves. I take quickly pictures around the top deck and run back inside, to contemplate the view behind the windows. John takes over and I keep the kids inside while he also goes for a quick look around. The view is magic with all the snow on the rooftops, but I don't even think of looking at Central Park. I'm so cold my brain doesn't seem to work properly. I just looked at the city skyline but lucky, I see the park on my pictures.

We walk to Grand Central and admire the beauty of the train station. Again, I recall all the movies I've seen featuring the magnificent place and I'm glad to be here with my little family. It's grandiose and we stay for a little while, in the middle of the station, looking around this beautiful architecture, surrounded by stairs, lights, a beautiful ceiling painted with stars constellations, the American flag and the old ticket offices. After a quick picture with the nicest cops we've seen in the US so far, securing one exit, we have a coffee in a sort of food court on the side of the main concourse and leave the building to walk to Time Square. The kids have been pretty good all day and I'm stunned they stayed that long in the pram without too much fuss. They love to visit and look around new places, be outside discovering. They definitely take after me. We are amazed to walk through Time Square with hundreds of lighted advertising screens. It's astonishing. I imagine all the people who were probably there for New Year's Eve a week ago; looking at the countdown…I'm here. Finally. We take a picture while the snow is falling again and walk undercover for some crazy shopping at M&M's World. I must have the giant mugs of Yellow and Red, the nighty, the lanyard, I get a couple of tees for John and some blankets for the kids and we are out of the three levels building of one of my favourite confectionery brand.

The 9th of January is our last day in town. Times flies when you're having fun, and we are. I go for more shopping at the Levi' s Store on Time Square, prices are mad and it would have been silly not to get anything out of the half-price sale. We get two pairs of jeans, three tops, a belt and two track pants. It's with two monster bags that we're going to spend the day out...We take the metro in Times Square to the closest disabled accessible station to Little Italy, where we all eat two beautiful wood fire pizzas. We also get some Chinese bakery in China Town before walking through City Hall District. I'm glad to see the court where they film the series *Law and Order* before reaching Brooklyn Bridge. Jason and Rose are asleep by then and John and I can really savour the moment together. We take some selfies and pictures of the beautiful bridge and its views. From there, we can see the other bridge on the Hudson River, City Hall District, and One World. The architecture of the bridge with all the ropes and wood flooring is stunning, I love it.

After walking across the 9/11 Memorial and Museum, we walk down to Battery Park to take the free ferry to Staten Island. Jason plays with a squirrel and doesn't want to leave the little guy but we manage to get to the terminal where hundreds of people are waiting. It's impressive to see all these people embarking on the boat and, once on board, Jason and Rose love it. Another transport added to their collection. The Statue of Liberty seems quite small from the ferry windows but still bigger than the one we've seen in Paris. I also notice that her little island is quite far away from the city. We don't stay in Staten Island and go straight back into the ferry to return to the city by an amazing sunset. The sun going down is leaving an orange and pink sky and beautiful colours reflected on the city skyline buildings. The lights of the city start to shine and it's night time when we get off the boat. We quickly drop by Wall Street before taking the metro back to Time Square. We enjoy the last dinner in New York at Applebee's, a famous pub where we have a massive cocktail each, kids meals, burger for John and mac 'n' cheese for me —there was no way I'd leave the US without trying this dish. We admire the lights of Time Square one last time before sleeping our last night in the city that never sleeps.

The last morning, I finish packing our stuff and we walk around the block to see Rockefeller Centre. Lucky we saw the gigantic tree they had here a couple of days ago, because now it's gone. We see the Lego Land store and decide to enter per curiosity and spend two hours in there. They have this gigantic Lego sculpture of the Rockefeller Centre and a spy game associated to it. So John and I had to find out all the enigmas. We find Batman, how many dogs, bicycles, cameras, and famous characters there are and the rest of them and get rewarded by three little characters we can create ourselves and a Batman set. Jason and Rose are walking around, playing with everything they can touch and it's tough to go through all the little heads, bodies, accessories and pants displayed in small boxes while looking after the kids. But we have a great time and after our last hot dog, our driver picks us up at the hotel at 1.30pm for our last transfer to the airport. Our flight takes off at 6 pm.

We are pretty happy to go back home after such a big trip around the world with our two babies. It's been exhausting but I'm glad I had the chance to see all my friends and family, all the people I love, my country, my hometown, and discover a city I dreamt of for so long. Now, when I will watch a movie filmed in New York, it won't be the same anymore; it will look more familiar and it will remind me of this magic trip.

21

We're back in Sydney and John and I have a week off together as we drop the kids off at day-care every morning. But what's supposed to be a great romantic week ends up being a dreadful time for us. I have scans and doctor appointments three days out of the five and John doesn't really want to waste his time coming with me. I don't feel his support. Finally, he comes for the PET scan and I leave him in the waiting room once the doctor calls me. While lying in the radiation room for an hour, I update him by text messages to let him know at what time I should be out and also that my phone is running out of battery. When I come out two hours later after a crappy time of radioactivity loneliness, I'm expecting to see him but he isn't there and when I go outside, he's not at the car either. Without any cell phone, I have to go back inside the hospital and ask the lady at the reception of the nuclear centre to call him, twice, to finally hear that he is at the car but wasn't there when I was. I'm very disappointed and feel heartbroken. He knows these scans make me anxious and I was just hoping to be able to hold his hand once out, him asking me how I felt, walking me to the car. Instead, we argue when we are finally seated and ready to drive back home.

"Where were you?" I ask upset.

"I was at the car."

"No, you weren't. I came to the car as soon as I got out and didn't see you in the waiting room." I am furious.

"I was but then I saw this lady who had a flat tyre and helped her change it."

"Well that's very nice of you but I also needed your help, and you weren't there. Why weren't you in the waiting room? I sent you text messages to update you up until thirty minutes before I was out, so you knew when to come back." I am saddened, I need his support and I feel sorry not to be understood. I am missing my friends so badly now.

"I didn't want to wait two hours there, okay? And I don't know I thought you would come to the car anyway," he yells at me.

"But I needed you there, so we could go back to the car together, so you would be there to talk to me. You know how hard these scans are for me and what's the point of you coming with me for once and not being there once I'm out? I don't need a driver. I want my hubby by my side. Great for the lady, but today I was the one who needed your help. You know how bad I felt not seeing you, and my phone was dead; I couldn't reach you and you knew that. I don't understand why you were at the car. I thought it was obvious you would be in the waiting room." I am yelling and heartbroken.

"Okay, alright. Okay Alright. Enough." He shouts and shuts himself down.

"You know if you don't want to be here for me, you don't have to. I can do it by myself, like I usually do. You don't have to come with me tomorrow for my CT and my MRI. I can drive myself. I don't want to share my stupid cancer journey with you anymore because if it's to make me feel worse with you than without you, I'd rather do it without you. That way, you won't waste your time driving me."

He doesn't insist to come the next day, which breaks my heart. I wish he would have jumped in the car without asking me, coming with or without me being happy about it. Of course, I would be happy to have his support. I feel that love isn't enough sometimes. It's not because you love someone that it's enough to stay together. We need so much more to make it work. I'm also pissed off because he seemed grumpy for our trip overseas, because he couldn't handle the kids full time, or because of the small space we were living in, not to mention the cold, the snow, the planes, travel time and jet lag. At some point, I was thinking that I should have done it by myself but I really wanted to introduce the kids to my friends and family. I just wish he would have been more thoughtful, thinking that I was doing that because it could be the last time I see all my loved ones, my country and New York. It wasn't constantly bad, but the overall feeling was that he wasn't happy and I felt guilty about it because for once, it was all about me. But he should have also made an effort, as we don't go back often and I may never go back at all. I make efforts daily living in his country without my friends or family, dealing with his unreliable family and no support. I wish he could put himself in my shoes sometimes. But even if he did, he wouldn't understand as he doesn't care to have any friends and is used to his family. He doesn't understand what I'm missing.

I'm sad and lonely back at home. I'm already missing my family and friends, missing all the emotional support I could get there, and I take it out on my partner. I'm sorry he wasn't as excited as I was, I'm heartbroken he's dodgy in supporting me through my cancer journey, but I still love him and I want to believe that we just have to improve our communication skills in order to go through rough times. He won't change anyway so I have to deal with it and hope that one day, he will realise that I may not be here forever, and that he has to savour the moments we have together as much as he can.

Finally, John comes with me to discuss the results of my scans the following day. The good thing is that they are great. I'm still NED, even if the tumours are still there, there's no activity on the PET scan. I will have scans every three months from now on. Who knows how long this can go for? I hope for a lifetime. But my oncologist seems pretty stunned by these results, again. I decide to use the next three months to finish all the family photo books, exercise even more and find my next move. I want to have some kind of activity, maybe even go back to work. Having cancer is challenging enough on our couple, and financial pressure is definitely not helping us. Working would help, money-wise, but put more pressure on us to take care of the kids and the house. I will require more help at home from John after a day at work. I want to help my family financially but avoid the stress, I'm just not quite sure how. I've always wanted to be my own boss but never found any idea to start a business. Starting my own business will be too much stress and won't help with the finances so I'm starting to think about going back to my previous job. If my next scan is okay, I will. For now, I need to finalise everything that I started.

We have a barbecue with Jason and Rose for Australia Day, and John is working the next day. Jason gets sick that night and doesn't sleep for two nights in a row, and of course I'm in charge. So I try to sleep in to recover but John doesn't understand or accept it because he works during the week and I'm not. And we argue again. Not long this time because I'm tired of arguing.

I don't say anything when the kids are still in their pyjamas at 10 am, hadn't any breakfast, nothing is planned for lunch, and the dishwasher is still full of clean dishes. I don't say anything. Usually, I would say the same thing, like every Saturday morning and mention all the things he didn't do, again. But I don't and I dress up the kids and I feed them. I play with them and I prepare lunch. I barely have the time to sit for a coffee. Sometimes I wonder why I sleep in if it's to be running around like a chicken with his head cut off as soon as I'm awake? In the afternoon, I take the kids outside, in our backyard to play in the little above the ground pool we bought before Australia Day. A good thing, we finally have a pool, not an in-ground heated one, but we have one.

John is playing games with guns on his Xbox and I don't want the kids to look at the screen. After an hour I have to remind him that he has a family playing outside and he finally comes out, forced and resigned. By the end of the day, he packs a bag and leaves without explanations, just saying that he's tired of being treated like shit. I don't feel treated like a princess either. I'm more like Cinderella these days, before meeting Prince Charming. I don't know what to think anymore. Am I falling out of love? I'm not really proud of him anymore. There has been too many arguments unsolved, slept on, too many mornings pretending nothing happened the night before. I'm tired. Now that I have cancer, I'm thinking: do I want to spend the rest of my life unhappy? Because I feel like it's been a while since he made me feel truly happy. Okay.

This shitty cancer gets on my mood and it's always on the back of my mind, putting a sort of veil over my happiness, like all the light in the world is filtered through it and I'm unable to see things the way I used to anymore. Or maybe more like sunglasses. My vision is changed forever. But I don't want it to be for the worse. I want to make the most out of these new glasses, since I can't live without them anymore. I'm stuck with them. I'm condemned to see things differently now. Things have changed forever. I have a sword over my head and it can drop at any time. I'm subject to a death sentence, wondering what I've done wrong, it's unfair.

John isn't a bad man. He works hard, even if he doesn't seem to like his job anymore. He's a good-hearted man. But I always feel like a nagging wife with him. He never says anything nice to me anymore, never apologises when he's being rude, yelling at me or calling me names, never thanks me for all the hard work I'm doing in the house and with the kids. Our mutual respect is on the road to extinction. The four legs of any relationship stool –pride, respect, desire, and love– are falling apart and we are going down. I am not sure how I can save us anymore but I know I want to. They say cancer either brings you closer or tears you apart. Once again, I'm afraid we are in the second case scenario.

From day one I knew this relationship would be challenging: different backgrounds, different beliefs, from different countries but we had the same values, hopes and the same expectations in life, the same idea of the life we wanted to have together. I also had faith in him, since he left everything for me to follow me in my picking quest, since he had quit smoking for me, since he had left his bachelor way of life and he was caring for me like no other man has ever care for me before. But now I feel ripped off. Because if I knew he would rather spend time on his Xbox or on his phone than with his family, I'm not sure I would have married him. The night before he left, I told him that I was deeply saddened about our relationship situation lately and he replied with something along "whatever you want"... for real? It didn't even make sense. And my heart broke, like the faith I had he could change. Mister *"I don't care"* is demonstrating once again that he isn't the man I fell in love with anymore. And the worst part is that I start to open my eyes on all the things that I can't stand anymore.

Since he left, I didn't cry. Like my eyes are dried after all the tears I had the past six years, I can't find any left. He texts me the next day and even if I don't want to answer—because he always tries to solve our conflicts by text messages and I hate it—I do. Just so I'm sure he knows what I think is wrong and what I'm fed up with. All these chores I'm doing by myself, and all the things I have to ask him to do in order for them to be done, as if I'm asking my teenage son. He even has the guts to say that it's normal for me to do it all because I'm not working. But I was working before, for years and it was the same, I was doing it all back then too. He can pretend that he's doing his best; it's not enough for me. It's not that he isn't good enough but he isn't helping me enough. This, on top of his whining, swearing—I hate how much he swears—and the fact that he's never talking to me about anything deep, important, interesting, unless I bring up the subject myself. Even the election of the US President caused us arguments. John thought that because it was the Americans' decision, it wasn't affecting us…in an interconnected world of globalisation? Really? Of course, we have to be worried about the silly decisions this rude guy makes. But again he took out the *"I don't care"* card. I'm so over him not caring for anything, not even me or my feelings. I used to be hurt but since he left, I'm numb. I'm not sure to be sad. Of course, I'm sad that our relationship has issues, but I'm not sure I'm sad to lose him. Sometimes I feel like he's just waiting for me to die, so then he won't have to deal with me anymore. It's horrible to feel that way. No wonder why I'm not happy. But I am not sure about what will make me happy anymore, except for my kids; they are my world, my happy bubble, my pride and the best reason I have to live for.

John comes home every night for the next four nights but he won't say anything. He stands there looking at me feeding and bathing the kids and doesn't even help. I tell him I need time to think about us, about our lives, find some kind of miracle solution for us to be a happier couple and that unless he finds one, it was pointless coming back. I don't want to talk about our issues in front of the kids either, ending with arguments, him yelling at me with either "okay, all right," or "I'm not good enough anyway, you'd better find someone else." On the third night he comes with six red roses and says "Just to say I'm sorry and stuff." Really? He adds "I love you, tell the kids I love them too" and he leaves after taking something he needed in his shed and the mail in the letterbox. I find it nice but it doesn't cut it. It's too easy. No discussion at all, he pretty much wasted a bunch of flowers then. He should have developed his apologies; *"stuff"* isn't the best problem solving and I actually find it disrespectful, like he was forced to apologise. Is it all I deserved? All we are worthy of?

He finally comes back the next day and we have a heated conversation at home about everything and the help I need, not only in doing things but also in thinking about what needs to be done. It doesn't help. He's still yelling and I don't want to be yelled at. I leave to pick up the kids at day-care. I think he will leave again. But he's there when I come back and tells me "I will do whatever it takes even if I'm not happy about it, just ask me." I have to ask, but it's a start. I hate asking though, that's what makes me feel like a nagging wife.

Since then, I have done lots of thinking. After being overwhelmed with so much love and support from my family and friends during our big trip, I guess it's been hard for me to come back to the harsh reality of my loneliness here. I have no one to really count on, a few mates but not one I can really rely on, except for John. He's everything for me here, I'm depending on him. It's sad and this simple thought is depressing. But living in France is out of the question, since he doesn't speak French...so I have to deal with it and make the most out of my days here from now on. John isn't perfect and yes, I have to tell him everything I want him to help me with, but he's trying his best—his real best—to help since then, with the kids and the house. I can tell he's making efforts and that all that matters to me. Okay, I'm still waiting for us to get some quality romantic time, but without reliable babysitters it's tough. Our couple has been through so much in only six years, and we got married after knowing each other for only a few months. Yet, we are still there, working hard on our relationship, going through life together without much family support, enduring the loss of our first unborn child, dealing with the arrival of a thirty-week premature baby, and coping with terminal cancer during our first pregnancy. Some couples don't go through half of it in twenty years. But we did and we still love each other. Life is hectic and we may doubt sometimes but our love has been intensified and our faith in each other, growing stronger. We need to work through these overwhelming times though.

And now that my health is getting better, we want to enjoy our new *"normal"*, worry less about what the future holds for us and embrace the few happy times we can get out of our busy young parent's life. It's hard enough. Hopefully, I will stay healthy for many years and defy the odds until I die, my hair white and my skin wrinkly, in my sleep, holding my husband's hand.

By the end of February, I tick another item off my bucket list: I get a cover-up tattoo for the tribal butterfly and Chinese love sign I had on my left shoulder blade since I was eighteen that John hated. After about fourteen hours of suffering, I have a colourful tattoo representing an angel wing embracing a hibiscus and two frangipani flowers—a symbol of femininity and strength—with a black feather in a black ribbon shape finishing in flying birds and the name of my kids above it all. I'm quite happy with the results and glad I have my kids literally under my skin. Also, I've finished the birthday letters for them and the first two photo books for 2016. I will need a third one as it's been a captivating year, full of events. After these books, I will have to find out what will be my next step. I'd like to see my kids more often but I have to figure out if I will go back to work first. I don't feel comfortable not knowing what will happen with my health in the future. It's difficult to make a decision work wise. I don't really want to go back to my previous job and I don't know if going back to work will affect negatively my health, because of the stress and pressure that could affect me and my family. Uncertainty doesn't help the decision-making process. Trying to make decisions, anticipating what could happen, and coming from planning the end of the road to finally living in a future in expansion makes surviving cancer an anxious and stressful journey.

22

It's April 2017, I'm starving for comfort and very anxious. Surviving is exhausting and emotionally draining. I've spent eighteen months watching the Internet for melanoma research articles, new treatments, and also other melanoma patients' stories. And I've seen so many people dying around me. Too many. Every couple of days someone is having bad results or dying of melanoma. It's devastating and I can't help but think that I could be the next. A twenty-five-year-old woman had melanoma in Queensland and she wrote a very successful blog. I asked her what kind of treatment she was on back when I was diagnosed and she never replied to me. But since, I've been following her journey from a distance. Amanda told me not to be too close and avoid this kind of social media activity as it could depress me quickly and she was right. I had to remove myself from a lot of groups because, at some point, it was overwhelming and increased the negative thoughts in my head. But when I learned that this particular girl passed away, after two years fighting the disease, it hurt more than ever.

Of course, I knew it would happen but having seen her posts for the past two years, I thought she would have some more time, fighting, like all of us. But her time was up, she didn't have any treatment options left and she was gone in a couple of months. Like that. Again, when treatment options are out, you go fast, very fast from there. That's also the reason why I've done my boxes, the cards, the photo albums, planned my funerals, all of it, just to avoid doing it when I will lack time, when I'd like to cuddle my kids and my husband instead. Since Emma passed away, I feel like I'm slipping down this thread, my fragile thread of life, but I'm trying to keep on holding it, with all my strength and hopes. I try to keep focus and remember that I'm lucky where I am today, and I slowly climb back up on the thread. Staying on top of it helps because if I have to slip again, I won't fall out. My arms are getting sore and it's harder when I lose energy crying, letting go my fears and sadness. But I'm not at the end of it...not yet.

It's always difficult for me when one of my melanoma mates dies; it makes my mortality even more real. Every time I see people dying from melanoma around me, falling like flies so quickly, I'm scared. I feel closer to my own death. It's a constant reminder of my disease, of the danger of my condition and it usually occurs just when I start to get comfortable in my new *"normal"* life. I have a sword over my head, hanging by such a light thread too. I'm hoping that the more I stay positive and live mindfully, the more chances I have to survive and strengthen the thread, so the sword never cuts my neck.

I've been so lucky. I got it easy compared to some of my melanoma mates. The worst side effects I had were extreme fevers and joint pains. But it's now eight months I don't take any treatment, and somehow my immune system took over and is fighting efficiently against the black beast. I'm still with *"No evidence of disease"* on my last PET scan. I'm one of the very rare lucky ones and I intend to stay that way. I hope I won't have to give any of the birthday cards I've prepared for my children and write each and every single one of them again, close to the date and give them myself, with a kiss. I'm waiting to write the 21st birthday card, if I don't have much time left to live, I will have the time for this card, the last one. I will wait until the cancer is back, until the day I'm not able to get any treatment or clinical trial, until I run out of options, and hopefully that day will never come.

This book is another of my bucket list ticks and I'm glad to write it. After all the things I have done and ticked off this list, that's another one that I've finally started. I've also obtained my citizenship, getting a score of hundred per cent on the test that I passed in five minutes. My next step will be to take some time off with the kids and maybe go back to work. I want to help my family again. Also, if I survive ten years, I can't spend ten years without doing anything. That would drive me crazy. Meanwhile, I'm spending my days writing or going to the doctors.

I book an appointment with a private Ears Nose and Throat specialist for Jason as I'm not waiting for September; he's waking up every night now and having tonsillitis monthly, I want his tonsils and adenoids removed ASAP. And I enjoy playing with my babies of course. Rose wants to use the potty already and they are growing so fast. Jason is definitely not growing enough as people think they are twins; I can't wait for him to get better and finally thrive. She's also talking a lot more and is definitely a smart cookie. Jason is about to go to pre-school. He's naughty and cheeky, the typical *threenager*... and they love each other so much. I'm a happy mother and I love my family. I'm living an emotional roller coaster but I'm lucky.

My oncologist reassured me that the more time I'm spending without active tumours, the more chances I have to survive longer. And that changed everything. Before, I used to think the opposite, that the longer I stayed out of treatment, the more chances I had to get the cancer back. But I was wrong. Dealing with surviving has been tough emotionally but I'm stable and obviously my immune system is fighting for me. It apparently happens to a handful of people but usually the cancer would come back after three months for fifty per cent of them, the other two and half fingers are like me...Lucky bitches. I'm a freaking miracle. Since they told me that I feel like I can live a *normal* life again. I'm not worried as much anymore. Of course cancer will always be on the back of my mind —as long as there is no cure for it– but I'm not scared of dying on a daily basis anymore. I feel free for the first time in the last year and half. I'm not as stressed as I used to be, thinking that every little pain I get in my body is the cancer coming back. And I'm feeling pretty good, for the first time in what feels like a very, very long time. My last results show a new uptake lymph node but my oncologist doesn't think it's cancer. So I will have to do another PET scan in a couple of months. Meanwhile, I'm socialising again and I found a nice group of expatriate mums living in my area to go out and about with, and that's just what I needed.

Now that I'm clear for the past nine months, I start thinking it could be a lifetime thing. I could live like any other person on Earth. I can go back to work and pretend nothing happened. But it did. And cancer changed me forever. I get it now: I must live my life like I will be hit by a car the next day, with no regrets, to the fullest. Since I've had cancer, I can see clearly for the first time in my life. I have a terrible vision and require glasses but I can see the details and the depth in everything, like never before. I was blind and now

I see. Life is beautiful, in poverty or wealth, in health or sickness, trust me, I've experienced all of it, to a certain extent. But where life is even more beautiful is in love. Love helps me to fill my anger and desperation with peace and hope. The love for my family gives me wings to fight and I will hopefully remain a fucking miracle, keeping this cancer away from me. Terminal is my condition, but my life is far from over. And somehow, through pain and anger, my husband and I got better at communicating and helping each other. He's helping me so much now at home and with our children; I'm sure that he would be better at supporting me emotionally if the black beast comes back. Our bond is stronger than ever and we are very hopeful for our future.

The hardest part of cancer is really the emotional journey I've been through, a very lonely one. At first, when I told everyone, I was overwhelmed by support and attention, people bringing me pasta home, offering their help and helping with fundraisers. But after a few months, I found myself to be very lonely. No one came anymore, no one was offering help. I felt lonely and misunderstood, even by my family and friends. At times I actually wondered if people were waiting for me to die and because I wasn't, they were keeping quiet, forgetting. I was still there, but I wasn't breaking news anymore. People like drama. They like fresh news and I was getting better. It was like because I was surviving and had a better outcome than expected, I wasn't worthy of love and attention anymore? I was in a *too good* shape? I even felt that way with my melanoma mates at the Melanoma fundraiser this year. For the first one I was dying and people cared so much, but when I participated to this one, it was like I wasn't interesting enough because I was NED with no treatment. I can't believe the nature of humans. A story of hope isn't better than a story of death? I've been shocked and saddened.

I still need emotional support, who knows how long I will stay in such a good position? But like my best friend John said: "the most important is that you're surviving, you have more time and too bad if they're not happy about it." Because on top of that, I feel guilty I'm surviving with no treatment and they aren't. Somewhere, I lost my place in the *"normal"* people society and it doesn't seem like I've got one in the cancer patients' either. I'm like an outcast and that makes me feel even lonelier. But I have my family to lean on; at least, they give me a big place in their heart and that's the best place I can be. But if I have to meet new people I will avoid the subject, so they won't feel like they're starting a relationship with a potential dead body. I don't want pity, I want love and friendship. I guess everybody thinks that because you're better and you're not dying anymore, they can stop supporting you emotionally—because you're back to normal—but they don't realise that normal is over; now it's all about survival. It's like I have another chance in life and I don't want to waste it or use it like if I didn't learn any lessons from this journey, because otherwise my life could be taken away again. I feel like I have to live by my values and respect the honour I've been given to live again, otherwise I may lose my health again, and my life with it. I have to prove to whoever is in charge upstairs that I deserve to live somehow.

I've changed. I became more humble maybe, more cautious of what I am doing and why I'm doing it for sure. I am expecting even more from myself and I feel like I owe my life so I want to make sure I'm not screwing up with *Karma*. I have been pretty lucky so far and I managed to get all the things I've ever wanted, I am blessed with my guardian angel; my grandma Lucienne is watching over me and I don't want to disappoint her. I'm still adjusting to the new version of myself, but it's a better version for sure. Lucie 2.0 is now operational and I'll try not to crash again because I don't really want to go through another reboot. I guess I feel like my entire life was a succession of cycles. I have so many stories, I've re-born so many times; this time is definitely different though because it wasn't my choice. I feel lucky being where I am today, because I'm free.

I feel like the nightmare is gone. I know it can come back anytime soon but for now it's not there. Living in the present is okay for me. I can enjoy my life mindfully, the sky is clear for now but I'm ready for the storm, if it comes back one day. At the moment, I'm enjoying a blue sky and a happy life with my beautiful family. We left the umbrellas at home and it's with our hats and sunscreen on that we enjoy the warmth of a sunny sky, playing together in our backyard. Rain may come, but not today. Today is beautiful.